RESEARCH AND INFORMATION GUIDES IN BUSINESS, INDUSTRY, AND ECONOMIC INSTITUTIONS
(VOL. 11)

THE INTERNATIONAL FINANCIAL STATISTICS LOCATOR

GARLAND REFERENCE LIBRARY
OF SOCIAL SCIENCE
(VOL. 924)

Research and Information Guides in Business, Industry, and Economic Institutions

General Editor: Wahib Nasrallah

FRANCHISING IN BUSINESS
A Guide to Information
Services
by Lucy Heckman

THE INFORMAL ECONOMY
A Research Guide
by Abol Hassan Danesh

STAFF TRADING
An Annual Review of the Literature
by William Crimando and
T.F. Riggar

THE WORLD BANK GROUP
A Guide to Information
Services
edited by Carol R. Wilson

GLOBAL COUNTERTRADE
An Annotated Bibliography
by Leon Zurawicki and
Louis Suichmezian

THE NEW YORK STOCK EXCHANGE
A Guide to Information Services
by Lucy Heckman

**U.S. SECURITIES AND EXCHANGE
COMMISSION**
A Research and Information Guide
by John W. Graham

**THE INTERNATIONAL MONETARY
FUND, 1944–1992**
A Research Guide
by Mary Elizabeth Johnson

**THE INTERNATIONAL FINANCIAL
STATISTICS LOCATOR**
A Research and Information Guide
by Domenica M. Barbuto

THE INTERNATIONAL FINANCIAL STATISTICS LOCATOR

A Research and Information Guide

Domenica M. Barbuto

GARLAND PUBLISHING, Inc.
New York & London / 1995

Library of Congress Cataloging-in-Publication Data

Barbuto, Domenica M., 1951–
    The international financial statistics locator : a research and
information guide / Domenica M. Barbuto
        p. cm. — (Research and information guides in business,
industry, and economic institutions ; vol. 11) (Garland reference
library of social science ; vol. 924
    ISBN 0-8153-1483-3 (alk. paper)
    1. Finance—Statistics—Information services. 2. Finance—
Statistics—Bibliography. I. Title. II. Series: Research and
information guides in business, industry, and economic institutions ; 11.
III. Series: Garland reference library of social science ; v. 924.
HG151.7.B37   1995
016.332—dc20   94-19999

Printed on acid-free, 250-year-life paper
Manufactured in the United States of America

Contents

Series Foreword

The new information society has exceeded everyone's expectations in providing new and exciting media for the collection and dissemination of data. Such proliferation has been matched by a similar increase in the number of providers of business literature. Furthermore, many emerging technologies, financial fields, and management processes have amassed an amazing body of knowledge in a short period of time. Indicators are that packaging of information will continue its trend of diversification, confounding even the experienced researcher. How then will information seekers identify and assess the adequacy and relevancy of various packages to their research needs?

It is my hope that Garland's Research and Information Guides in Business, Industry, and Economic Institutions series will bridge the gap between classical forms of literature and new alternative formats. Each guide will be devoted to an industry, a profession, a managerial process, or a field of study. Organization of the guides will emphasize subject access to formats such as bibliographic and numeric databases on-line, distributed databases, CD-Rom products, loose-leaf services, government publications and books, and periodical articles. Although most of the guides will serve as locators and bridges to bodies of knowledge, some may be reference books with self-contained information.

Since compiling such guides requires substantial knowledge in the organization of information or the field of study, authors are selected on the basis of their expertise as information professionals or subject specialists. Inquiries about the series and its content should be addressed to the Series Editor.

Wahib Nasrallah
Langsam Library
University of Cincinnati

Introduction

In the current, increasingly global economy, investors require quick access to a wide range of financial and investment-related statistics to assist them in better understanding the macroeconomic environment in which their investments will operate. *The International Financial Statistics Locator* eliminates the need to search through a number of sources to identify those that contain much of this statistical information. It is intended for use by librarians, students, individual investors, and the business community and provides access to twenty-two resources, print and electronic, that contain current and historical financial and economic statistics investors need to appreciate and profit from evolving and established international markets.

Today, there is a broad range of statistical sources in various formats available to the researcher. The twenty-two sources included in *The International Financial Statistics Locator* were selected because they are widely available, easy to use, produced by companies or organizations that are generally considered to be reliable and accurate, and not unreasonably expensive, so that academic, public, and special libraries as well as individual investors can afford access to them.

The International Financial Statistics Locator is arranged in two sections. The first section contains a listing of acronyms used to identify the sources where information may be found. This listing is followed by annotated entries for the twenty-two selected sources. These annotations include a description of the kind, frequency, and scope of information presented, as well as information about format: print, on-line, CD-ROM, or magnetic tape. This section also includes instructions on how to use *The International Financial Statistics Locator*.

The second section is an alphabetically arranged topical listing that provides geographic and subject access points. Information is provided on approximately 175 countries. This geographic arrangement allows the reader to quickly identify country-related statistics; standardized, country-specific entries assist in cross-country comparisons. The data elements in each entry are followed by an acronym which indicates which of the selected sources contain the required information. These acronyms correspond to the acronyms listed in the first section of the locator.

The Appendix is a directory of world securities markets and contains the name, address, telephone and facsimile numbers for more than 125 securities markets. This information has been included to assist the reader who requires information that is not available in the twenty-two sources selected for inclusion in *The International Financial Statistics Locator*, and for the reader who requires information beyond the scope of this publication such as specific, detailed information about the performance of individual securities markets or certain companies. Many of these markets publish factbooks or yearbooks and some provide electronic access to information about their operations.

I wish to thank Wahib Nasrallah of the University of Cincinnati for his advice during the preparation of this manuscript and Amanda and Kenny Kaplan for their assistance. Special thanks go to my colleagues in the Reference Department of the Joan and Donald E. Axinn Library at Hofstra University for their interest and support, particularly Martha Kreisel and Janet Wagner for their thoughtful and useful suggestions. I am especially indebted to Elena Cevallos for her interest, encouragement, and expert technical advice. Finally, and most importantly, I want to acknowledge the support and assistance of my family, particularly my sister, Frances, in this and in so many other projects I have undertaken and completed because I knew that they were always there for me.

Geographic Note

Users of this locator need to be aware of the tremendous changes that are occurring in the global geo-political situation because these changes may affect the way in which this resource is used. In some instances independent nations have united to form new republics. This is illustrated by the unification of the Federal Republic of Germany (FRG, West Germany) and the German Democratic Republic (GDR, East Germany). In October 1990 under international law the former GDR became part of the FRG. According to the terms of the treaty on German Economic, Monetary, and Social Union (GEMSU), the deutsche mark was adopted as the currency of the GEMSU. This change and others are reflected in the information reported in the sources selected for inclusion in this locator. The reader should consult the explanatory notes that appear in the selected sources to determine any variations in the reporting of information.

In some instances existing nations have been divided into two or more independent states. This is the case with the former Czechoslovakia which was divided into two independent states, the Czech Republic and the Slovak Republic in January 1993. Beginning in 1990 the geographic entity known as Yugoslavia was partitioned into the following independent republics: Bosnia and Hercegovina, Croatia, Macedonia, Serbia and Montenegro, and Slovenia. When the Soviet Union collapsed in December 1991, the fifteen former republics of Armenia, Azerbaijan, Belarus, Estonia, Georgia, Kazakhstan, Kyrgyzstan, Latvia, Lithuania, Moldova, Russia, Tajikistan, Turkmenistan, Ukraine, and Uzbekistan became independent states. All but five of these nations, Azerbaijan, Estonia, Georgia, Latvia, and Lithuania established a voluntary association known as The Commonwealth of Independent States. Even though these countries are part of the global landscape, they all have not been fully integrated into the international finance reporting structure. In most cases, due to reporting delays, information relating to these geo-political entities continues to be reported under the designations Czechoslovakia, Yugoslavia, and the Soviet Union. Because of this, I have relied on authoritative sources (i.e., the International Monetary Fund, the United Nations, the Organization for Economic Cooperation and Development) for place names and have retained the older designations. The reader should be aware that in the next few years the financial information highlighted in this locator may be reported under different geographic place names.

Section One

How to Use *The International Financial Statistics Locator*

The International Financial Statistics Locator indicates where statistical data may be found in one or more of the twenty-two sources which are described below. This locator is generally arranged alphabetically by country. Within each country entry there are up to fifty data elements followed by a listing of acronyms of sources where information may be found. In cases where none of the sources contains the statistical data indicated, the acronym *N/A* indicates that information is *Not Available* for this data element in any of the twenty-two selected sources.

For example, to locate sources for exchange rates for the French Franc, turn to France. Within this entry find the heading "Exchange Rates"

France

Exchange Rates

Currency—French Franc
Cross Rates—FTI, WSJ
Forward Exchange Rate—FTI
Per ECU—FTI
Per SDR—FSM*, FSY*, FTI
Per U.S. Dollar—BAR, DJN, DRF, FRB, FSM*, FSY*, MEI*, NYT, WSJ

This entry indicates that exchange rates for the French Franc per U.S. Dollar appear in nine sources. The complete listing of acronyms and sources appears below. The frequency and format of these sources are indicated in the source annotations below.

3

Topics which are not necessarily country specific, such as commodity prices, are interfiled alphabetically and cross referenced. All data elements within the country entries are also cross referenced.

Source Key for Acronyms

Acronym	Source
BAR	Barron's
BOP*	Balance of Payments
CSI	CSI Market Statistics (MARSTAT)
DJN	Tradeline (on Dow Jones News/ Retrieval)
DRC	DRI Commodities Data Base (DRICOM)
DRF	DRI Financial and Credit Statistics Data Base (DRIFACS)
DRI	DRI Financial Market Indexes Data Base (INDEX)
ECI	Economic Indicators
FRB	Federal Reserve Bulletin
FS1	OECD Financial Statistics Monthly Part One, Section One
FS2*	OECD Financial Statistics Monthly Part One, Section Two
FSM*	International Financial Statistics (Monthly)
FSY*	International Financial Statistics (Yearbook)
FTI	Financial Times
GSY*	Government Finance Statistics Yearbook
MEI*	OECD Main Economic Indicators
N/A	Not Available
NYT	The New York Times
UNN	United Nations National Accounts
UNY	United Nations Statistical Yearbook

*indicates title in more than one format
For brief descriptions, consult annotations below.

WSJ	The Wall Street Journal
WTA*	World Debt Tables
WDR	World Development Report

Source Annotations

Balance of Payments Statistics Yearbook.
Washington, D.C.: International Monetary Fund.

Acronym: *BOP**
Formats: Print, magnetic tape

This annual publication presents a series of alphabetically-arranged country tables that include transactions data for approximately 140 countries. Tables in the presented version include eight years of data. The magnetic tape version contains 50,000 annual and quarterly time series for 140 countries and annual data is available from 1965 to the present. Data groupings include transfers, investments, current account, long and short-term capital, and reserves. The tape format, which is updated monthly, corresponds to the print version of the International Monetary Fund's *Balance of Payments Statistics Yearbook.*

Barron's National Business and Financial Weekly.
Chicopee, Massachusetts: Dow Jones & Company, Inc.

Acronym: *BAR*
Format: Print

This weekly publication presents an extensive variety of both United States and international investment statistics. In addition to regular columns there are articles and special features most of which are illustrated with graphs and charts. Price quotations from the major United States stock exchanges are included as well as selected listings from foreign stock exchanges. The Market Week section, which has an index of the statistics reported in it, includes economic indicators, foreign exchange rates, bond prices and yields, commodities prices, and worldwide stock exchange indexes.

CSI Market Statistics (MARSTAT).
Boca Raton, Florida: Commodity Systems Inc.

Acronym: *CSI*
Formats: On-line, magnetic tape, diskette

The MARSTAT database includes a wide selection of data such as commodity futures and options and stock index options. For most commodities forty years of data are available. Data sources include Commodity News Service, Commodity World News, Allied Bunker Ramo's Quotation, and Reuters.

DRI Commodities Data Base (DRICOM).
Lexington, Massachusetts: DRI/McGraw-Hill.

Acronym: *DRC*
Format: On-line

DRICOM provides worldwide coverage of Asian, European, Canadian and United States commodity markets. More than 50,000 time series on financials, indexes, crops, food, oil and gas, metals and currencies are available. Information in this database is derived from several commodities exchanges and from Telekurs, N.A. and from the Commodity Research Bureau. Generally, DRICOM supplies data from 1980 to the present although some series extend back to the 1960s. This database is updated daily.

DRI Financial and Credit Statistics Data Base (DRIFACS).
Lexington, Massachusetts: DRI/McGraw-Hill.

Acronym: *DRF*
Format: On-line

DRIFACS includes over 15,000 time series and provides worldwide coverage of currency exchange, fixed income, and money market rates. Information is drawn from the Federal Reserve System, the United States Treasury, Moody's, Telerate, and from private banks. Data is available from 1970 to the present, and the database is updated daily, weekly, or monthly as available.

DRI Financial Market Indexes Data Base (INDEX).
Lexington, Massachusetts: DRI/McGraw-Hill

Acronym: *DRI*
Format: On-line

This database, referred to as INDEX, contains an extensive amount of information. It provides coverage of major United States securities markets as well as a substantial number of international markets. More than 1,000 equity stock indexes and commodity futures indexes are presented on a daily, weekly, or monthly basis. Material is drawn from a number of sources including Telerate, Reuters, regional United States stock exchanges, and a number of international exchanges and is updated daily. Coverage includes 1970 to the present.

Economic Indicators.
Washington D.C.: Council of Economic Advisors

Acronym: *ECI*
Format: Print

This monthly publication is a statistical digest that includes a variety of statistics including gross domestic product, national income, consumption, exports, and imports. Ten years of data are presented on an annual or monthly basis using tables, graphs, and charts. Sources of information include various departments of the United States government such as the Treasury Department, the Board of Governors of the Federal Reserve System, the Department of Agriculture, and the Department of Labor.

Federal Reserve Bulletin.
Washington D.C.: The Board of Governors of the Federal Reserve
  System.

Acronym: *FRB*
Format: Print

This monthly publication includes articles on the United States Banking Industry as well as the text of statements related to the banking system that were delivered before Congressional Committees. There is a section entitled "Financial and Business Statistics" which presents information on an annual, monthly, weekly, or daily basis. Statistics included cover financial markets, money stock, and United States Federal government finances.

The Financial Times
London: The Financial Times Limited

Acronym: *FTI*
Format: Print

The first section of this daily (Monday–Saturday) newspaper contains articles and special reports on international current events. The Companies & Markets section includes a variety of investment statistics such as foreign exchange rates, commodity prices, and stock market indexes and share prices for major European, North American, and selected foreign exchanges.

Government Finance Statistics Yearbook.
Washington D.C.: International Monetary Fund.

Acronym: *GSY**
Formats: Print, magnetic tape

The print version of this annual publication presents detailed statistics in tabular format for 122 countries. It covers central government revenues and expenditures, financing, lending, and debt. Data for state, local, and general governments that parallel the central government statistical tables are presented but in less detail. The magnetic tape version corresponds to the print version of the International Monetary Fund's *Government Finance Statistics Yearbook*. It contains approximately 35,000 time series for the same 122 countries, and it is updated monthly. Coverage includes central government expenditures and revenue, financing, lending, grants, and debt as well as data on government-owned financial institutions and government operations. Tables of data for state and local government operations are included for selected countries.

International Financial Statistics.
Washington D.C.: International Monetary Fund.

Acronyms: *FSY** (Yearbook)
             FSM* (Monthly)
Formats: Print, magnetic tape, CD-ROM, on-line

This is an important source of current and historical statistics for approximately 200 countries. Information on individual countries is supplemented with comparative country tables and graphs. The yearbook presents thirty years of annual statistics. The monthly issue presents information on a daily, monthly, quarterly, or annual basis. Statistics include: exchange rates, prices, production, money and banking, balance of payments, government finance, international liquidity, and national accounts. The electronic versions present more than 24,000 time series for approximately 200 countries and data is reported annually, monthly, and quarterly. The CD-ROM and magnetic tape formats are updated monthly. Updating of the on-line product depends on the provider, but data is generally updated every one to two months. Topics include: interest rates, prices and production, exchange rates, consumption, and government expenditures and revenue. The electronic versions correspond to the International Monetary Fund's *International Financial Statistics* print version which provides supplemental information such as definitions of terms and details on sources of information.

National Accounts Statistics: Main Aggregates and Detailed Tables.
New York: United Nations Statistical Division of the Department of Economic and Social Development of the United Nations.

Acronym: *UNN*
Format: Print

This two-volume, annual publication is arranged alphabetically by country. It presents statistics on 170 countries and areas of the world. Tables include information on consumption, national income, gross domestic product, gross national product, imports, and exports.

The New York Times.
New York: The New York Times.

Acronym: *NYT*
Format: Print

The first section of this daily newspaper contains articles and special reports on national and international current events. A variety of investment statistics are in a separate Business Section. These include foreign exchange rates, commodities prices, stock market indexes for both the United States and international securities markets, and stock prices for shares traded on major United States and selected foreign exchanges.

OECD Financial Statistics Monthly Part One, Section One: International Markets.

Paris: Organisation for Economic Co-Operation and Development

Acronym: *FS1*
Format: Print

   This publication presents information on selected international transactions of the countries that are members of the Organisation for Economic Co-Operation and Development. Arranged by country, it presents tables that include information on international issues of bonds (Eurobonds) by issuer and by currency of issue and information on traditional foreign bonds by issuer and by country of issue. A separate *Methodological Supplement* provides definitions of terms and explanations of calculations.

OECD Financial Statistics Monthly Part One, Section Two: Domestic Markets.

Paris: Organisation for Economic Co-Operation and Development

Acronym: *FS2**
Formats: Print, diskette

   This publication presents information on the domestic markets of the countries that are members of the Organisation for Economic Co-Operation and Development. Arranged by country, it presents tables that include information on security market issues, stock exchange turnover, stock exchange capitalization, interest rates, and consumer credit outstanding. A separate *Methodological Supplement* provides definitions of terms and explanations of calculations. The diskette version of this publication includes selected interest rates on the domestic and international markets of OECD countries. Data is available from 1960 to the present.

OECD Main Economic Indicators.

Paris: Organisation for Economic Co-Operation and Development.

Acronym: *MEI**
Formats: Print, magnetic tape, diskette

This monthly publication uses tables and graphs to present statistics on developments in OECD countries from 1960 to date. It is arranged in two parts, by country and by subject. The economic indicators presented include wages, prices, interest rates, national accounts, and industrial production. Information is presented on an annual, monthly, and quarterly basis. This source corresponds to the *OECD Main Economic Indicators* print version. It includes nearly 7,200 monthly, quarterly, and annual time series for OECD member countries. In addition, selected totals are presented for OECD-Europe, all OECD countries, the European Community, and North America. Contains information on national income, balance of payments, international liquidity, prices and wages, and industrial production.

Statistical Yearbook.

New York: United Nations Department of Economic and Social Information and Policy Analysis Statistical Division

Acronym: *UNY*
Format: Print

This yearbook, which is arranged in four parts, contains a wide range of social and economic statistics. The first part contains a worldwide and regional statistical summary; the second presents population and social statistics; the third includes statistics on economic activity; and the fourth focuses on international economic relations. Information in this yearbook is sometimes several years old. Some current statistics may be found in the United Nations *Monthly Bulletin of Statistics.*

Tradeline.

New York: IDD Information Services

Acronym: *DJN*
Format: On-line

This database contains up to fifteen years of daily pricing data for more than 120,000 United States and Canadian securities, foreign exchange rates, and a variety of security market indexes. *Tradeline* also includes historical information on approximately 25,000 international issues and more than 300 international indexes. This database is available through IDD Information Services and through the Dow Jones News/Retrieval System.

The Wall Street Journal.
Princeton, New Jersey: Dow Jones & Company.

Acronym: *WSJ*
Format: Print

Section One of this daily newspaper includes articles and special features on business and finance-related topics as well as coverage of worldwide economic, social, and political events. Section Two, Money and Investing, contains United States and international stock and bond indexes, prices for shares traded on major United States and selected international stock markets, commodities prices, and exchange rates.

World Debt Tables.
Washington, D.C.: The World Bank.

Acronym: *WTA**
Formats: Print, magnetic tape, Diskette

This annual publication is arranged in two volumes. The first includes an analysis of recent developments in international finance for 146 countries. Data is arranged in country tables that include a twenty-one-year time series. The second volume contains statistical tables for these countries arranged by topic. Data is expressed as ratios or growth rates. The diskette version does not correspond exactly to the printed version of this source but includes most of the information included in the country tables. The magnetic tape version presents approximately 20,300 annual time series for developing countries and six world regions. Coverage of selected data elements extends back to 1950. Some long-term forecasts on external debt are also included. Data is arranged by category of debt and type of creditor.

World Development Report.
Washington, D.C.: The World Bank.

Acronym: *WDR*
Format: Print

This annual publication is arranged in two parts. The first is an in-depth report on a topic of special interest in the developing countries, such as the environment or health care, that has a significant impact on public finance and public policy in the developing world. The second part, "World Development Indicators" includes economic indicators for selected periods or years. Specific data is presented for 125 developing and industrialized countries. There is also a limited data set of basic indicators for approximately sixty countries. Data is generally presented as ratios or rates of growth. Coverage varies, but some data is available from 1970 to date.

Section Two:
Country and Subject Listings

A

Affarsvariden General Index - *see* **- Sweden - Securities Markets**

Afghanis - *see* **- Afghanistan - Exchange Rates**

Afghanistan

Banking, Finance, and Money

Banking Institutions - Assets/Liabilities - *FSM*, FSY**
Monetary Authorities - Assets/Liabilities - *FSM*, FSY**
Money Supply - *FSM*, FSY*, UNY*

Exchange Rates

Currency - *Afghanis*
Cross Rates - *N/A*
Forward Exchange Rate - *N/A*
Per ECU - *N/A*
Per SDR - *FSM*, FSY**
Per U.S. Dollar - *DRF, FSM*, FSY*, UNY*

Government Finance

Debt - *N/A*
Deficit/Surplus - *N/A*
Expenditure - *N/A*
Revenue - *N/A*

Interest Rates

Bank Rate - *N/A*
Discount Rate - *N/A*
Government Bonds - *N/A*
Money Market - *N/A*
Treasury Bills - *N/A*

International Liquidity

Reserves Minus Gold - *FSM*, FSY*, UNY*
Gold - *FSM*, FSY*, UNY*

International Transactions

Balance of Payments - *BOP*, FSM*, FSY*, UNY, WDR*
Exports - *FSM*, FSY**
Imports - *FSM*, FSY**

National Accounts

Consumption
 Government - *N/A*
 Private - *N/A*
Gross Domestic Product - *WDR*
Gross National Product - *N/A*
National Income - *N/A*

Prices, Production, Employment

Consumer Credit Outstanding - *N/A*
Consumer Prices - *FSM*, FSY*, UNY, WDR*
Earning/Wages - *N/A*
Employment - *N/A*
Production - *N/A*
Wholesale/Producer Prices - *N/A*

Securities Markets - *N/A*

Aibor - *see* - Netherlands - Interest Rates

Albania

Banking, Finance, and Money

Banking Institutions - Assets/Liabilities - *N/A*
Monetary Authorities - Assets/Liabilities - *N/A*
Money Supply - *N/A*

Exchange Rates

Currency - *Lek*
Cross Rates - *N/A*
Forward Exchange Rate - *N/A*
Per ECU - *N/A*
Per SDR - *N/A*
Per U.S. Dollar - *DJN, UNY*

Interest Rates

Bank Rate - *N/A*
Discount Rate - *N/A*
Government Bonds - *N/A*
Money Market - *N/A*
Treasury Bills - *N/A*

International Liquidity

Reserves Minus Gold - *N/A*
Gold - *N/A*

International Transactions

Balance of Payments - *BOP*, WDR*
Exports - *N/A*
Imports - *N/A*

National Accounts

Consumption
  Government - *N/A*
  Private - *N/A*
Gross Domestic Product - *UNY*
Gross National Product - *N/A*
National Income - *N/A*

Prices, Production, Employment

Consumer Credit Outstanding - *N/A*
Consumer Prices - *UNY*
Earnings/Wages - *UNY*
Employment - *UNY*
Production - *N/A*
Wholesale/Producer Prices - *N/A*

Securities Markets - *N/A*

Algeria

Banking, Finance, and Money

Banking Institutions - Assets/Liabilities - *FSM*, FSY**
Monetary Authorities - Assets/Liabilities - *FSM*, FSY**
Money Supply - *FSM*, FSY*, UNY, WTA**

Exchange Rates

Currency - *Algerian Dinars*

Cross Rates - *N/A*
Forward Exchange Rate - *N/A*
Per ECU - *N/A*
Per SDR - *FSM*, FSY**
Per U.S. Dollar - *DJN, DRF, FSM*, FSY*, UNY*

Government Finance

Debt - *WTA**
Deficit/Surplus - *FSY**
Expenditure - *N/A*
Revenue - *N/A*

Interest Rates

Bank Rate - *N/A*
Discount Rate - *N/A*
Government Bonds - *N/A*
Money Market - *N/A*
Treasury Bills - *N/A*

International Liquidity

Reserves Minus Gold - *FSM*, FSY*, UNY, WTA**
Gold - *FSM*, FSY*, UNY, WTA**

International Transactions

Balance of Payments - *BOP*, FSM*, FSY*, UNY, WDR, WTA**
Exports - FSM*, *FSY*, UNN, UNY, WTA**
Imports - *FSM*, FSY*, UNN, WTA**

National Accounts

Consumption
  Government - *FSM*, FSY*, UNN, WDR, WTA**
  Private - *FSM*, FSY*, UNN, WDR, WTA**
Gross Domestic Product - *FSM*, FSY*, UNN, UNY, WDR, WTA**
Gross National Product - *UNN, WDR, WTA**
National Income - *UNN, WTA**

Prices, Production, Employment

Consumer Credit Outstanding - *N/A*
Consumer Prices - *FSM*, FSY*, UNY, WDR, WTA**
Earnings/Wages - *WDR, WTA**

Production
    Crude Petroleum - *FSM*, FSY**
    Industrial - *UNY*
    Wholesale/Producer Prices - *N/A*
  Securities Markets - *N/A*

Algerian Dinars - *see* **- Algeria**

All-Mining Price Index - *see* **- Australia - Securities Markets**

All-Ordinaries Price Index - *see* **- Australia - Securities Markets;** *see also* **- Commodities**

All Share Index - *see* **- South Africa - Securities Markets**

Aluminum - *see* **- Commodities**

American Stock Exchange (AMEX) - *see* **- United States - Securities Markets**

AMEX (American Stock Exchange) - *see* **- United States - Securities Markets**

AMEX Value Index - *see* **- United States - Securities Markets**

Amsterdam Stock Exchange - *see* **- Netherlands - Securities Markets**

Angola
  Banking, Finance, and Money
    Banking Institutions - Assets/Liabilities - *N/A*
    Monetary Authorities - Assets/Liabilities - *N/A*
    Money Supply - *N/A*
  Exchange Rates
    Currency - *Kwanza*
    Cross Rates - *N/A*
    Forward Exchange Rate - *N/A*
    Per ECU - *N/A*
    Per SDR - *N/A*
    Per U.S. Dollar - *DRF*
  International Transactions
    Balance of Payments - *BOP**
    Exports - *UNY*

Imports - *UNY*

National Accounts

Consumption
   Government - *N/A*
   Private - *N/A*
Gross Domestic Product - *UNN, UNY, WDR*
Gross National Product - *UNN*
National Income - *N/A*

Prices, Production, Employment

Consumer Credit Outstanding - *N/A*
Consumer Prices - *UNY*
Earnings/Wages - *N/A*
Employment - *UNY*
Production - *N/A*
Wholesale/Producer Prices - *N/A*

Securities Markets - *N/A*

Anguilla

Banking, Finance, and Money

Banking Institutions - Assets/Liabilities - *N/A*
Monetary Authorities - Assets/Liabilities - *N/A*
Money Supply - *N/A*

Exchange Rates

Currency - *East Caribbean Dollar*
Cross Rates - *N/A*
Forward Exchange Rate - *N/A*
Per ECU - *N/A*
Per SDR - *N/A*
Per U.S. Dollar - *N/A*

Government Finance

Debt - *N/A*
Deficit/Surplus - *N/A*
Expenditure - *N/A*
Revenue - *N/A*

Interest Rates

Bank Rate - *N/A*
Discount Rate - *N/A*

Government Bonds - *N/A*
Money Market - *N/A*
Treasury Bills - *N/A*

International Liquidity

Reserves Minus Gold - *N/A*
Gold - *N/A*

International Transactions

Balance of Payments - *N/A*
Exports - *UNN*
Imports - *UNN*

National Accounts

Consumption
  Government - *UNN*
  Private - *UNN*
Gross Domestic Product - *UNN, UNY*
Gross National Product - *N/A*
National Income - *N/A*
Wholesale/Producer Prices - *N/A*

Securities Markets - *N/A*

ANP-CBS General Index - *see* - **Netherlands - Securities Markets**

Antigua and Barbuda

Banking, Finance, and Money

Banking Institutions - Assets/Liabilities - *FSM*, FSY**
Monetary Authorities - Assets/Liabilities - *FSM*, FSY**
Money Supply - *FSM*, FSY*, WTA*, UNY*

Exchange Rates

Currency - *East Caribbean Dollar*
Cross Rates - *N/A*
Forward Exchange Rate - *N/A*
Per ECU - *N/A*
Per SDR - *FSM*, FSY**
Per U.S. Dollar - *DRF, FSM*, FSY*, UNY*

Government Finance

Debt - *N/A*
Deficit/Surplus - *N/A*

Expenditure - *N/A*
Revenue - *N/A*

Interest Rates

Bank Rate - *N/A*
Discount Rate - *N/A*
Government Bonds - *N/A*
Money Market - *N/A*
Treasury Bills - *FSM*, FSY*, UNY*

International Liquidity

Reserves Minus Gold - *FSM*, FSY*, UNY, WTA**
Gold - *N/A*

International Transactions

Balance of Payments - *BOP*, FSM*, FSY*, UNY, WTA**
Exports - *FSM*, FSY*, UNN, UNY*
Imports - *FSM*, FSY*, UNN, UNY*

National Accounts

Consumption
  Government - *FSY*, UNN*
  Private - *FSY*, UNN*
Gross Domestic Product - *FSM*, FSY*, UNN, UNY, WTA**
Gross National Product - *WTA**
National Income - *N/A*

Prices, Production, Employment

Consumer Credit Outstanding - *N/A*
Consumer Prices - *FSY*, UNY*
Earnings/Wages - *UNY*
Employment - *N/A*
Production - *N/A*
Wholesale/Producer Prices - *N/A*

Securities Markets - *N/A*

Argentina

Banking, Finance, and Money

Banking Institutions - Assets/Liabilities - *FSM*, FSY**
Monetary Authorities - Assets/Liabilities - *FSM*, FSY**
Money Supply - *FSM*, FSY*, UNY, WTA**

Exchange Rates

Currency - *Argentine Australe*
Cross Rates - *N/A*
Forward Exchange Rates - *N/A*
Per ECU - *N/A*
Per SDR - *FSY**
Per U.S. Dollar - *BAR, DJN, DRF, FSY*, FTI, NYT, WSJ*
Currency - *Peso*
Cross Rates - *N/A*
Forward Exchange Rate - *N/A*
Per ECU - *N/A*
Per SDR - *FSM**
Per U.S. Dollar - *FSM**

Government Finance

Debt - *FSM*, FSY*, GSY*, WTA**
Deficit/Surplus - *FSM*, FSY*, GSY*, WDR, WTA**
Expenditure - *GSY*, WDR*
Revenue - *GSY*, WDR*

Interest Rates

Bank Rate - *N/A*
Discount Rate - *N/A*
Government Bonds - *N/A*
Money Market - *N/A*
Treasury Bills - *N/A*

International Liquidity

Reserves Minus Gold - *FSM*, FSY*, UNY, WTA**
Gold - *FSM*, FSY*, UNY, WTA**

International Transactions

Balance of Payments - *BOP*, FSM*, FSY*, UNY, WDR, WTA**
Exports - *FSM*, FSY*, UNN, WTA**
Imports - *FSM*, FSY*, UNN, WTA**

National Accounts

Consumption
  Government - *FSM*, FSY*, UNN, WDR, WTA**
  Private - *FSM*, FSY*, UNN, WDR, WTA**

Gross Domestic Product - *FSM*, FSY*, GSY*, UNN, UNY, WDR, WTA**
Gross National Product - *FSM*, FSY*, WDR, WTA**
National Income - *N/A*

Prices, Production, Employment

Consumer Credit Outstanding - *N/A*
Consumer Prices - *FSM*, FSY*, GSY*, UNY, WDR, WTA**
Earnings/Wages - *UNY, WDR, WTA**
Employment - *WTA**
Production
  Manufacturing - *FSM*, FSY*, UNN, UNY*
  Crude Petroleum - *FSM*, FSY**
  Industrial - *UNY*
Wholesale/Producer Prices - *FSM*, FSY*, UNY*

Securities Markets

Stock Exchange - *Buenos Aires Stock Exchange*
Index - *Buenos Aires Stock Exchange Share Price Index*
Foreign Bonds
  Value of bonds issued - *FS1*
Shares
  Price Index - *BAR*
  Prices - Selected Issues - *NYT*

Argentine Australe - *see* - Argentina - Exchange Rates

Aruba

Banking, Finance, and Money

Banking Institutions - Assets/Liabilities - *FSM*, FSY**
Monetary Authorities - Assets/Liabilities - *FSM*, FSY**
Money Supply - *FSM*, FSY*, UNY*

Exchange Rates

Currency - *Florin*
Cross Rates - *N/A*
Forward Exchange Rate - *N/A*
Per ECU - *N/A*
Per SDR - *FSY**
Per U.S. Dollar - *DRF, FSM*, FSY**

Government Finance

Debt - *N/A*
Deficit/Surplus - *N/A*
Expenditure - *N/A*
Revenue - *N/A*

Interest Rates

Bank Rate - *N/A*
Discount Rate - *FSM*, FSY*, UNY*
Government Bonds - *N/A*
Money Market - *N/A*
Treasury Bills - *N/A*

International Liquidity

Reserves Minus Gold - *FSM*, FSY*, UNY*
Gold - *FSM*, FSY*, UNY*

International Transactions

Balance of Payments - *BOP*, FSM*, FSY*, UNY*
Exports - *FSM*, FSY*, UNY*
Imports - *FSM*, FSY*, UNY*

Prices, Production, Employment

Consumer Credit Outstanding - *N/A*
Consumer Prices - *FSM*, FSY*, UNY*
Earnings/Wages - *N/A*
Employment - *N/A*
Production - *N/A*
Wholesale/Producer Prices - *N/A*

Securities Markets - *N/A*

ASE (Athens Stock Exchange) - *see* **- Greece - Securities Markets**

ASX (Australian Stock Exchange) - *see* **- Australia - Securities Markets**

Athens Stock Exchange - *see* **- Greece - Securities Markets**

Athens Stock Exchange Share Price Index - *see* **- Greece - Securities Markets**

Australe - *see* **- Argentina - Exchange Rates**

Australia

Banking, Finance, and Money

Banking Institutions - Assets/Liabilities - *FSM*, FSY**
Monetary Authorities - Assets/Liabilities - *FSM*, FSY**
Money Supply - *FSM*, FSY*, UNY, WDR, WTA**

Exchange Rates

Currency - *Australian Dollar*
Cross Rates - *N/A*
Currency Futures - *BAR*
Currency Options - *BAR*
Forward Exchange Rate - *DRF*
Per ECU - *N/A*
Per SDR - *FSM*, FSY**
Per U.S. Dollar - *BAR, DJN, DRF, FRB, FSM*, FSY*, FTI, MEI*, NYT, UNY, WSJ*

Government Finance

Debt - *FSM*, FSY*, GSY*, WTA**
Deficit/Surplus - *FSM*, FSY*, GSY*, WDR, WTA**
Expenditure - *GSY*, WDR, WTA**
Revenue - *GSY*, WDR, WTA**

Interest Rates

Bank Rate - *N/A*
Discount Rate - *FSM*, FSY*, UNY*
Government Bonds - *BAR, DRF, FS1, FSM*, FSY*, FTI, UNY*
Money Market - *FSM*, FSY**
Treasury Bills - *FS1, FSM*, FSY*, UNY*

International Liquidity

Reserves Minus Gold - *FSM*, FSY*, MEI*, UNY, WTA**
Gold - *FSM*, FSY*, UNY, WTA**

International Transactions

Balance of Payments - *BOP*, FSM*, FSY*, MEI*, UNY, WDR, WTA**
Exports - *FSM*, FSY*, MEI*, UNN, UNY, WTA**
Imports - *FSM*, FSY*, MEI*, UNN, UNY, WTA**

National Accounts

Consumption
  Government - *FSM*, FSY*, GSY*, UNN, WDR, WTA**
  Private - *FSM*, FSY*, UNN, WDR, WTA**
  Gross Domestic Product - *FSM*, FS1*, GSY*, MEI*, UNN, UNY, WDR, WTA**
  Gross National Product - *FSM*, FSY*, UNN, WDR, WTA**
  National Income - *FSM*, FSY*, UNN, WTA**

Prices, Production, Employment

Consumer Credit Outstanding - *FS2**
Consumer Prices - *FSM*, FSY*, FS1, MEI*, UNY, WTA**
Earnings/Wages - *FSM*, FSY*, MEI*, UNY, WDR, WTA**
Employment - *FSM*, FSY*, MEI*, UNY, WTA**
Production
  Manufacturing - *FSM*, FSY*, MEI*, UNN, UNY*
  Industrial - *MEI*, UNY*
Wholesale/Producer Prices - *FSM*, GSY*, MEI*, UNY*

Securities Markets

Stock Exchange - *Australian Stock Exchange (Sydney)*
Indexes
  All-Mining Price Index
  All-Ordinaries Price Index
Bonds
  Yield - *FS2**
Eurobonds
  Value of bonds issued - *FS1*
Foreign Bonds
  Value of bonds issued - *FS1*
Shares
  Dividend yield - *FS1*
  Last day of month - *MEI**
  Price/Earnings Ratio - *FS1, FS2**
  Price Indexes
    All-Mining - FTI
    All-Ordinaries - BAR, DJN, DRI, FS1, FS2*, FSM*, FSY*, MEI,* NYT, UNY, WSJ
  Prices - Selected Issues - *BAR, FTI, NYT, WSJ*
  Yield - *FS2**

Stock Exchange Capitalization - *FS2**

Australian Dollar - *see* - **Australia** - **Exchange Rates;** *see also* **Commodities**

Australian Stock Exchange - *see* - **Australia** - **Securities Markets**

Australian Stock Exchange All-Mining Price Index - *see* - **Australia** - **Securities Markets**

Australian Stock Exchange All-Ordinaries Price Index - *see* - **Australia** - **Securities Markets**

Austria

Banking, Finance, and Money

Banking Institutions - Assets/Liabilities - *FSM*, FSY**
Monetary Authorities - Assets/Liabilities - *FSM*, FSY**
Money Supply - *FSM*, FSY*, MEI*, UNY, WTA**

Exchange Rates

Currency - *Austrian Schilling*
Cross Rates - *N/A*
Forward Exchange Rate - *FTI*
Per ECU - *FTI*
Per SDR - *FSM*, FSY*, FTI*
Per U.S. Dollar - *BAR, DJN, DRF, FRB, FSM*, FSY*, MEI*, NYT, UNY, WSJ*

Government Finance

Debt - *FSM*, FSY*, GSY**
Deficit/Surplus - *FSM*, FSY*, GSY*, WDR, WTA**
Expenditure - *GSY*, WDR, WTA**
Revenue - *GSY*, WDR, WTA**

Interest Rates

Bank Rate - *N/A*
Discount Rate - *FRB, FSM*, FSY*, FS1, FS2*, MEI*, UNY*
Government Bonds - *FSM*, FSY*, UNY*
Money Market - *FSM*, FSY**
Treasury Bills - *N/A*
Vibor - *FS1, MEI**

International Liquidity

Reserves Minus Gold - *FSM*, MEI*, UNY, WTA**
Gold - *FSM*, UNY, WTA**

International Transactions

Balance of Payments - *BOP*, FSM*, FSY*, MEI*, UNN, UNY, WTA**
Exports - *FSM*, FSY*, MEI*, UNN, UNY, WTA**
Imports - *FSM*, FSY*, MEI*, UNN, UNY, WTA**

National Accounts

Consumption
Government - *FSM*, FSY*, UNN, WDR, WTA**
Private - *FSM*, FSY*, UNN, WDR, WTA**
Gross Domestic Product - *FSM*, FSY*, GSY*, UNN, UNY, WDR, WTA**
Gross National Product - *FSM*, FSY*, UNN, WDR, WTA**
National Income - *FSM*, FSY*, UNN, WTA**

Prices, Production, Employment

Consumer Credit Outstanding - *FS2**
Consumer Prices - *FSM*, FSY*, FS1, GSY*, MEI*, UNY, WDR, WTA**
Earnings/Wages - *FSM*, FSY*, MEI*, UNY, WDR, WTA**
Employment - *FSM*, FSY*, MEI*, UNY, WTA**
Production
Industrial - *FSM*, FSY*, MEI*, UNY*
Manufacturing - *UNN*
Wholesale/Producer Prices - *FSM*, FSY*, MEI*, UNY*

Securities Markets

Stock Exchange - *Weiner Borse* (Vienna Stock Exchange)
Index - *Credit Aktien* (CA Index)
Bonds
Yield - *FS2**
Eurobonds
Value of bonds issued - *FS1*
Foreign Bonds
Value of bonds issued - *FS1*
Shares
Last day of month - *FS1*

Price/Earnings Ratio - *FS1, FS2**
Price Index - *BAR, DRI, FS1, FS2*, FSM*, FSY*, FTI, MEI*,
UNY*
Prices - Selected Issues - *FTI*
Stock Exchange Capitalization - *FS2**

Austrian Schilling - *see* **- Austria - Exchange Rates**

B

Bahamas

Banking, Finance, and Money

Banking Institutions - Assets/Liabilities - *FSM*, FSY**
Monetary Authorities - Assets/Liabilities - *FSM*, FSY**
Money Supply - *FSM*, FSY*, UNY, WTA**

Exchange Rates

Currency - *Bahamian Dollars*
Cross Rates - *N/A*
Forward Exchange Rate - *N/A*
Per ECU - *N/A*
Per SDR - *FSM*, FSY**
Per U.S. Dollar - *FSM*, FSY*, UNY*

Government Finance

Debt - *FSM*, FSY*, GSY**
Deficit/Surplus - *FSM*, FSY*, GSY*, WTA**
Expenditure - *GSY*, WTA**
Revenue - *GSY*, WTA**

Interest Rates

Bank Rate - *FSM*, FSY**
Discount Rate - *UNY*
Government Bonds - *N/A*
Money Market - *N/A*
Treasury Bills - *FSM*, FSY*, UNY*

International Liquidity

Reserves Minus Gold - *FSM*, FSY*, UNY, WTA**
Gold - *FSM**

International Transactions

Balance of Payments - *BOP*, FSM*, FSY*, UNY, WTA**
Exports - *FSM*, FSY*, UNN, UNY, WTA**
Imports - *FSM*, FSY*, UNN, UNY, WTA**

National Accounts

Consumption
  Government - *FSM*, UNN, WTA**
  Private - *FSY*, UNN, WTA**
Gross Domestic Product - *FSM*, GSY*, UNN, UNY, WTA**
Gross National Product - *UNN, WTA**
National Income - *UNN, WTA**

Prices, Production, Employment

Consumer Credit Outstanding - *N/A*
Consumer Prices - *FSM*, FSY*, GSY*, UNY, WTA**
Earnings/Wages - *N/A*
Employment - *N/A*
Production - *N/A*
Wholesale/Producer Prices - *N/A*

Securities Markets - *N/A*

Bahamian Dollar - *see* - Bahamas - Exchange Rates

Bahrain

Banking, Finance, and Money

Banking Institutions - Assets/Liabilities - *FSM*, FSY**
Monetary Authorities - Assets/Liabilities - *FSM*, FSY**
Money Supply - *FSM*, FSY*, UNY, WTA**

Exchange Rates

Currency - *Bahrain Dinar*
Cross Rates - *N/A*
Forward Exchange Rate - *N/A*
Per ECU - *N/A*
Per SDR - *FSY**
Per U.S. Dollar - *BAR, DJN, DRF, FSY*, UNY, WSJ*

Government Finance

Debt - *FSM*, FSY*, GSY**
Deficit/Surplus - *FSM*, FSY*, GSY*, WTA**

Expenditure - *GSY*, WTA**
Revenue - *GSY*, WTA**

Interest Rates

Bank Rate - *N/A*
Discount Rate - *N/A*
Government Bonds - *N/A*
Money Market - *FSM*, FSY**
Treasury Bills - *FSM*, FSY*, UNY*

International Liquidity

Reserves Minus Gold - *FSM*, FSY*, UNY, WTA**
Gold - *FSM*, FSY*, UNY, WTA**

International Transactions

Balance of Payments - *BOP*, FSM*, FSY*, UNY, WTA**
Exports - *FSM*, FSY*, UNN, UNY, WTA**
Imports - *FSM*, FSY*, UNN, UNY, WTA**

National Accounts

Consumption
  Government - *FSM*, FSY*, UNN, WTA**
  Private - *FSM*, FSY*, UNN, WTA**
Gross Domestic Product - *FSM*, FSY*, GSY*, UNN, UNY, WTA**
Gross National Product - *FSM*, FSY*, UNN, WTA**
National Income - *FSY*, UNN, WTA**

Prices, Production, Employment

Consumer Credit Outstanding - *N/A*
Consumer Prices - *FSM*, FSY*, GSY*, UNY, WTA**
Earnings/Wages - *N/A*
Employment - *UNY*
Production
  Crude Petroleum - *FSM*, FSY**
  Refined Petroleum - *FSM*, FSY**
Wholesale/Producer Prices - *N/A*

Securities Markets - *N/A*

Bahrain Dinar - *see* - Bahrain - Exchange Rates

Baht - *see* - Thailand - Exchange Rates

Balance of Payments - *see* - **Individual Countries** - **International Transactions**

Balboa - *see* - **Panama** - **Exchange Rates**

Bangkok SET Index - *see* - **Thailand** - **Securities Markets**

Bangladesh

Banking, Finance, and Money

Banking Institutions - Assets/Liabilities - *FSM*, FSY**
Monetary Authorities - Assets/Liabilities - *FSM*, FSY**
Money Supply - *FSM*, FSY*, UNY, WTA**

Exchange Rates

Currency - *Bangladesh Taxa*
Cross Rates - *N/A*
Forward Exchange Rate - *N/A*
Per ECU - *N/A*
Per SDR - *FSM*, FSY**
Per U.S. Dollar - *FSM*, FSY*, UNY*

Government Finance

Debt - *WTA**
Deficit/Surplus - FSY*, GSY*, WDR, WTA*
Expenditure - *GSY*, WDR*
Revenue - GSY*, WDR, WTA*

Interest Rates

Bank Rate - *N/A*
Discount Rate - *FSY*, FSM*, UNY*
Government Bonds - *N/A*
Money Market - *N/A*
Treasury Bills - *N/A*

International Liquidity

Reserves Minus Gold - *FSM*, FSY*, UNY, WTA**
Gold - FSM*, FSY*, UNY, WTA*

International Transactions

Balance of Payments - *BOP*, FSM*, FSY*, FS1, UNY, WTA**
Exports - *FSM*, FSY*, UNY, WTA**
Imports - *FSM*, FSY*, UNY, WTA**

National Accounts

Consumption
  Government - *UNN, WTA**
  Private - *UNN, WDR*
Gross Domestic Product - *FSM*, FSY*, GSY*, UNN, WDR, WTA**
Gross National Product - *WDR, WTA**
National Income - *WTA**

Prices, Production, Employment

Consumer Credit Outstanding - *N/A*
Consumer Prices - *FSM*, FSY*, GSY*, UNY, WDR, WTA**
Earnings/Wages - *WDR, WTA**
Employment - *WTA**
Production
  Industrial - *FSM*, FSY*, UNY*
Wholesale/Producer Prices - *UNY*

Securities Markets - *N/A*

Bangladesh Taxa - *see* - **Bangladesh - Exchange Rates**

Bank Rate - *see* - **Individual Countries - Interest Rates**

Banking Institutions - Assets/Liabilities - *see* - **Individual Countries - Banking, Finance, and Money**

Barbados

Banking, Finance, and Money

Banking Institutions - Assets/Liabilities - *FSM*, FSY**
Monetary Authorities - Assets/Liabilities - *FSM*, FSY**
Money Supply - *FSM*, FSY*, UNY, WTA**

Exchange Rates

Currency - *Barbados Dollar*
Cross Rates - *N/A*
Forward Exchange Rate - *N/A*
Per ECU - *N/A*
Per SDR - *FSM*, FSY**
Per U.S. Dollar - *DJN, DRF, FSM*, FSY*, UNY*

Government Finance

Debt - *FSM*, FSY*, GSY**

Deficit/Surplus - *FSM*, FSY*, GSY*, WTA**
Expenditure - *GSY*, WTA**
Revenue - *GSY*, WTA**

Interest Rates

Bank Rate - *FSM*, FSY**
Discount Rate - *UNY*
Government Bonds - *N/A*
Money Market - *N/A*
Treasury Bills - *FSM*, FSY*, UNY*

International Liquidity

Reserves Minus Gold - *FSM*, FSY*, UNY, WTA**
Gold - *FSM*, FSY*, UNY, WTA**

International Transactions

Balance of Payments - *BOP*, FSM*, FSY*, UNY, WTA**
Exports - *FSM*, FSY*, UNN, UNY, WTA**
Imports - *FSM*, FSY*, UNN, UNY, WTA**

National Accounts

Consumption
  Government - *FSM*, FSY*, UNN*
  Private - *FSM*, FSY*, UNN*
Gross Domestic Product - *FSM*, FSY*, GSY*, UNN, UNY, WTA**
Gross National Product - *FSY*, WTA**
National Income - *N/A*

Prices, Production, Employment

Consumer Credit Outstanding - *N/A*
Consumer Prices - *FSM*, FSY*, GSY*, WTA**
Earnings/Wages - *UNY, WTA**
Employment - *UNY, WTA**
Production
  Industrial - *FSM*, FSY*, UNY*
Wholesale/Producer Prices - *N/A*

Securities Markets - *N/A*

Barbados Dollar - *see* - **Barbados - Exchange Rates**

BCI (Banca Commerciale Italiana) Index - *see* - **Italy - Securities Markets**

Bel 20 - *see* **- Belgium - Securities Markets**

Belgian Franc - *see* **- Belgium - Exchange Rates**

Belgium

Banking, Finance, and Money

Banking Institutions - Assets/Liabilities - *FSM**, *FSY**
Monetary Authorities - Assets/Liabilities - *FSM**, *FSY**
Money Supply - *FSM**, *FSY**, *UNY, WDR*

Exchange Rates

Currency - *Belgian Francs*
Cross Rates - *FTI*
Forward Exchange Rate - *DRF, FTI, MEI**
Per ECU - *FSM**, *FSY**, *FTI*
Per SDR - *FSY**, *FTI*
Per U.S. Dollar - *BAR, DJN, DRF, FRB, FSM**, *FSY**, *MEI**, *NYT, UNY, WSJ*

Government Finance

Debt - *FSM**, *FSY**, *GSY**
Deficit/Surplus - *FSM**, *FSY**, *GSY**, *WDR, WTA**
Expenditure - *GSY**, *WDR, WTA**
Revenue - *GSY**, *WDR, WTA**

Interest Rates

Bank Rate - *MEI**
Discount Rate - DRF, FRB, FSM*, FSY*, FS2*, UNY
Government Bonds - *BAR, DRF, FSM**, *FSY**, *FS1, FTI, MEI**, *UNY*
Money Market - *FSM**, *FSY**
Prime Rate - *DRF*
Treasury Bills - *DRF, FSY**, *FS1, UNY*

International Liquidity

Reserves Minus Gold - *FSM**, *FSY**, *MEI**, *UNY*
Gold - FSM*, FSY*, UNY, WTA*

International Transactions

Balance of Payments - *BOP**, *FSM**, *FSY**, *MEI**, *UNY, WDR, WTA**
Exports - *FSM**, *FSY**, *MEI**, *UNN, UNY, WTA**

Imports - *FSM*, FSY*, MEI*, UNN, UNY, WTA**

National Accounts

Consumption
   Government - *FSM*, FSY*, UNN, UNY, WDR, WTA**
   Private - *FSM*, FSY*, UNN, WDR, WTA**
Gross Domestic Product - *FSM*, FSY*, GSY*, UNN, UNY, WDR WTA**
Gross National Product - *FSM*, FSY*, UNN, WDR, WTA**
National Income - *FSM*, FSY*, UNN, WTA**

Prices, Production, Employment

Consumer Credit Outstanding - *FS2**
Consumer Prices - *FSM*, FSY, FS1, GSY*, MEI*, UNY, WTA**
Earnings/Wages - *FSM*, FSY*, MEI*, UNY, WDR, WTA**
Employment - *UNY, WTA**
Production
   Industrial - *FSM*, FSY*, MEI*, UNY*
   Manufacturing - *UNN*
Wholesale/Producer Prices - *FSM*, FSY*, MEI*, UNY*

Securities Markets

Stock Exchange - *Bourse de Bruxelles (Brussels Stock Exchange)*
Index - *Bel 20*
Bonds
   Yield - *FS2**
Eurobonds
   Value of bonds issued - *FS1*
Foreign Bonds
   Value of bonds issued - *FS1*
Shares
   Price/Earnings Ratio - *FS1, FS2**
   Price Index - *BAR, FS2*, FS1, FSY*, FSM*, FTI, DJN, DRI, NYT, UNY, WSJ*
   Prices - Selected Issues - *BAR, FTI, NYT, WSJ*
   Yield - *FS1, FS2**
Stock Exchange Capitalization - *FS2**

Belize

Banking, Finance, and Money

Banking Institutions - Assets/Liabilities - *FSM*, FSY**
Monetary Authorities - Assets/Liabilities - *FSM*, FSY**
Money Supply - *FSM*, FSY*, UNY, WTA**

Exchange Rates

Currency - *Belize Dollar*
Cross Rates - *N/A*
Forward Exchange Rate - *N/A*
Per ECU - *N/A*
Per SDR - *FSM*, FSY**
Per U.S. Dollar - *DRF, FSM*, FSY*, UNY*

Government Finance

Debt - *FSM*, FSY*, GSY*, WTA**
Deficit/Surplus - *FSM*, FSY*, GSY*, WTA**
Expenditure - *GSY*, WTA**
Revenue - *GSY*, WTA**

Interest Rates

Bank Rate - *N/A*
Discount Rate - *FSM*, FSY*, UNY*
Government Bonds - *FSY**
Money Market - *FSY**
Treasury Bills - *FSM*, FSY*, UNY*

International Liquidity

Reserves Minus Gold - *FSM*, FSY*, UNY, WTA**
Gold - *FSM**

International Transactions

Balance of Payments - *BOP*, FSM*, FSY*, UNY, WTA**
Exports - *FSM*, FSY*, UNN, UNY, WTA**
Imports - *FSM*, FSY*, UNN, UNY, WTA**

National Accounts

Consumption
  Government - *FSM*, FSY*, UNN*
  Private - *FSM*, FSY*, UNN*
Gross Domestic Product - *FSM*, FSY*, GSY*, UNN, WTA**
Gross National Product - *UNN, WTA**

National Income - *UNN, WTA**

Prices, Production, Employment

Consumer Credit Outstanding - *N/A*
Consumer Prices - *FSM*, FSY*, GSY*, UNY, WTA**
Earnings/Wages - *N/A*
Employment - *N/A*
Production - *N/A*
Wholesale/Producer Prices - *N/A*

Securities Markets - *N/A*

Belize Dollar - *see* - Belize - Exchange Rates

Benin

Banking, Finance, and Money

Banking Institutions - Assets/Liabilities - *FSM*, FSY**
Monetary Authorities - Assets/Liabilities - *FSM*, FSY**
Money Supply - *FSM*, FSY*, UNY, WTA**

Exchange Rates

Currency - *CFA Franc*
Cross Rates - *N/A*
Forward Exchange Rate - *N/A*
Per ECU - *N/A*
Per SDR - *FSM*, FSY**
Per U.S. Dollar - *DRF, FSM*, FSY*, UNY*

Government Finance

Debt - *WTA**
Deficit/Surplus - *FSY*, GSY*, WTA**
Expenditure - *WTA**
Revenue - *WTA**

Interest Rates

Bank Rate - *N/A*
Discount Rate - *FSM*, FSY*, UNY*
Government Bonds - *FSY**
Money Market - *FSM*, FSY**
Treasury Bills - *FSY**

International Liquidity

Reserves Minus Gold - *FSM*, FSY*, UNY, WTA**

Gold - *FSM*, FSY*, UNY, WTA**

International Transactions

Balance of Payments - *BOP*, FSM*, FSY*, UNY, WDR, WTA**

Exports - *FSM*, FSY*, UNN, UNY, WTA**

Imports - *FSM*, FSY*, UNN, UNY, WTA**

National Accounts

Consumption
Government - *FSM*, FSY*, UNN, WDR, WTA**
Private - *FSM*, FSY*, UNN, WDR, WTA**
Gross Domestic Product - *FSM*, FSY*, GSY*, UNY, WDR, WTA**
Gross National Product - *FSM*, FSY*, UNN, WDR, WTA**
National Income - *FSM*, FSY*, UNN, WTA**

Prices, Production, Employment

Consumer Credit Outstanding - *N/A*
Consumer Prices - *WTA**
Earnings/Wages - *WTA**
Employment - *UNY, WTA**
Production
Manufacturing - *UNN*
Wholesale/Producer Prices - *N/A*

Securities Markets - *N/A*

Bhutan

Banking, Finance, and Money

Banking Institutions - Assets/Liabilities - *FSM**
Monetary Authorities - Assets/Liabilities - *FSM**
Money Supply - *FSM*, UNY*

Exchange Rates

Currency - *Bhutanese Ngultrum*
Cross Rates - *N/A*
Forward Exchange Rate - *N/A*
Per ECU - *N/A*
Per SDR - *FSM**
Per U.S. Dollar - *DRF, FSM*, UNY*

Government Finance

Debt - *FSM*, GSY*, WTA**
Deficit/Surplus - *FSM*, GSY*, WDR, WTA**
Expenditure - *GSY*, WDR, WTA**
Revenue - *GSY*, WDR, WTA**

Interest Rates

Bank Rate - *N/A*
Discount Rate - *N/A*
Government Bonds - *N/A*
Money Market - *N/A*
Treasury Bills - *N/A*

International Liquidity

Reserves Minus Gold - *FSM*, UNY, WTA**
Gold - *N/A*

International Transactions

Balance of Payments - *MEI*, UNY, WTA**
Exports - *FSM*, UNN, WTA**
Imports - *FSM*, UNN, WTA**

National Accounts

Consumption
  Government - *FSM*, UNN*
  Private - *FSM*, UNN*
Gross Domestic Product - *FSM*, GSY*, UNN, UNY, WDR, WTA**
Gross National Product - *FSM*, UNN, WDR, WTA**
National Income - *UNN*

Prices, Production, Employment

Consumer Credit Outstanding - *N/A*
Consumer Prices - *FSM*, GSY*, WDR, WTA**
Earnings/Wages - *N/A*
Employment - *N/A*
Production - *N/A*
Wholesale/Producer Prices - *N/A*

Securities Markets - *N/A*

Bhutanese Ngultrum - *see* - **Bhutan - Exchange Rates**

Bipkwele - *see* - **Equatorial Guinea - Exchange Rates**

Birr - *see* - **Ethopia - Exchange Rates**

BMV Index (Bolsa Mexicana de Valores Index) - *see* - **Mexico - Securities Markets**

Bolivar - *see* - **Venezuela - Exchange Rates**

Bolivia

Banking, Finance, and Money

Banking Institutions - Assets/Liabilities - *FSM*, FSY**
Monetary Authorities - Assets/Liabilities - *FSM*, FSY**
Money Supply - *FSM*, FSY*, UNY, WTA**

Exchange Rates

Currency - *Boliviano*
Cross Rates - *N/A*
Forward Exchange Rate - *N/A*
Per ECU - *N/A*
Per SDR - *FSM*, FSY**
Per U.S. Dollar - *DJN, DRF, FSM*, FSY*, UNY*

Government Finance

Debt - *FSM*, WTA**
Deficit/Surplus - *FSM*, FSY*, GSY*, WDR, WTA**
Expenditure - *GSY*, WDR, WTA**
Revenue - *GSY*, WDR, WTA**

Interest Rates

Bank Rate - *N/A*
Discount Rate - *FSY**
Government Bonds - *N/A*
Money Market - *N/A*
Treasury Bills - *N/A*

International Liquidity

Reserves Minus Gold - *FSM*, UNY, WTA**
Gold - FSM*, WTA*

International Transactions

Balance of Payments - *BOP*, FSM*, FSY*, UNY, WDR, WTA**

Exports - *FSM*, FSY*, UNN, WTA**
Imports - *FSM*, FSY*, UNN, WTA**

National Accounts

Consumption
  Government - FSM*, FSY*, UNN, WDR, WTA*
  Private - FSM*, FSY*, UNN, WDR, WTA*
  Gross Domestic Product - *FSM*, FSY*, GSY*, UNN, WDR, WTA**
  Gross National Product - *FSY*, UNN, WDR, WTA**
  National Income - *FSY*, UNN, WTA**

Prices, Production, Employment

Consumer Credit Outstanding - *N/A*
Consumer Prices - *FSM*, FSY*, GSY*, UNY, WDR, WTA**
Earnings/Wages - *WDR, WTA**
Employment - *UNY, WTA**
Production
  Crude Petroleum - *FSM*, FSY*, UNN*
  Industry - *UNY*
  Manufacturing - *UNN, UNY*
Wholesale/Producer Prices - *N/A*

Securities Markets - *N/A*

Boliviana - *see* - **Bolivia - Exchange Rates**

Bolsa de Bogotá - *see* - **Colombia - Securities Markets**

Bolsa de Comercio de Madrid (Madrid Stock Exchange) - *see* - **Spain - Securities Markets**

Bolsa de Comercio de Santiago, Bolsa de Valores (Santiago Stock Exchange) - *see* - **Chile - Securities Markets**

Bolsa de Medellín (Medellín Stock Exchange) - *see* - **Colombia - Securities Markets**

Bolsa Mexicana de Valores (Mexican Stock Exchange) - *see* - **Mexico - Securities Markets**

Bolsa Nacional de Valores - *see* - **Costa Rica - Securities Markets**

Bombay Stock Exchange - *see* - **India - Securities Markets**

Bonds - *see* - **Individual Countries - Securities Markets**

Borsa Valori di Milano (Milan Stock Exchange) - *see* - **Italy - Securities Markets**

Boston Stock Exchange - *see* - **United States - Securities Markets**

Botswana

Banking, Finance, and Money

Banking Institutions - Assets/Liabilities - *FSM*, FSY**
Monetary Authorities - Assets/Liabilities - *FSM*, FSY**
Money Supply - *FSM*, FSY*, UNY, WTA**

Exchange Rates

Currency - *Botswana Pula*
Cross Rates - *N/A*
Forward Exchange Rate - *N/A*
Per ECU - *N/A*
Per SDR - *FSM*, FSY**
Per U.S. Dollar - *DJN, DRF, FSM*, FSY*, UNY*

Government Finance

Debt - *FSM*, FSY*, GSY*, WTA**
Deficit/Surplus - *FSM*, FSY*, GSY*, WDR, WTA**
Expenditure - *GSY*, WDR, WTA**
Revenue - *GSY*, WDR, WTA**

Interest Rates

Bank Rate - *FSM*, FSY**
Discount Rate - *UNY*
Government Bonds - *N/A*
Money Market - *N/A*
Treasury Bills - *N/A*

International Liquidity

Reserves Minus Gold - *FSM*, FSY*, UNY, WTA**
Gold - *N/A*

International Transactions

Balance of Payments - *BOP*, FSM*, FSY*, UNY, WDR, WTA**
Exports - *FSM*, FSY*, UNN, WTA**
Imports - *FSM*, FSY*, UNN, WTA**

National Accounts

Consumption
Government - *FSM*, FSY*, UNN, WDR, WTA**
Private - *FSM*, FSY*, UNN, WDR, WTA**
Gross Domestic Product - FSM*, FSY*, GSY*, UNN, UNY, WDR, WTA*
Gross National Product - *FSY*, UNN, WDR, WTA**
National Income - *FSY*, UNN, WTA**

Prices, Production, Employment

Consumer Credit Outstanding - *N/A*
Consumer Prices - *FSM*, FSY*, GSY*, UNY, WDR, WTA**
Earnings/Wages - *UNN, WDR, WTA**
Employment - *UNY, WTA**
Production
Manufacturing - *UNN*
Mining - *FSM*, FSY*, UNN*
Wholesale/Producer Prices - *N/A*

Securities Markets - *N/A*

Botswana Pula - *see* - **Botswana - Exchange Rates**

Bourse de Bruxelles (Brussels Stock Exchange) - *see* - **Belgium - Securities Markets**

Bourse de Luxembourg SA - *see* - **Luxembourg - Securities Markets**

Bourse de Montréal (Montreal Stock Exchange) - *see* - **Canada - Securities Markets**

Brazil

Banking, Finance, and Money

Banking Institutions - Assets/Liabilities - *FSM*, FSY**
Monetary Authorities - Assets/Liabilities - *FSM*, FSY**
Money Supply - *FSM*, FSY*, UNY, WTA**

Exchange Rates

Currency - *Cruziero Real*
Cross Rates - *N/A*
Forward Exchange Rate - *N/A*
Per ECU - *N/A*

Per SDR - *FSY**
Per U.S. Dollar - *DRF, FTI, FSM*, FSY*, WSJ*
Currency - *Brazilian Cruzeiro*
Cross Rates - *N/A*
Forward Exchange Rate - *N/A*
Per ECU - *N/A*
Per SDR - *N/A*
Per U.S. Dollar - *BAR, DJN, DRF, FSM*, NYT, UNY*

Government Finance

Debt - *FSY*, GSY*, WTA**
Deficit/Surplus - *FSM*, FSY*, GSY*, WDR, WTA**
Expenditure - *GSY*, WDR, WTA**
Revenue - *GSY*, WTA**

Interest Rates

Bank Rate - *FSM*, FSY**
Discount Rate - *UNY*
Government Bonds - *N/A*
Money Market - *N/A*
Treasury Bills - *FSM*, FSY*, UNY*

International Liquidity

Reserves Minus Gold - *FSM*, FSY*, UNY, WTA**
Gold - *FSM*, FSY*, UNY, WTA**

International Transactions

Balance of Payments - *BOP*, FSM*, FSY*, UNY, WDR*
Exports - *FSM*, FSY*, UNN*
Imports - *FSM*, FSY*, UNN*

National Accounts

Consumption
  Government - *FSM*, FSY*, UNN, WDR, WTA**
  Private - *FSM*, FSY*, UNN, WDR*
Gross Domestic Product - *FSM*, FS1, GSY*, UNN, UNY, WDR, WTA**
Gross National Product - *FSM*, FSY*, GSY*, UNN, WDR, WTA**
National Income - *FSY*, UNN, WTA**

Prices, Production, Employment

Consumer Credit Outstanding - *N/A*
Consumer Prices - *FSM*, FSY*, GSY*, UNY, WTA**
Earnings/Wages - *UNY, WDR, WTA**
Employment - *UNY, WTA**
Production
  Industrial - *UNY*
  Manufacturing - *UNY*
  Wholesale/Producer Prices - *FSM*, FSY*, UNY*

Securities Markets - *N/A*

Brazilian Cruzeiro Real - *see* - Brazil - Exchange Rates

Brazilian Cruzeiro - *see* - Brazil - Exchange Rates

British Pound - *see* - United Kingdom - Exchange Rates - Pound Sterling

Brunei Darussalam

Banking, Finance, and Money

Banking Institutions - Assets/Liabilities - *N/A*
Monetary Authorities - Assets/Liabilities - *N/A*
Money Supply - *N/A*

Exchange Rates

Currency - *Brunei Dollar*
Cross Rates - *N/A*
Forward Exchange Rate - *N/A*
Per SDR - *N/A*
Per U.S. Dollar - *DJN, DRF*

Government Finance

Debt - *N/A*
Deficit/Surplus - *N/A*
Expenditure - *N/A*
Revenue - *N/A*

Interest Rates

Bank Rate - *N/A*
Discount Rate - *N/A*
Government Bonds - *N/A*
Money Market - *N/A*

Treasury Bills - *N/A*

International Liquidity

Reserves Minus Gold - *N/A*
Gold - *N/A*

International Transactions

Balance of Payments - *N/A*
Exports - *UNY*
Imports - *UNY*

National Accounts

Consumption
  Government - *N/A*
  Private - *N/A*
Gross Domestic Product - *UNY*
Gross National Product - *UNN*
National Income - *N/A*

Prices, Production, Employment

Consumer Credit Outstanding - *N/A*
Consumer Prices - *UNY*
Earnings/Wages - *N/A*
Employment - *UNY*
Production - *N/A*
Wholesale/Producer Prices - *N/A*

Securities Markets - *N/A*

Brunei Dollar - *see* - **Brunei Darussalam - Exchange Rates**

Brussels Stock Exchange - *see* - **Belgium - Securities Markets**

Budapest Stock Exchange - *see* - **Hungary - Securities Markets**

Budapesti Ertekpapir Tozsde (Budapest Stock Exchange) - *see* - **Hungary - Securities Markets**

Buenos Aires Stock Exchange - *see* - **Argentina - Securities Markets**

Buenos Aires Stock Exchange Share Price Index - *see* - **Argentina - Securities Markets**

Bulgaria

Banking, Finance, and Money

Banking Institutions - Assets/Liabilities - *N/A*
Monetary Authorities - Assets/Liabilities - *N/A*
Money Supply - *N/A*

Exchange Rates

Currency - *Bulgarian Leva*
Cross Rates - *N/A*
Forward Exchange Rates - *N/A*
Per ECU - *N/A*
Per SDR - *N/A*
Per U.S. Dollar - *DJN, DRF, UNY*

Government Finance

Debt - *GSY**
Deficit/Surplus - *GSY*, WDR*
Expenditure - *GSY*, WDR*
Revenue - *GSY*, WDR*

Interest Rates

Bank Rate - *N/A*
Discount Rate - *N/A*
Government Bonds - *N/A*
Money Market - *N/A*
Treasury Bills - *N/A*

International Liquidity

Reserves Minus Gold - *N/A*
Gold - *N/A*

International Transactions

Balance of Payments - *BOP*, WDR*
Exports - *UNY, WTA**
Imports - *UNY, WTA**

National Accounts

Consumption
  Government - *WDR, WTA**
  Private - *WDR, WTA**
Gross Domestic Product - *UNY, WDR, WTA**
Gross National Product - *WDR, WTA**

National Income - *WTA**

Prices, Production, Employment

Consumer Credit Outstanding - *N/A*
Consumer Prices - *UNY, WDR*
Earnings/Wages - *UNY*
Employment - *UNY, WTA**
Production
Industrial - *UNY*
Wholesale/Producer Prices - *N/A*

Securities Markets - *N/A*

Bulgarian Leva - *see* - **Bulgaria** - **Exchange Rates**

Burkina Faso

Banking, Finance, and Money

Banking Institutions - Assets/Liabilities - *FSM*, FSY**
Monetary Authorities - Assets/Liabilities - *FSM*, FSY**
Money Supply - *FSM*, FSY*, UNY, WTA**

Exchange Rates

Currency - *CFA Franc*
Cross Rates - *N/A*
Forward Exchange Rate - *N/A*
Per ECU - *N/A*
Per SDR - *FSM*, FSY**
Per U.S. Dollar - *DRF, FSM*, FSY*, UNY*

Government Finance

Debt - *WTA**
Deficit/Surplus - *FSM*, FSY*, GSY*, WDR, WTA**
Expenditure - *GSY*, WDR, WTA**
Revenue - *GSY*, WDR, WTA**

Interest Rates

Bank Rate - *N/A*
Discount Rate - *FSM*, FSY**
Government Bonds - *N/A*
Money Market - *FSM*, FSY**
Treasury Bills - *N/A*

International Liquidity

Reserves Minus Gold - *FSM*, FSY*, UNY, WTA**
Gold - *FSM*, FSY*, UNY, WTA**

International Transactions

Balance of Payments - *BOP*, FSM*, FSY*, UMY, WDR, WTA**
Exports - *FSM*, FSY*, UNN, UNY, WTA**
Imports - *FSM*, FSY*, UNN, UNY, WTA**

National Accounts

Consumption
  Government - *FSY*, UNN, WDR, WTA**
  Private - *FSY*, UNN, WDR, WTA**
Gross Domestic Product - *FSM*, FSY*, GSY*, UNN, WDR, WTA**
Gross National Product - *FSY*, UNN, WDR, WTA**
National Income - *WTA**

Prices, Production, Employment

Consumer Credit Outstanding - *N/A*
Consumer Prices - *FSM*, FSY*, GSY*, UNY, WDR, WTA**
Earnings/Wages - *WTA**
Employment - *N/A*
Production - *N/A*
Wholesale/Producer Prices - *N/A*

Securities Markets - *N/A*

Burma - *see* - Myanmar

Bursa Efek Indonesia (The Jakarta Stock Exchange) - *see* - Indonesia - Securities Markets

Burundi

Banking, Finance, and Money

Banking Institutions - Assets/Liabilities - *FSM*, FSY**
Monetary Authorities - Assets/Liabilities - *FSM*, FSY**
Money Supply - *FSM*, FSY*, UNY*

Exchange Rates

Currency - *Burundi Franc*
Cross Rates - *N/A*

Forward Exchange Rate - *N/A*
Per ECU - *N/A*
Per SDR - *FSM*, FSY**
Per U.S. Dollar - *DRF, FSM*, FSY*, UNY*

Government Finance

Debt - *FSM*, FSY*, WTA**
Deficit/Surplus - *FSM*, FSY*, GSY*, WDR, WTA**
Expenditure - *GSY*, WDR, WTA**
Revenue - *GSY*, WDR, WTA**

Interest Rates

Bank Rate - *N/A*
Discount Rate - *FSM*, FSY*, UNY*
Government Bonds - *N/A*
Money Market - *N/A*
Treasury Bills - *N/A*

International Liquidity

Reserves Minus Gold - *FSM*, FSY*, UNY, WTA**
Gold - *FSM*, FSY*, UNY, WTA**

International Transactions

Balance of Payments - *BOP*, FSM*, FSY*, UNY, WTA**
Exports - *FSM*, FSY*, UNN, UNY, WTA**
Imports - *FSM*, FSY*, UNN, UNY, WTA**

National Accounts

Consumption
  Government - *FSM*, FSY*, UNN, WDR, WTA**
  Private - *FSM*, FSY*, UNN, WDR, WTA**
Gross Domestic Product - *FSM*, FSY*, GSY*, UNY, UNN, WDR, WTA**
Gross National Product - *WDR, UNN, WTA**
National Income - *UNN, WTA**

Prices, Production, Employment

Consumer Credit Outstanding - *N/A*
Consumer Prices - *FSM*, FSY*, GSY*, UNY, WDR, WTA**
Earnings/Wages - *UNY, WDR, WTA**
Employment - *UNY*
Production - *N/A*

Wholesale/Producer Prices - *N/A*
Securities Markets - *N/A*

Burundi Franc - *see* - **Burundi - Exchange Rates**

C

CA (Credit Aktien) Index - *see* - **Austria - Securities Markets**

CAC40 Index - *see* - **France - Securities Markets;** *see also* - **Commodities**

CAC General - *see* - **France - Securities Markets**

Cambodia

Banking, Finance, and Money

Banking Institutions - Assets/Liabilities - *N/A*
Monetary Authorities - Assets/Liabilities - *N/A*
Money Supply - *N/A*

Exchange Rates

Currency - *New Riel*
Cross Rates - *N/A*
Forward Exchange Rate - *N/A*
Per ECU - *N/A*
Per SDR - *N/A*
Per U.S. Dollar - *DRF*

Government Finance

Debt - *N/A*
Deficit/Surplus - *N/A*
Expenditure - *N/A*
Revenue - *N/A*

Interest Rates

Bank Rate - *N/A*
Discount Rate - *N/A*
Government Bonds - *N/A*

Money Market - *N/A*
Treasury Bills - *N/A*

International Liquidity

Reserves Minus Gold - *N/A*
Gold - *N/A*

International Transactions

Balance of Payments - *N/A*
Exports - *N/A*
Imports - *N/A*

National Accounts

Consumption
  Government - *N/A*
  Private - *N/A*
Gross Domestic Product - *N/A*
Gross National Product - *N/A*
National Income - *N/A*

Prices, Production, Employment

Consumer Credit Outstanding - *N/A*
Consumer Prices - *N/A*
Earnings/Wages - *N/A*
Production - *N/A*
Wholesale/Producer Prices - *N/A*

Securities Markets - *N/A*

Cameroon

Banking, Finance, and Money

Banking Institutions - Assets/Liabilities - *FSM*, FSY**
Monetary Authorities - Assets/Liabilities - *FSM*, FSY**
Money Supply - *FSM*, FSY*, UNY, WTA**

Exchange Rates

Currency *CFA Franc*
Cross Rates - *N/A*
Forward Exchange Rate - *N/A*
Per ECU - *N/A*
Per SDR - *FSM*, FSY**
Per U.S. Dollar - *FSM*, FSY*, UNY*

Government Finance

Debt - *FSM*, FSY*, GSY*, WTA**
Deficit/Surplus - *FSM*, FSY*, GSY*, WDR, WTA**
Expenditure - *GSY*, WDR, WTA**
Revenue - *GSY*, WDR, WTA**

Interest Rates

Bank Rate - *N/A*
Discount Rate - *FSM*, FSY*, UNY*
Government Bonds - *FSM*, FSY*, UNY*
Money Market - *N/A*
Treasury Bills - *N/A*

International Liquidity

Reserves Minus Gold - *FSM*, FSY*, UNY, WTA**
Gold - *FSM*, FSY*, UNY, WTA**

International Transactions

Balance of Payments - *FSM*, FSY*, UNY, WDR, WTA**
Exports - *FSM*, FSY*, UNN, UNY, WTA**
Imports - *FSM*, FSY*, UNN, UNY, WTA**

National Accounts

Consumption
Government - *FSY*, UNN, WDR, WTA**
Private - *FSY*, UNN, WDR, WTA**
Gross Domestic Product - *FSM*, FSY*, GSY*, UNN, UNY, WDR, WTA**
Gross National Product - *FSY*, UNN, WDR, WTA**
National Income - *FSY*, UNN, WTA**

Prices, Production, Employment

Consumer Credit Outstanding - *N/A*
Consumer Prices - *FSM*, FSY*, GSY*, UNY, WDR, WTA**
Earnings/Wages - *WDR, WTA**
Employment - *N/A*
Production
Manufacturing - *UNN*
Wholesale/Producer Prices - *N/A*

Securities Markets - *N/A*

Canada

Banking, Finance, and Money

Banking Institutions - Assets/Liabilities - *FSM*, FSY**
Monetary Authorities - Assets/Liabilities - *FSM*, FSY**
Money Supply - *FSM*, FSY*, MEI*, UNY, WTA**

Exchange Rates

Currency - *Canadian Dollar*
Cross Rates - *FTI, WSJ*
Currency Futures - *BAR, NYT*
Currency Options - *BAR, NYT, WSJ*
Forward Exchange Rate - *FTI, MEI**
Per ECU - *FTI*
Per SDR - *FSM*, FSY*, FTI*
Per U.S. Dollar - *BAR, DJN, DRF, FRB, FSM*, FSY*, MEI*, NYT, UNY, WSJ*

Government Finance

Debt - *FSM*, FSY*, GSY**
Deficit/Surplus - *FSM*, FSY*, GSY*, WDR, WTA**
Expenditure - *GSY*, WDR*
Revenue - *GSY*, WDR, WTA**

Interest Rates

Bank Rate - *FSM*, FSY**
Discount Rate - *FRB, FS1, FS2*, MEI*, UNY*
Government Bonds - *BAR, DRF, FSM*, FSY*, FS1, FTI, MEI*, UNY*
Money Market - *FSM*, FSY**
Prime Rate - *BAR, DJN, MEI*, WSJ*
Treasury Bills - *DRF, FSM*, FSY*, FS1, UNY*

International Liquidity

Reserves Minus Gold - *FSM*, FSY*, MEI*, UNY, WTA**
Gold - *FSM*, FSY*, UNY, WTA**

International Transactions

Balance of Payments - *BOP*, FSM*, FSY*, MEI*, UNY, WDR, WTA**
Exports - *FSM*, FSY*, MEI*, UNN, UNY, WTA**
Imports - *FSM*, FSY*, MEI*, UNN, UNY, WTA**

National Accounts

Consumption
  Government - *FSM*, FSY*, UNN, WDR, WTA**
  Private - *FSM*, FSY*, UNN, WDR, WTA**
  Gross Domestic Product - *FSM*, FSY*, GSY*, MEI*, UNN, UNY, WDR, WTA**
  Gross National Product - *FSM*, FSY*, UNN, WDR, WTA**
  National Income - *FSM*, FSY*, UNN, WTA**

Prices, Production, Employment

Consumer Credit Outstanding - *FS2**
Consumer Prices - *FSM*, FSY*, FS1, GSY*, MEI*, UNY, WDR, WTA**
Earnings/Wages - *FSM*, FSY*, MEI*, UNY, WDR, WTA**
Employment - *FSM*, MEI*, UNY, WTA**
Production
  Crude Petroleum - *FSM*, FSY**
  Industrial - *FSM*, FSY*, MEI*, UNA, UNY*
  Manufacturing - *MEI*, UNY*
  Mining - *UNY*
Wholesale/Producer Prices - *FSM*, FSY*, MEI*, UNY*

Securities Markets

Stock Exchange - *Toronto Stock Exchange (TSE)*
Index - *Toronto 300 Composite Index*
Bonds
  Yield - *FS1*
Eurobonds
  Value of bonds issued - *FS1*
Foreign Bonds
  Value of bonds issued - *FS1*
Shares
  Last day of month - *FS1*
  Price/Earnings Ratio - *FS1, FS2**
  Price Index - *BAR FTI, NYT, DJN, FSM*, FSY*, MEI*, UNY*
  Prices - Selected Issues - *BAR, FTI, NYT, WSJ*
  Yield - *FS1, FS2**
Stock Exchange Capitalization - *FS2**
Stock Exchange - *Bourse de Montréal (Montreal Stock Exchange)*

Index - *Montreal Portfolio*
Shares
   Price Index - *FTI*
   Prices - Selected Issues - *BAR, FTI, NYT, WSJ*

Canadian Dollar - *see* - **Canada** - **Exchange Rates;** *see also* - **Commodities**

Cape Verde

Banking, Finance, and Money

Banking Institutions - Assets/Liabilities - *FSM**
Monetary Authorities - Assets/Liabilities - *FSM**
Money Supply - *FSM*, WTA**

Exchange Rates

Currency - *Escudo*
Cross Rates - *N/A*
Forward Exchange Rate - *N/A*
Per ECU - *N/A*
Per SDR - *FSM**
Per U.S. Dollar - *DRF, FSM*, UNY*

Government Finance

Debt - *WTA**
Deficit/Surplus - *N/A*
Expenditure - *N/A*
Revenue - *N/A*

International Liquidity

Reserves Minus Gold - *FSM*, UNY, WTA**
Gold - *N/A*

International Transactions

Balance of Payments - *BOP*, FSM*, UNY, WTA**
Exports - *FSM*, UNN, UNY, WTA**
Imports - *FSM*, UNN, UNY, WTA**

National Accounts

Consumption
   Government - *FSM*, UNN, WTA**
   Private - *FSM*, UNN, WTA**
Gross Domestic Product - *FSM*, UNN, UNY, WTA**

Gross National Product - *UNN, WTA**
National Income - *N/A*

Prices, Production, Employment

Consumer Credit Outstanding - *N/A*
Consumer Prices - *FSM*, UNY, WTA**
Earnings/ Wages - *N/A*
Employment - *N/A*
Production - *N/A*
Wholesale/Producer Prices - *N/A*

Securities Markets - *N/A*

Cattle - *see* - Commodities

Cayman Islands

Banking, Finance, and Money

Banking Institutions - Assets/Liabilities - *N/A*
Monetary Authorities - Assets/Liabilities - *N/A*
Money Supply - *N/A*

Exchange Rates

Currency - *Cayman Island Dollar*
Cross Rates - *N/A*
Forward Exchange Rate - *N/A*
Per ECU - *N/A*
Per SDR - *N/A*
Per U.S. Dollar - *DJN, DRF*

Government Finance

Debt - *N/A*
Deficit/Surplus - *GSY*
Expenditure - *UNN*
Revenue - *UNN*

Interest Rates

Bank Rate - *N/A*
Discount Rate - *N/A*
Government Bonds - *N/A*
Money Market - *N/A*
Treasury Bills - *N/A*

International Liquidity

Reserves Minus Gold - *N/A*
Gold - *N/A*

International Transactions

Balance of Payments - *N/A*
Exports - *UNN*
Imports - *UNN*

National Accounts

Consumption
  Government - *UNN*
  Private - *UNN*
Gross Domestic Product - *UNN, UNY*
Gross National Product - *UNN*
National Income - *UNN*

Prices, Production, Employment

Consumer Credit Outstanding - *N/A*
Consumer Prices - *UNY*
Earnings/Wages - *N/A*
Employment - *N/A*
Production
  Manufacturing - *UNN*
  Mining - *UNN*

Securities Markets - *N/A*

CBS All Share Index - *see* - Netherlands - Securities Markets

CBS Stock Trend Index - *see* - Netherlands - Securities Markets

Cedi - *see* - Ghanda - Exchange Rates

Central African Republic

Banking, Finance, and Money

Banking Institutions - Assets/Liabilities - *FSM*, FSY**
Monetary Authorities - Assets/Liabilities - *FSM*, FSY**
Money Supply - *FSM*, FSY*, UNY*

Exchange Rates

Currency - *CFA Franc*
Cross Rates - *N/A*

Forward Exchange Rate - *N/A*
Per ECU - *N/A*
Per SDR - *FSM*, FSY**
Per U.S. Dollar - *DRF, FSM*, FSY*, UNY*

Government Finance

Debt - *WTA**
Deficit/Surplus - *FSY*, WTA**
Expenditure - *WDR, WTA**
Revenue - *WDR, WTA**

Interest Rates

Bank Rate - *N/A*
Discount Rate - *FSM*, FSY*, UNY*
Government Bonds - *N/A*
Money Market - *N/A*
Treasury Bills - *N/A*

International Liquidity

Reserves Minus Gold - *FSM*, FSY*, UNY, WTA**
Gold - *FSM*, FSY*, UNY, WTA**

International Transactions

Balance of Payments - *BOP*, FSM*, FSY*, UNY, WDR, WTA**
Exports - *FSM*, FSY*, UNY, WTA**
Imports - *FSM*, FSY*, UNY, WTA**

National Accounts

Consumption
  Government - *WDR, WTA**
  Private - *WDR, WTA**
Gross Domestic Product - *FSM*, FSY*, WDR, WTA**
Gross National Product - *WDR, WTA**
National Income - *WTA**

Prices, Production, Employment

Consumer Credit Outstanding - *N/A*
Consumer Prices - *FSM*, FSY*, UNY, WDR, WTA**
Earnings/Wages - *WTA**
Employment - *UNY*
Production - *N/A*

Wholesale/Producer Prices - *FSM*, FSY**

Securities Markets - *N/A*

CFA Franc (Communauté Financiére Africaine) - *see* - **Benin - Exchange Rates; Burkina Faso - Exchange Rates; Côte d'Ivoire - Exchange Rates; Mali - Exchange Rates; Niger - Exchange Rates; Senegal - Exchange Rates; Togo - Exchange Rates**

CFA Franc (Coopération Financière en Afrique Central - *see* - **Cameroon - Exchange Rates; Central African Republic - Exchange Rates; Chad - Exchange Rates; Congo - Exchange Rates; Equatorial Guinea - Exchange Rates; Gabon - Exchange Rates**

Chad

Banking, Finance, and Money

Banking Institutions - Assets/Liabilities - *FSM*, FSY**
Monetary Authorities - Assets/Liabilities - *FSM*, FSY**
Money Supply - *FSM*, FSY*, UNY, WTA**

Exchange Rates

Currency - *CFA Franc*
Cross Rates - *N/A*
Forward Exchange Rate - *N/A*
Per ECU - *N/A*
Per SDR - *FSM*, FSY**
Per U.S. Dollar - *DRF, FSM*, FSY*, UNY*

Government Finance

Debt - *FSM*, WTA**
Deficit/Surplus - *FSM*, FSY*, WDR, WTA**
Expenditure - *WDR, WTA**
Revenue - *WDR, WTA**

Interest Rates

Bank Rate - *N/A*
Discount Rate - *UNY*
Government Bonds - *N/A*
Money Market - *N/A*
Treasury Bills - *N/A*

International Liquidity

Reserves Minus Gold - *FSM*, FSY*, UNY, WTA**
Gold - *FSM*, FSY*, UNY, WTA**

International Transactions

Balance of Payments - *BOP*, FSM*, FSY*, MEI*, UNY, WTA**
Exports - *FSM*, FSY*, UNY, WTA**
Imports - *FSM*, FSY*, UNY, WTA**

National Accounts

Consumption
  Government - *WTA**
  Private - *WTA**
Gross Domestic Product - *WDR, WTA**
Gross National Product - *WDR, WTA**
National Income - *WTA**

Prices, Production, Employment

Consumer Credit Outstanding - *N/A*
Consumer Prices - *FSM*, FSY*, UNY, WDR, WTA**
Earnings/Wages - *N/A*
Employment - *UNY*
Production - *N/A*
Wholesale/Producer Prices - *N/A*

Securities Markets - *N/A*

Chile

Banking, Finance, and Money

Banking Institutions - Assets/Liabilities - *FSM*, FSY**
Monetary Authorities - Assets/Liabilities - *FSM*, FSY**
Money Supply - *FSM*, FSY*, UNY, WTA**

Exchange Rates

Currency - *Chilean Peso*
Cross Rates - *N/A*
Forward Exchange Rate - *N/A*
Per ECU - *N/A*
Per SDR - *FSM*, FSY**
Per U.S. Dollar - *BAR, DJN, DRF, FSM*, FSY*, NYT, UNY, WSJ*

Government Finance

Debt - *FSY*, WTA**
Deficit/Surplus - *FSY*, GSY*, WDR, WTA**
Expenditure - *GSY*, WDR, WTA**
Revenue - *GSY*, WDR, WTA**

International Liquidity

Reserves Minus Gold - *FSM*, FSY*, UNY, WTA**
Gold - *FSM*, FSY*, UNY, WTA**

International Transactions

Balance of Payments - *BOP*, FSM*, FSY*, UNY, WDR, WTA**
Exports - *FSM*, FSY*, UNY, WTA**
Imports - *FSM*, FSY*, UNY, WTA**

National Accounts

Consumption
  Government - *FSM*, FSY*, UNN, WDR, WTA**
  Private - *FSM*, FSY*, UNN, WDR, WTA**
  Gross Domestic Product - *FSM*, FSY*, GSY*, UNN, UNY, WDR, WTA**
  Gross National Product - *FSM*, FSY*, UNN, WDR, WTA**
  National Income - *FSY*, UNN, UNY, WTA**

Prices, Production, Employment

Consumer Credit Outstanding - *N/A*
Consumer Prices - *FSM*, FSY*, UNY, WDR, WTA**
Earnings/Wages - *FSM*, FSY*, UNY, WDR, WTA**
Employment - *UNY, WTA**
Production
  Manufacturing - *FSM*, FSY*, UNA, UNY*
  Mining - *FSM*, FSY*, UNN, UNY*
Wholesale/Producer Prices - *FSM*, FSY*, UNY*

Securities Markets

Stock Exchange - *Bolsa de Comercio de Santiago, Bolsa de Valores* (Santiago Stock Exchange)
Index - *General Share Price Index (IGPA)*
Shares
  Price Index - BAR, FSM*, FSY*, UNY

Chilean Peso - *see* - **Chile - Exchange Rates**

China (People's Republic)

Banking, Finance, and Money

Banking Institutions - Assets/Liabilities - *FSM*, FSY**
Monetary Authorities - Assets/Liabilities - *FSM*, FSY**
Money Supply - *FSM*, FSY*, UNY, WTA**

Exchange Rates

Currency - *Chinese Yuan (Renminbiao,* also *People's Bank Dollar)*
Cross Rates - *N/A*
Forward Exchange Rate - *N/A*
Per ECU - *N/A*
Per SDR - *FSM*, FSY**
Per U.S. Dollar - *DRF, FRB, FSM*, FSY*, NYT, WDR, WSJ*

Government Finance

Debt - *WTA**
Deficit/Surplus - *FSM*, FSY**
Expenditure - *N/A*
Revenue - *N/A*

International Liquidity

Reserves Minus Gold - *FSM*, FSY*, UNY, WTA**
Gold - *FSM*, FSY*, UNY, WTA**

International Transactions

Balance of Payments - *BOP*, FSM*, FSY*, UNY, WSJ, WTA**
Exports - *FSM*, FSY*, UNN, UNY, WTA**
Imports - *FSM*, FSY*, UNN, WTA**

National Accounts

Consumption
  Government - *WDR, WTA**
  Private - *WDR, WTA**
Gross Domestic Product - *UNY, WDR, WTA**
Gross National Product - *FSM*, FSY*, UNY, WDR, WTA**
National Income - *FSM*, FSY*, UNY, WTA**

Prices, Production, Employment

Consumer Credit Outstanding - *N/A*
Consumer Prices - *FSM*, FSY*, UNY, WDR, WTA**
Earnings/Wages - *FSM*, FSY*, UNY, WDR*

Employment - *FSM*, FSY*, UNY*
Production
  Agriculture - *FSM*, FSY**
  Industrial - *FSM*, FSY**
  Wholesale/Producer Prices - *FSM*, FSY**

Securities Markets

Stock Exchange - *Shanghai Securities Exchange*

China (Republic of)

Banking, Finance, and Money

Banking Institutions - Assets/Liabilities - *N/A*
Monetary Authorities - Assets/Liabilities - *N/A*
Money Supply - *N/A*

Exchange Rates

Currency - *Taiwan Dollar*
Cross Rates - *N/A*
Forward Exchange Rate - *N/A*
Per ECU - *N/A*
Per SDR - *N/A*
Per U.S. Dollar - *BAR, DJN, DRF, FRB, FTI, NYT, WSJ*

Government Finance

Debt - *N/A*
Deficit/Surplus - *N/A*
Expenditure - *N/A*
Revenue - *N/A*

Interest Rates

Bank Rate - *N/A*
Discount Rate - *N/A*
Government Bonds - *N/A*
Money Market - *N/A*
Treasury Bills - *N/A*

International Liquidity

Reserves Minus Gold - *N/A*
Gold - *N/A*

International Transactions

Balance of Payments - *N/A*

Exports - *N/A*
Imports - *N/A*

National Accounts

Consumption
  Government - *N/A*
  Private - *N/A*
Gross Domestic Product - *N/A*
Gross National Product - *N/A*
National Income - *N/A*

Prices, Production, Employment

Consumer Credit Outstanding - *N/A*
Consumer Prices - *N/A*
Earnings/Wages - *N/A*
Employment - *N/A*
Production - *N/A*
Wholesale/Producer Prices - *N/A*

Securities Markets

Stock Exchange - *Taiwan Stock Exchange Corporation*
Index - *Taiwan Stock Exchange Weighted Price Index*
Shares
  Price Index - *BAR, DRF, FTI*

Chinese Renminbiao - *see* - **China (Peoples' Republic) - Exchange Rates - Chinese Yuan**

Chinese Yuan - *see* - **China (Peoples' Republic) - Exchange Rates**

Cocoa - *see* - **Commodities**

Coffee - *see* - **Commodities**

Colombia

Banking, Finance, and Money

Banking Institutions - Assets/Liabilities - *FSM*, FSY**
Monetary Authorities - Assets/Liabilities - *FSM*, FSY**
Money Supply - *FSM*, FSY*, UNY, WTA**

Exchange Rates

Currency - *Colombian Peso*
Cross Rates - *N/A*

Forward Exchange Rate - *N/A*
Per ECU - *N/A*
Per SDR - *FSM*, FSY**
Per U.S. Dollar - *BAR, DJN, DRF, FSM*, FSY*, NYT, UNY, WSJ*

Government Finance

Debt - *FSY*, GSY*, WTA**
Deficit/Surplus - *FSY*, GSY*, WDR, WTA**
Expenditure - *FSM*, FSY*, WDR, WTA**
Revenue - *FSM*, FSY*, WDR, WTA**

Interest Rates

Bank Rate - *N/A*
Discount Rate - *FSM*, FSY**
Government Bonds - *N/A*
Money Market - *N/A*
Treasury Bills - *N/A*

International Liquidity

Reserves Minus Gold - *FSM*, FSY*, UNY, WTA**
Gold - *FSM*, FSY*, UNY, WTA**

International Transactions

Balance of Payments - *BOP*, FSM*, FSY*, UNY, WDR, WTA**
Exports - *FSM*, FSY*, UNN, UNY, WTA**
Imports - *FSM*, FSY*, UNN, UNY, WTA**

National Accounts

Consumption
    Government - *FSM*, FSY*, UNN, WDR, WTA**
    Private - *FSM*, FSY*, UNN, WDR, WTA**
Gross Domestic Product - *FSM*, FSY*, GSY*, UNN, UNY, WDR, WTA**
Gross National Product - *FSM*, FSY*, UNN, WDR, WTA**
National Income - *UNN, WTA**

Prices, Production, Employment

Consumer Credit Outstanding - *N/A*
Consumer Prices - *FSM*, FSY*, UNY, WDR, WTA**
Earnings/Wages - *UNY, WDR, WTA**

Employment - *FSM*, UNY, WTA**
Production
  Crude Petroleum - *FSM*, FSY**
  Gold - *FSM*, FSY*, UNY*
  Industrial - *UNY*
  Manufacturing Production - *FSM*, UNN, UNY*
Wholesale/Producer Prices - *FSM*, FSY*, UNY*

Securities Markets

Stock Exchanges - *Bolsa de Bogotá, Bolsa de Medellín*
Shares
  Price Index - *BAR, FSM*, FSY*, UNY*

Colombian Peso - *see* - **Colombia - Exchange Rates**

Colon - *see* - **Costa Rica - Exchange Rates; El Salvador - Exchange Rates**

Commerzbank Index - *see* - **Germany (Federal Republic) - Securities Markets**

Commodities

All-Ordinaries Index - *CSI, DRC*
Aluminum - *CSI, DRC, FTI, NYT, WSJ*
Australian Dollar - *BAR, CSI, DRC, DJN*
CAC40 Index - *CSI, DRC*
Canadian Dollar - *BAR, CSI, DJN, DRC, WSJ*
Cattle - *BAR, CSI, DJN, DRC, FTI, NYT, WSJ*
Cocoa - *BAR, CSI, DJN, DRC, FTI, NYT, WSJ*
Coffee - *BAR, CSI, DJN, DRC, FTI, NYT, WSJ*
Copper - *BAR, CSI, DRC, FTI, WSJ*
Corn - *BAR, CSI, DJN, DRC, NYT, WSJ*
Cotton - *BAR, DJN, DRC, FTI, NYT, WSJ*
Crude Oil - *BAR, CSI, DRC, FTI, NYT, WSJ*
DAX Index - *CSI, DRC*
Deutsche Mark - *BAR, CSI, DJN, DRC, NYT, WSJ*
Eurodollar - *BAR, CSI, DRC, NYT, WSJ*
French Franc - *CSI, DJN*
FTSE 100 Index - *CSI, DRC, WSJ*
Gasoline - *BAR, CSI, DRC, NYT, WSJ*
Gold - *BAR, CSI, DRC, FTI, NYT, WSJ*
Hang Seng Index - *CSI, DRC*

Heating Oil - *BAR, DJN, DRC, FTI, NYT, WSJ*
Hogs - *BAR, CSI, DRC, FTI, NYT, WSJ*
Hong Kong Index - *CSI*
Japanese Yen - *BAR, CSI, DJN, DRC, NYT, WSJ*
Lead - *DJN, DRC, FTI, NYT, WSJ*
Libor Rate - *BAR, CSI, DRC, WSJ*
Natural Gas - *BAR, CSI, DRC, NYT, WSJ*
Nickel - *CSI, DRC, WSJ*
Nikkei Index - *BAR, CSI, DRC, WSJ*
Oats - *BAR, CSI, DJN, DRC, NYT, WSJ*
Orange Juice - *BAR, CSI, DRC, FTI, NYT, WSJ*
Palladium - *BAR, CSI, DJN, DRC, FTI, NYT, WSJ*
Pibor - *CSI, DRC*
Platinum - *BAR, CSI, DJN, DRC, FTI, NYT, WSJ*
Pork Bellies - *BAR, CSI, DRC, FTI, NYT, WSJ*
Pound Sterling - *BAR, CSI, DJN, DRC, NYT, WSJ*
Silver - *BAR, CSI, DJN, DRC, FTI, NYT, WSJ*
Soybeans - *BAR, CSI, DRC, FTI, NYT, WSJ*
Sugar - *BAR, CSI, DJN, DRC, FTI, NYT, WSJ*
Swiss Franc - *BAR, CSI, DJN, DRC, NYT, WSJ*
Swiss Market Index - *CSI, DRC*
Tin - *CSI, DJN, DRC, FTI, NYT, WSJ*
Topix Index - *CSI, DRC*
United States Treasury Bills - *BAR, CSI, DJN, DRC, WSJ*
United States Treasury Bonds - *BAR, CSI, DJN, DRC, NYT, WSJ*
United States Treasury Notes - *BAR, CSI, DJN, DRC, NYT, WSJ*
Wheat - *BAR, CSI, DRC, FTI, NYT, WSJ*
Zinc - *CSI, DRC, FTI, NYT, WSJ*

Commodity Indexes - *BAR, FTI, WSJ*

Comoros

Banking, Finance, and Money

Banking Institutions - Assets/Liabilities - *FSM*, FSY**
Monetary Authorities - Assets/Liabilities - *FSM*, FSY**
Money Supply - *FSM*, FSY*, UNY, WTA**

Exchange Rates

Currency - *Comoros Franc*
Cross Rates - *N/A*
Forward Exchange Rate - *N/A*
Per ECU - *N/A*
Per SDR - *FSM*, FSY**
Per U.S. Dollar - *DRF, FSM*, FSY*, UNY*

Government Finance

Debt - *FSM*, FSY*, WTA**
Deficit/Surplus - *FSM*, FSY*, GSY*, WTA**
Expenditure - *FSY*, WTA**
Revenue - *GSY*, WTA**

Interest Rates

Bank Rate - *N/A*
Discount Rate - *FSM*, FSY*, UNY*
Government Bonds - *N/A*
Money Market - *N/A*
Treasury Bills - *N/A*

International Liquidity

Reserves Minus Gold - *FSY*, UNY, WTA**
Gold - *FSM*, WTA**

International Transactions

Balance of Payments - *BOP*, FSM*, FSY*, UNY, WTA**
Exports - *FSM*, FSY*, WTA**
Imports - *FSM*, FSY*, UNY, WTA**

National Accounts

Consumption
  Government - *N/A*
  Private - *N/A*
Gross Domestic Product - *FSY*, WTA**
Gross National Product - *WTA**
National Income - *WTA**

Prices, Production, Employment

Consumer Credit Outstanding - *N/A*
Consumer Prices - *N/A*
Earnings/Wages - *N/A*

Employment - *N/A*
Production - *N/A*
Wholesale/Producer Prices - *N/A*

Securities Markets - *N/A*

Comoros Franc - *see* - **Comoros** - **Exchange Rates**

Congo

Banking, Finance, and Money

Banking Institutions - Assets/Liabilities - *FSM*, FSY**
Monetary Authorities - Assets/Liabilities - *FSM*, FSY**
Money Supply - *FSM*, FSY*, UNY, WTA**

Exchange Rates

Currency - *CFA Franc*
Cross Rates - *N/A*
Forward Exchange Rate - *N/A*
Per ECU - *N/A*
Per SDR - *N/A*
Per U.S. Dollar - *DRF, FSM*, FSY*, UNY*

Government Finance

Debt - *FSY*, WTA**
Deficit/Surplus - *FSY*, WTA**
Expenditure - *WTA**
Revenue - *WDR, WTA**

Interest Rates

Bank Rate - *N/A*
Discount Rate - *FSM*, FSY*, UNY*
Government Bonds - *FSM*, FSY*, UNY*
Money Market - *N/A*
Treasury Bills - *N/A*

International Liquidity

Reserves Minus Gold - *FSM*, FSY*, UNY, WTA**
Gold - *FSM*, FSY*, UNY, WTA**

International Transactions

Balance of Payments - *BOP*, FSM*, FSY*, UNY, WDR, WTA**
Exports - *FSM*, FSY*, UNN, UNY, WTA**

Imports - *FSM*, FSY*, UNY, WDR, WTA**

National Accounts

Consumption
  Government - *FSM*, FSY*, UNN, WDR, WTA**
  Private - *FSM*, FSY*, UNN, WDR·*
Gross Domestic Product - *FSM*, FSY*, UNN, UNY, WDR, WTA**
Gross National Product - *UNN, WDR, WTA**
National Income - *UNN, WTA**

Prices, Production, Employment

Consumer Credit Outstanding - *N/A*
Consumer Prices - *FSM*, FSY*, UNY, WDR, WTA**
Earnings/Wages - *WTA**
Employment - *N/A*
Production
  Crude Petroleum - *FSM*, FSY**
Wholesale/Producer Prices - *FSM*, FSY**

Securities Markets - *N/A*

Consumer Credit Outstanding - *see* **- Individual Countries - Prices, Production, Employment**

Consumer Prices - *see* **- Individual Countries - Prices, Production, Employment**

Consumption - *see* **- Individual Countries - National Accounts**

Copenhagen Stock Exchange Index - *see* **- Denmark - Securities Markets**

Copper - *see* **- Commodities**

Corn - *see* **- Commodities**

Costa Rica

Banking, Finance, and Money

Banking Institutions - Assets/Liabilities - *FSM*, FSY**
Monetary Authorities - Assets/Liabilities - *FSM*, FSY**
Money Supply - *FSM*, FSY*, UNY, WTA**

Exchange Rates

Currency - Costa Rican Colon
Cross Rates - N/A
Forward Exchange Rate - N/A
Per ECU - N/A
Per SDR - FSM*, FSY*
Per U.S. Dollar - FSM*, FSY*, UNY

Government Finance

Debt - *FSM*, *FSY*, *GSY*, *WTA**
Deficit/Surplus - *FSM*, *FSY*, *GSY*, *WDR*, *WTA**
Expenditure - *GSY*, *WDR*, *WTA**
Revenue - *GSY*, *WDR*, *WTA**

Interest Rates

Bank Rate - *N/A*
Discount Rate - *FSM*, *FSY*, *UNY*
Government Bonds - *N/A*
Money Market - *N/A*
Treasury Bills - *N/A*

International Liquidity

Reserves Minus Gold - *FSM*, *FSY*, *UNY*, *WTA**
Gold - FSM*, FSY*, GSY*, UNY

International Transactions

Balance of Payments - *BOP*, *FSM*, *FSY*, *UNY*, *WDR*, *WTA**
Exports - *FSM*, *FSY*, *UNN*, *UNY*, *WTA**
Imports - *FSM*, *FSY*, *UNN*, *UNY*, *WTA**

National Accounts

Consumption
 Government - *FSM*, *FSY*, *UNN*, *WDR*, *WTA**
 Private - *FSM*, *FSY*, *UNN*, *WDR*, *WTA**
Gross Domestic Product - *FSM*, *FSY*, *GSY*, *UNN*, *UNY*, *WDR*, *WTA**
Gross National Product - *FSM*, *FSY*, *UNN*, *WDR*, *WTA**
National Income - *FSM*, *FSY*, *UNN*, *WTA**

Prices, Production, Employment

Consumer Credit Outstanding - *N/A*

Consumer Prices - *FSM*, FSY*, UNY, WDR, WTA**
Earnings/Wages - *UNY, WTA**
Employment - *UNY, WTA**
Production
  Industrial - *UNY*
  Manufacturing - *UNA, UNY*
  Mining - *UNY*
  Wholesale/Producer Prices - *FSM*, FSY*, UNY*
Securities Markets - *N/A*

Costa Rican Colon - *see* - **Costa Rica - Exchange Rates**

Côte D'Ivoire

Banking, Finance, and Money

Banking Institutions - Assets/Liabilities - *FSM*, FSY**
Monetary Authorities - Assets/Liabilities - *FSM*, FSY**
Money Supply - *FSM*, FSY*, UNY*

Exchange Rates

Currency - *CFA Franc*
Cross Rates - *N/A*
Forward Exchange Rate - *N/A*
Per ECU - *N/A*
Per SDR - *FSM*, FSY**
Per U.S. Dollar - *DRF, FSM*, FSY*, UNY*

Government Finance

Debt - *FSY*, GSY*, WTA**
Deficit/Surplus - *FSY*, GSY*, WTA**
Expenditure - *GSY*, WTA**
Revenue - G*SY*, WTA**

Interest Rates

Bank Rate - *N/A*
Discount Rate - *FSM*, FSY*, UNY*
Government Bonds - *N/A*
Money Market - *FSM*, FSY**
Treasury Bills - *N/A*

International Liquidity

Reserves Minus Gold - *FSM*, FSY*, UNY, WTA**
Gold - *FSM*, FSY*, UNY, WTA**

International Transactions

Balance of Payments - *BOP*, FSM*, FSY*, UNY, WDR, WTA**
Exports - *FSM*, FSY*, UNY, WTA**
Imports - *FSM*, FSY*, UNY, WTA**

National Accounts

Consumption
  Government - *FSM*, FSY*, UNN, WDR, WTA**
  Private - *FSM*, FSY*, UNN, WDR, WTA**
  Gross Domestic Product - *FSM*, FSY*, GSY*, UNN, UNY, WTA**
  Gross National Product - *FSY*, UNN, WDR, WTA**
  National Income - *FSY*, UNN, WTA**

Prices, Production, Employment

Consumer Credit Outstanding - *N/A*
Consumer Prices - *FSM*, FSY*, GSY*, WDR, WTA**
Earnings/Wages - *WDR, WTA**
Employment - *UNY*
Production
  Industrial - *FSM*, FSY*, UNY*
  Manufacturing - *UNY*
  Mining - *UNY*
Wholesale/Producer Prices - *N/A*

Securities Markets - *N/A*

Cotton - *see* - Commodities

Credit Aktien - *see* - Austria - Securities Markets

Credit Suisse Stock Index - *see* - Switzerland - Securities Markets

Cross Rates - *see* - Individual Countries - Exchange Rates

Crude Oil - *see* - Commodities

Cruzeiro Real - *see* - Brazil - Exchange Rates

Cuba

Banking, Finance, and Money

Banking Institutions - Assets/Liabilities - *N/A*
Monetary Authorities - Assets/Liabilities - *N/A*

Money Supply - *N/A*

Exchange Rates

Currency - *Cuban Peso*
Cross Rates - *N/A*
Forward Exchange Rate - *N/A*
Per ECU - *N/A*
Per SDR - *N/A*
Per U.S. Dollar - *DRF*

Government Finance

Debt - *N/A*
Deficit/Surplus - *N/A*
Expenditure - *N/A*
Revenue - *N/A*

Interest Rates

Bank Rate - *N/A*
Discount Rate - *N/A*
Government Bonds - *N/A*
Money Market - *N/A*
Treasury Bills - *N/A*

International Liquidity

Reserves Minus Gold - *N/A*
Gold - *N/A*

International Transactions

Balance of Payments - *N/A*
Exports - *UNN, UNY*
Imports - *UNN, UNY*

National Accounts

Consumption
  Government - *N/A*
  Private - *N/A*
Gross Domestic Product - *UNN, UNY*
Gross National Product - *N/A*
National Income - *N/A*

Prices, Production, Employment

Consumer Credit Outstanding - *N/A*
Consumer Prices - *N/A*

Earnings/Wages - *UNY*
Employment - *UNY*
Production - *N/A*
Wholesale/Producer Prices - *N/A*

Securities Markets - *N/A*

Cuban Peso - *see* **- Cuba - Exchange Rates**

Currency - *see* **- Individual Countries - Exchange Rates**

Cyprus

Banking, Finance, and Money

Banking Institutions - Assets/Liabilities - *FSM*, FSY**
Monetary Authorities - Assets/Liabilities - *FSM*, FSY**
Money Supply - *FSM*, FSY*, UNY*

Exchange Rates

Currency - *Cyprus Pound*
Cross Rates - *N/A*
Forward Exchange Rate - *N/A*
Per ECU - N/A
Per SDR - FSM*, FSY*
Per U.S. Dollar - DJN, DRF, FSM*, FSY*, UNY

Government Finance

Debt - *FSM*, FSY*, GSY*, WTA**
Deficit/Surplus - *FSM*, FSY*, GSY*, WTA**
Expenditure - *GSY*, WTA**
Revenue - *GSY*, WTA**

Interest Rates

Bank Rate - *N/A*
Discount Rate - *FSM*, FSY*, UNY*
Government Bonds - *N/A*
Money Market - *N/A*
Treasury Bills - *N/A*

International Liquidity

Reserves Minus Gold - *FSM*, FSY*, UNY, WTA**
Gold - *FSM*, FSY*, UNY, WTA**

International Transactions

Balance of Payments - *BOP*, FSM*, FSY*, UNY, WTA**

Exports - *FSM*, FSY*, UNN, UNY, WTA**
Imports - *FSM*, FSY*, UNN, UNY, WTA**

National Accounts

Consumption
  Government - *FSM*, FSY*, UNN, WTA**
  Private - *FSM*, FSY*, UNN, WTA**
Gross Domestic Product - *FSM*, FSY*, GSY*, UNN, UNY, WTA**
Gross National Product - *FSM*, FSY*, UNN, WTA**
National Income - *FSM*, FSY*, UNN, WTA**

Prices, Production, Employment

Consumer Credit Outstanding - *N/A*
Consumer Prices - *FSM*, FSY*, GSY*, UNY, WTA**
Earnings/Wages - *UNY, WTA**
Employment - *UNY*
Production
  Industrial - *FSM*, FSY*, UNY*
  Manufacturing - *UNA, UNY*
  Mining - *FSM*, FSY*, UNN, UNY*
Wholesale/Producer Prices - *N/A*

Securities Markets - *N/A*

Cyprus Pound - *see* - **Cyprus - Exchange Rates**

Czechoslovak Crown - *see* - **Czechoslovakia - Exchange Rates - Koruna**

Czechoslovakia

Banking, Finance, and Money

Banking Institutions - Assets/Liabilities - *N/A*
Monetary Authorities - Assets/Liabilities - *N/A*
Money Supply - *UNY*

Exchange Rates

Currency - *Koruna*
Cross Rates - *N/A*
Forward Exchange Rate - *N/A*
Per ECU - *N/A*
Per SDR - *FSY*, WSJ*
Per U.S. Dollar - *BAR, DJN, DRF, FSM*, NYT, UNY*

Government Finance

Debt - *GSY**
Deficit/Surplus - *GSY*, WDR*
Expenditure - *GSY*, WDR*
Revenue - *GSY*, WDR*

Interest Rates

Bank Rate - *N/A*
Discount Rate - *UNY*
Government Bonds - *N/A*
Money Market - *N/A*
Treasury Bills - *N/A*

International Liquidity

Reserves Minus Gold - *FSM*, UNY*
Gold - *FSM*, UNY*

International Transactions

Balance of Payments - *BOP*, FSM*, UNY, WDR*
Exports - *FSM*, UNN, UNY*
Imports - *FSM*, UNN, UNY*

National Accounts

Consumption
  Government - *FSM*, WDR*
  Private - *FSM*, UNN, WDR*
Gross Domestic Product - *FSM*, GSY*, UNN, UNY, WDR*
Gross National Product - *WDR*
National Income - *N/A*

Prices, Production, Employment

Consumer Credit Outstanding - *N/A*
Consumer Prices - *FSM*, UNY, WDR*
Earnings/Wages - *FSM*, UNY*
Employment - *FSM*, UNY*
Production
  Industrial - *FSM*, UNY*
  Manufacturing - *UNY*
  Mining - *UNY*
Wholesale/Producer Prices - *N/A*

Securities Markets - *N/A*

D

Dalasi - *see* - **Gambia** - **Exchange Rates**

Danish Krone - *see* - **Denmark** - **Exchange Rates**

DAX Index (Deutscher Aktien Index) - *see* - **Germany (Federal Republic)** - **Securities Markets;** *see also* - **Commodities**

Debt - *see* - **Individual Countries** - **Government Finance**

Deficit/Surplus - *see* - **Individual Countries** - **Government Finance**

Denmark

Banking, Finance, and Money

Banking Institutions - Assets/Liabilities - *FSM*, FSY**
Monetary Authorities - Assets/Liabilities - *FSM*, FSY**
Money Supply - *FSM*, FSY*, MEI*, UNY, WTA**

Exchange Rates

Currency - *Danish Krone*
Cross Rates - *N/A*
Forward Exchange Rate - *FTI*
Per ECU - *FTI*
Per SDR - *FSM*, FSY*, FTI*
Per U.S. Dollar - *BAR, DJN, DRF, FRB, FSM*, FSY*, MEI*, NYT, UNY, WSJ*

Government Finance

Debt - *FSM*, FSY*, GSY**
Deficit/Surplus - *FSM*, FSY*, GSY*, WDR, WTA**
Expenditure - *GSY*, WDR, WTA**
Revenue - *GSY*, WDR, WTA**

Interest Rates

Bank Rate - *N/A*

Discount Rate - *DRF, FRB, FSM*, FSY, FS1, FS2*, MEI*, UNY*

Government Bonds - *BAR, DRF, FSM*, FSY*, FS1, MEI*, UNY*

Money Market - *FSM*, FSY**

Treasury Bills - *UNY*

International Liquidity

Reserves Minus Gold - *FSM*, FSY*, MEI*, UNY, WTA**

Gold - *FSM*, FSY*, UNY, WTA**

International Transactions

Balance of Payments - *BOP*, FSM*, FSY*, MEI*, UNY, WDR, WTA**

Exports - *FSM*, FSY*, MEI*, UNN, UNY, WTA**

Imports - *FSM*, FSY*, MEI*, UNN, UNY, WTA**

National Accounts

Consumption

Government - *FSM*, FSY*, UNN, WDR, WTA**

Private - *FSM*, FSY*, UNN, WDR, WTA**

Gross Domestic Product - *FSM*, FSY*, GSY*, UNN, UNY, WDR, WTA**

Gross National Product - *FSM*, FSY*, UNN, WDR, WTA**

National Income - *FSM*, FSY*, UNN, WTA**

Prices, Production, Employment

Consumer Credit Outstanding - *N/A*

Consumer Prices - *FSM*, FSY*, FS1, GSY*, MEI*, UNY, WDR, WTA**

Earnings/Wages - *FSM*, FSY*, MEI*, UNY, WDR, WTA**

Employment - *FSM*, MEI*, UNN, WTA**

Production

Agriculture - *FSM*, FSY*, UNN*

Industrial - *FSM*, FSY*, UNY*

Manufacturing - *FSY*, UNN, UNY*

Mining - *UNY*

Wholesale/Producer Prices - *FSM*, MEI*, UNY*

Securities Markets

Stock Exchange - *København Føndsbørs Stock Exchange*
(The Copenhagen Stock Exchange)
Index - *Copenhagen Stock Exchange Index*
Bonds
  Yield - *FS2**
Eurobonds
  Value of bonds issued - *FS1*
Foreign Bonds
  Value of bonds issued - *FS1*
Shares
  Price Index - *BAR, FSM, FSY, FS1, FS2*, FTI, DRI, MEI**
  Prices - Selected Issues - *FTI*
  Stock Exchange Capitalization - *FS2**
  Stock Exchange Turnover - *FS2**

Deutsche Mark - *see* - **Germany (Federal Republic)** - **Exchange Rates;** *see also* - **Commodities**

Deutscher Aktien Index (DAX Index) - *see* - **Germany (Federal Republic)** - **Securities Markets**

Dinar - *see* - **Algeria** - **Exchange Rates; Bahrain** - **Exchange Rates; Iraq** - **Exchange Rates; Jordan** - **Exchange Rates; Kuwait** - **Exchange Rates; Libya** - **Exchange Rates; Moroccan Dirham** - **Exchange Rates; Tunisia** - **Exchange Rates; Yemen (People's Democratic Republic)** - **Exchange Rates; Yemen (Republic of)** - **Exchange Rates; Yugoslavia** - **Exchange Rates**

Dirham - *see* - **United Arab Emirates** - **Exchange Rates**

Discount Rate - *see* - **Individual Countries** - **Interest Rates**

Djibouti

Banking, Finance, and Money

Banking Institutions - Assets/Liabilities - *FSM*, FSY**
Monetary Authorities - Assets/Liabilities - *FSM*, FSY**
Money Supply - *FSM*, FSY*, UNY*

Exchange Rates

Currency - *Djibouti Franc*
Cross Rates - *N/A*

Forward Exchange Rates - *N/A*
Per ECU - *N/A*
Per SDR - *FSM*, FSY**
Per U.S. Dollar - *DRF, FSM*, FSY*, UNY*

Government Finance

Debt - *N/A*
Deficit/Surplus - *FSM*, FSY*, GSY**
Expenditure - *GSY**
Revenue - *GSY**

International Liquidity

Reserves Minus Gold - *FSM*, FSY*, UNY*
Gold - *N/A*

International Transactions

Balance of Payments - *N/A*
Exports - *FSM*, FSY*, UNY*
Imports - *FSM*, FSY*, UNY*

National Accounts

Consumption
   Government - *UNN*
   Private - *UNN*
Gross Domestic Product - *FSY*, GSY*, UNN*
Gross National Product - *UNN*
National Income - *UNN*

Prices, Production, Employment

Consumer Credit Outstanding - *N/A*
Consumer Prices - *N/A*
Earnings/Wages - *N/A*
Employment - *N/A*
Production - *N/A*
Wholesale/Producer Prices - *N/A*

Securities Markets - *N/A*

Djibouti Franc - *see* - **Djibouti - Exchange Rates**

Dobra - *see* - **Sao Tome and Principe - Exchange Rates**

Dollar - *see* - **Australia - Exchange Rates; Bahama - Exchange Rates; Barbados - Exchange Rates; Belize - Exchange Rates;**

Brunei - Exchange Rates; Canada - Exchange Rates; Cayman Islands - Exchange Rates; Figi - Exchange Rates; Guyana - Exchange Rates; Hong Kong - Exchange Rates; Jamaica - Exchange Rates; Liberia - Exchange Rates; New Zealand - Exchange Rates; Singapore - Exchange Rates; Solomon Islands - Exchange Rates; Trinidad and Tobago - Exchange Rates; United States - Exchange Rates; Zimbabwe - Exchange Rates

Dominica

Banking, Finance, and Money

Banking Institutions - Assets/Liabilities - *FSM*, FSY**
Monetary Authorities - Assets/Liabilities - *FSM*, FSY**
Money Supply - *FSM*, FSY*, WTA**

Exchange Rates

Currency - *East Caribbean Dollar*
Cross Rates - *N/A*
Forward Exchange Rate - *N/A*
Per ECU - *N/A*
Per SDR - *FSM*, FSY**
Per U.S. Dollar - *DRF, FSM*, FSY*, UNY*

Government Finance

Debt - *N/A*
Deficit/Surplus - *FSY*, WTA**
Expenditure - *WTA**
Revenue - *WTA**

Interest Rates

Bank Rate - *N/A*
Discount Rate - *N/A*
Government Bonds - *N/A*
Money Market - *N/A*
Treasury Bills - *FSM*, FSY*, UNY*

International Liquidity

Reserves Minus Gold - *FSM*, FSY*, UNY, WTA**
Gold - *N/A*

International Transactions

Balance of Payments - *BOP*, FSM*, FSY*, UNY, WTA**
Exports - *FSM*, FSY*, UNN, UNY, WTA**
Imports - *FSM*, FSY*, UNN, UNY, WTA**

National Accounts

Consumption
  Government - *FSY*, UNN*
  Private - *FSY*, UNN*
Gross Domestic Product - *FSM*, FSY*, UNN, UNY, WTA**
Gross National Product - *UNN, WTA**
National Income - *N/A*

Prices, Production, Employment

Consumer Credit Outstanding - *N/A*
Consumer Prices - *FSM*, FSY*, UNY, WTA**
Earnings/Wages - *N/A*
Employment - *N/A*
Production - *N/A*
Wholesale/Producer Prices - *N/A*

Securities Markets - *N/A*

Dominican Peso - *see* - Dominican Republic - Exchange Rates

Dominican Republic

Banking, Finance, and Money

Banking Institutions - Assets/Liabilities - *FSM**
Monetary Authorities - Assets/Liabilities - *FSM*, FSY**
Money Supply - *FSM*, FSY*, UNY, WTA**

Exchange Rates

Currency - *Dominician Peso*
Cross Rates - *N/A*
Forward Exchange Rate - *N/A*
Per ECU - *N/A*
Per SDR - *FSM*, FSY**
Per U.S. Dollar - *DRF, FSM*, FSY*, UNY*

Government Finance

Debt - *FSY*, GSY*, WTA**
Deficit/Surplus - *FSM*, FSY*, GSY*, WDR, WTA**

Expenditure - *GSY*, WDR, WTA**
Revenue - *GSY*, WDR, WTA**

Interest Rates

Bank Rate - *N/A*
Discount Rate - *N/A*
Government Bonds - *N/A*
Money Market - *N/A*
Treasury Bills - *N/A*

International Liquidity

Reserves Minus Gold - *FSM*, UNY, WTA**
Gold - *FSM*, UNY, WTA**

International Transactions

Balance of Payments - *BOP*, FSM*, FSY*, UNY, WDR, WTA**
Exports - *FSM*, FSY*, UNN, UNY, WTA**
Imports - *FSM*, FSY*, UNN, UNY, WTA**

National Accounts

Consumption
  Government - *FSM*, FSY*, UNN, WDR, WTA**
  Private - *FSM*, FSY*, UNN, WDR, WTA**
Gross Domestic Product - *FSM*, FSY*, GSY*, UNN, UNY, WDR, WTA**
Gross National Product - *FSM*, FSY*, UNN, WDR, WTA**
National Income - *FSM*, FSY*, UNN, WTA**

Prices, Production, Employment

Consumer Credit Outstanding - *N/A*
Consumer Prices - *FSM*, FSY*, GSY*, UNY, WDR, WTA**
Earnings/Wages - *UNY, WDR*
Production
  Manufacturing - *UNN*
  Mining - *UNN*
Wholesale/Producer Prices - *UNY*

Securities Markets - *N/A*

Dong - *see* **- Vietnam - Exchange Rates**

Dow Jones World Stock Index - *BAR, FTI, NYT, WSJ*

Drachma - *see* - **Greece** - **Exchange Rates**

Dutch Guilder - *see* - **Netherlands** - **Exchange Rates** - **Netherlands Guilder**

E

EAFE - *see* - **Europe Australia Far East Index**

Earnings/Wages - *see* - **Individual Countries - Prices, Production, Employment**

East Caribbean Dollar - *see* - **Anguilla - Exchange Rates; Antigua and Barbuda - Exchange Rates; Dominica - Exchange Rates; Grenada - Exchange Rates; St. Kitts and Nevis - Exchange Rates; St. Lucia - Exchange Rates; St. Vincent - Exchange Rates**

EC Dollar - *see* - **East Caribbean Dollar**

Economic Times Index of Ordinary Shares - *see* - **India - Securities Markets**

ECU - *see* - **European Currency Unit**

Ecuador

    Banking, Finance, and Money

        Banking Institutions - Assets/Liabilities - *FSM*, FSY**
        Monetary Authorities - Assets/Liabilities - *FSM*, FSY**
        Money Supply - *FSM*, FSY*, UNY, WTA**

    Exchange Rates

        Currency - *Ecuadoran Sucre*
        Cross Rates - *N/A*
        Forward Exchange Rate - *N/A*
        Per ECU - *N/A*
        Per SDR - *FSM*, FSY**
        Per U.S. Dollar - *BAR, DRF, FSM*, FSY*, NYT, UNY, WSJ*

Government Finance

Debt - *FSY*, WTA**
Deficit/Surplus - *FSM*, FSY*, GSY*, WDR, WTA**
Expenditure - *GSY*, WDR, WTA**
Revenue - *GSY*, WDR, WTA**

Interest Rates

Bank Rate - *N/A*
Discount Rate - *FSY*, UNY*
Government Bonds - *N/A*
Money Market - *N/A*
Treasury Bills - *N/A*

International Liquidity

Reserves Minus Gold - *FSM*, FSY*, UNY, WTA**
Gold - *FSM*, FSY*, UNY, WTA**

International Transactions

Balance of Payments - *BOP, FSM*, FSY*, UNY, WDR, WTA**
Exports - *FSM*, FSY*, UNN, UNY, WTA**
Imports - *FSM*, FSY*, UNN, UNY, WTA**

National Accounts

Consumption
  Government - *FSM*, FSY*, UNN, WDR, WTA**
  Private - *FSM*, FSY*, UNN, WDR, WTA**
Gross Domestic Product - *FSM*, FSY*, GSY*, UNN, UNY, WDR, WTA**
Gross National Product - *FSM, FSY, WDR, WTA**
National Income - *FSM*, FSY*, UNN, WTA**

Prices, Production, Employment

Consumer Credit Outstanding - *N/A*
Consumer Prices - *FSM*, FSY*, GSY*, UNY, WDR, WTA**
Earnings/Wages - *WTA**
Employment - *UNY, WTA**
Production
  Crude Petroleum - *FSM*, FSY*, UNN*
  Industrial - *WTA**
  Manufacturing - *UNN, UNY*
  Mining - *UNN*

Wholesale/Producer Prices - *FSM**, *FSY**, *UNY*
Securities Markets - *N/A*

Ecuadoran Sucre - *see* - **Ecuador** - **Exchange Rates**

Egypt

Banking, Finance, and Money

Banking Institutions - Assets/Liabilities - *FSM**, *FSY**
Monetary Authorities - Assets/Liabilities - *FSM**, *FSY**
Money Supply - *FSM**, *FSY**, *UNY*, *WTA**

Exchange Rates

Currency - *Egyptian Pound*
Cross Rates - *N/A*
Forward Exchange Rate - *N/A*
Per ECU - *N/A*
Per SDR - *FSM**, *FSY**
Per U.S. Dollar - *DJN, DRF, FSM**, *FSY**, *NYT, UNY*

Government Finance

Debt - *FSM**, *GSY**, *WTA**
Deficit/Surplus - *FSM**, *FSY**, *GSY**, *WDR, WTA**
Expenditure - *GSY**, *WDR, WTA**
Revenue - *GSY**, *WDR, WTA**

Interest Rates

Bank Rate - *N/A*
Discount Rate - *FSM**, *FSY**, *UNY*
Government Bonds - *N/A*
Money Market - *N/A*
Treasury Bills - *N/A*

International Liquidity

Reserves Minus Gold - *FSM**, *FSY**, *UNY, WTA**
Gold - *FSM**, *FSY**, *UNY, WTA**

International Transactions

Balance of Payments - *BOP**, *FSM**, *FSY**, *UNY, WDR,*
WTA*
Exports - *FSM**, *FSY**, *UNN, UNY, WTA**
Imports - *FSM**, *FSY**, *UNN, UNY, WTA**

National Accounts

Consumption
  Government - FSM*, FSY*, UNN, WTA*
  Private - FSM*, FSY*, UNN, WDR, WTA*
  Gross Domestic Product - *FSM*, FSY*, GSY*, UNN, UNY, WTA**
  Gross National Product - *FSM*, FSY*, UNN, WDR, WTA**
  National Income - *WTA**

Prices, Production, Employment

Consumer Credit Outstanding - *N/A*
Consumer Prices - *FSM*, FSY*, GSY*, UNY, WDR, WTA**
Earnings/Wages - *UNY, WDR, WTA**
Employment - *UNY*
Production
  Industrial - *UNY*
  Manufacturing - *UNY, WTA**
  Mining - *UNY*
Wholesale/Producer Prices - *FSM*, FSY*, UNY*

Securities Markets - *N/A*

Egyptian Pound - *see* - Egypt - Exchange Rates

El Salvador

Banking, Finance, and Money

Banking Institutions - Assets/Liabilities - *FSM*, FSY**
Monetary Authorities - Assets/Liabilities - *FSM*, FSY**
Money Supply - *FSM*, FSY*, UNY, WTA**

Exchange Rates

Currency - *Salvadoran Colon*
Cross Rates - *N/A*
Forward Exchange Rate - *N/A*
Per ECU - *N/A*
Per SDR - *FSM*, FSY**
Per U.S. Dollar - *DRF, FSM*, FSY*, UNY*

Government Finance

Debt - *FSM*, FSY*, GSY*, WTA**
Deficit/Surplus - *FSM*, FSY*, GSY*, WDR, WTA**
Expenditure - *GSY*, WDR, WTA**

Revenue - *GSY*, WDR, WTA**

International Liquidity

Reserves Minus Gold - *FSM*, FSY*, UNY, WTA**
Gold - *FSM*, FSY*, UNY, WTA**

International Transactions

Balance of Payments - *BOP*, FSM*, FSY*, WDR, WTA**
Exports - *FSM*, FSY*, UNN, UNY, WTA**
Imports - *FSM*, FSY*, UNN, UNY, WTA**

National Accounts

Consumption
Government - *FSM*, FSY*, UNN, WDR, WTA**
Private - *FSM*, FSY*, UNN, WDR, WTA**
Gross Domestic Product - *FSM*, FSY*, GSY*, UNN, UNY, WDR, WTA**
Gross National Product - *FSM*, FSY*, UNN, WDR, WTA**
National Income - *FSM*, FSY*, UNN, WTA**

Prices, Production, Employment

Consumer Credit Outstanding - *N/A*
Consumer Prices - *FSM*, FSY*, GSY*, UNY, WDR, WTA**
Earnings/Wages - *WDR*
Production
Industrial - *UNY, WTA**
Manufacturing - *UNN, UNY, WTA**
Wholesale/Producer Prices - *FSM*, FSY*, UNY*

Securities Markets - *N/A*

Emalangeni - *see* - Swaziland - Exchange Rates

Employment - *see* - Individual Countries - Prices, Production, Employment

England - *see* - United Kingdom

Equatorial Guinea

Banking, Finance, and Money

Banking Institutions - Assets/Liabilities - *FSM*, FSY**
Monetary Authorities - Assets/Liabilities - *FSM*, FSY**
Money Supply - *FSM*, FSY*, UNY, WTA**

Exchange Rates

Currency - *CFA Franc*
Cross Rates - *N/A*
Forward Exchange Rate - *N/A*
Per ECU - *N/A*
Per SDR - *FSM*, FSY**
Per U.S. Dollar - *DRF, FSM*, FSY*, UNY*
Currency - *Bipkwele*
Cross Rates - *N/A*
Forward Exchange Rate - *N/A*
Per ECU - *N/A*
Per SDR - *FSM*, FSY**
Per U.S. Dollar - *FSM*, FSY**

Interest Rates

Bank Rate - *N/A*
Discount Rate - *FSY*, UNY*
Government Bonds - *N/A*
Money Market - *N/A*
Treasury Bills - *N/A*

International Liquidity

Reserves Minus Gold - *FSM*, FSY*, UNY, WTA**
Gold - *N/A*

International Transactions

Balance of Payments - *BOP*, FSM*, UNY, WTA**
Exports - *FSY*, WTA**
Imports - *WTA**

National Accounts

Consumption
  Government - *UNN*
  Private - *UNN*
Gross Domestic Product - *UNN, UNY, WTA**
Gross National Product - *WTA**
National Income - *WTA**

Prices, Production, Employment

Consumer Credit Outstanding - *N/A*
Consumer Prices - *FSM*, FSY*, WTA**
Earnings/Wages - *N/A*

Employment - *N/A*
Production
 Industrial - *WTA**
 Manufacturing - *UNY, WTA**
 Wholesale/Producer Prices - *N/A*

Securities Markets - *N/A*

Escudo - *see -* **Cape Verde - Exchange Rates; Portugal - Exchange Rates**

Ethiopia

Banking, Finance, and Money

Banking Institutions - Assets/Liabilities - *FSM*, FSY**
Monetary Authorities - Assets/Liabilities - *FSM*, FSY**
Money Supply - *FSM*, FSY*, UNY, WTA**

Exchange Rates

Currency - *Ethiopian Birr*
Cross Rates - *N/A*
Forward Exchange Rate - *N/A*
Per ECU - *N/A*
Per SDR - *FSM*, FSY**
Per U.S. Dollar - *DRF, FSM*, FSY*, UNY*

Government Finance

Debt - *FSY*, GSY*, WTA**
Deficit/Surplus - *FSY*, GSY*, WTA**
Expenditure - *GSY*, WDR, WTA**
Revenue - *GSY*, WDR, WTA**

Interest Rates

Bank Rate - *N/A*
Discount Rate - *FSY*, UNY*
Government Bonds - *FSY*, UNY*
Treasury Bills - *FSY*, UNY*

International Liquidity

Reserves Minus Gold - *FSM*, FSY*, UNY, WTA**
Gold - *FSM*, FSY*, UNY, WTA**

International Transactions

Balance of Payments - *BOP*, FSM*, FSY*, UNY, WDR, WTA**
Exports - *FSM*, FSY*, UNN, UNY, WTA**
Imports - *FSM*, FSY*, UNN, WTA**

National Accounts

Consumption
Government - *FSM*, FSY*, UNN, WDR, WTA**
Private - *FSM*, FSY*, UNN, WDR, WTA**
Gross Domestic Product - *FSM*, FSY*, GSY*, UNN, UNY, WDR, WTA**
Gross National Product - *FSM*, FSY*, WDR, WTA**
National Income - *WTA**

Prices, Production, Employment

Consumer Credit Outstanding - *N/A*
Consumer Prices - *FSM*, FSY*, GSY*, UNY, WDR, WTA**
Earnings/Wages - *WDR, WTA**
Employment - *WTA**
Production
Industrial - *UNY, WTA**
Wholesale/Producer Prices - *N/A*

Securities Markets - *N/A*

Ethiopian Birr - *see* **- Ethiopia - Exchange Rates**

Eurodollar

Futures - *BAR*
Rates - *BAR, DJN, DRF, FSY*, NYT, WSJ*
Time Deposits - *BAR, FTI, NYT, WSJ*

Eurodollar Bonds

Price Indexes - *DRF*
Yield - *DRF, WSJ*

Europe Australia Far East Index - *BAR*

European Currency Unit

Deposit Rates - *DRF*
Exchange Rates - *BAR, DRF, FSY*, FRI, NYT, WSJ*

Forward Exchange Rate - *FTI*
Interest Rates - *FTI, FS2**

Exchange Rates - Per ECU - *see* **- Individual Countries - Exchange Rates**

Exchange Rates - Per SDR - *see* **- Individual Countries - Exchange Rates**

Exchange Rates - Per U.S. Dollar - *see* **- Individual Countries - Exchange Rates**

Expenditure - *see* **- Individual Countries - Government Finance**

Exports - *see* **- Individual Countries - International Transactions**

F

FAZ Aktien (Frankfurter Allgemeine Zeitung Stock Index) - *see* - **Germany (Federal Republic) - Securities Markets**

Fibor - *see* - **Germany (Federal Republic) - Interest Rates**

Fiji

Banking, Finance, and Money

Banking Institutions - Assets/Liabilities - *FSM*, FSY**
Monetary Authorities - Assets/Liabilities - *FSM*, FSY**
Money Supply - *FSM*, FSY*, UNY, WTA**

Exchange Rates

Currency - *Fiji Dollar*
Cross Rates - *N/A*
Forward Exchange Rate - *N/A*
Per ECU - *N/A*
Per SDR - *FSM*, FSY**
Per U.S. Dollar - *DRF, FSM*, FSY*, UNY*

Government Finance

Debt - *FSM*, FSY*, GSY*, WTA**
Deficit/Surplus - *FSM*, FSY*, GSY*, WTA**
Expenditure - *GSY*, WTA**
Revenue - *GSY*, WTA**

Interest Rates

Bank Rate - *FSM*, FSY**
Discount Rate - *UNY*
Money Market - *FSM*, FSY**
Treasury Bills - *FSM*, FSY*, UNY*

International Liquidity

Reserves Minus Gold - *FSM*, FSY*, UNY, WTA**
Gold - *FSM*, FSY*, UNY*

International Transactions

Balance of Payments - *BOP*, FSM*, FSY*, UNY, WTA**
Exports - *FSM*, FSY*, UNN, UNY, WTA**
Imports - *FSM*, FSY*, UNN, UNY, WTA**

National Accounts

Consumption
Government - *FSM*, FSY*, UNN, WTA**
Private - *FSM*, FSY*, UNN, WTA**
Gross Domestic Product - *FSM*, FSY*, GSY*, UNN, UNY, WTA**
Gross National Product - *FSM*, FSY*, UNN, WTA**
National Income - *FSM*, FSY*, UNN, WTA**

Prices, Production, Employment

Consumer Credit Outstanding - *N/A*
Consumer Prices - *FSM*, FSY*, GSY*, UNY, WTA**
Earnings/Wages - *FSM*, FSY*, UNY, WTA**
Employment - *FSM*, FSY*, UNY, WTA**
Production
Industrial - *FSM*, FSY*, UNY*
Manufacturing - *UNN, UNY*
Mining - *UNY*
Wholesale/Producer Prices - *N/A*

Securities Markets - *N/A*

Fiji Dollar - *see* - Fiji - Exchange Rates

Financial Times Stock Exchange Indexes - *see* - United Kingdom - Securities Markets

Finland

Banking, Finance, and Money

Banking Institutions - Assets/Liabilities - *FSM*, FSY**
Monetary Authorities - Assets/Liabilities - *FSM*, FSY**
Money Supply - *FSM*, FSY*, MEI*, UNY, WTA**

Exchange Rates

Currency - *Finnish Markka*
Cross Rates - *N/A*
Forward Exchange Rate - *N/A*
Per ECU - *N/A*
Per SDR - *FSM*, FSY**
Per U.S. Dollar - *DJN, DRF, FRB, FSM*, FSY*, FTI, MEI*, NYT, UNY, WSJ*

Government Finance

Debt - *FSY*, GSY**
Deficit/Surplus - *FSM*, FSY*, GSY*, WDR, WTA**
Expenditure - *GSY*, WDR, WTA**
Revenue - *GSY*, WDR, WTA**

Interest Rates

Bank Rate - *N/A*
Discount Rate - *FSM*, FSY*, FS2, MEI**
Government Bonds - *FS1*
Helibor - *FS2*, MEI**
Money Market - *FSM*, FSY**
Treasury Bills - *N/A*

International Liquidity

Reserves Minus Gold - *FSM*, FSY*, MEI*, WTA**
Gold - *FSM*, FSY*, UNY, WTA**

International Transactions

Balance of Payments - *BOP*, FSM*, FSY*, MEI*, UNY, WDR, WTA**
Exports - *FSM*, FSY*, MEI*, UNN, UNY, WTA**
Imports - *FSM*, FSY*, MEI*, UNN, UNY, WTA**

National Accounts

Consumption
  Government - *FSM*, FSY*, UNN, WDR, WTA**
  Private - *FSM*, FSY*, UNN, WDR, WTA**
Gross Domestic Product - *FSM*, FSY*, GSY*, UNN, UNY, WDR, WTA**
Gross National Product - *FSM*, FSY*, UNN, WDR, WTA**
National Income - *FSM*, FSY*, UNN*

Prices, Production, Employment

Consumer Credit Outstanding - *FS2*
Consumer Prices - *FSM*, FSY*, FS1, GSY*, MEI*, UNY, WDR, WTA**
Earnings/Wages - *FSM*, FSY*, MEI*, UNY, WDR, WTA**
Employment - *FSM*, FSY*, MEI*, UNY, WTA**
Production
  Industrial - *FSM*, FSY*, MEI*, UNY*
  Manufacturing - *MEI*, UNN, UNY*
  Mining - *UNN, UNY*
Wholesale/Producer Prices - *FSM*, FSY*, MEI*, UNY*

Securities Markets

Stock Exchange - *Helsinki Stock Exchange*
Index - Hex General
Bonds
  Yield - *FS1*
Eurobonds
  Value of bonds issued - *FS1*
Foreign Bonds
  Value of bonds issued - *FS1*
Shares
  Price Index - *BAR, FSM*, FSY*, FS1, FS2*, FTI, MEI*, UNY*
  Prices - *FSM*, FSY*, FS1, MEI*, UNY*
  Prices - Selected Issues - *FTI*
  Yield - *FS1, FS2**
Stock Exchange Capitalization - *FS2**
Stock Exchange Turnover - *FS2**

Finnish Markka - *see* **- Finland - Exchange Rates**

Florin - *see* **- Aruba - Exchange Rates**

Florint - *see* **- Hungary - Exchange Rates**

Forward Exchange Rate - *see* **- Individual Countries - Exchange Rates**

Franc - *see* **- Belgium - Exchange Rates; Burundi - Exchange Rates; Comoros - Exchange Rates; Djibouti - Exchange Rates; France - Exchange Rates; Luxembourg - Exchange Rates;**

Madagascar - Exchange Rates; Rwanda - Exchange Rates; Switzerland - Exchange Rates

Franc Belge - *see* - **Belgium - Exchange Rates**

Franc Luxembourg - *see* - **Luxembourg - Exchange Rates**

Franc - Madagasy - *see* - **Madagascar - Exchange Rates**

France

Banking, Finance, and Money

Banking Institutions - Assets/Liabilities - *FSM*, FSY**
Monetary Authorities - Assets/Liabilities - *FSM*, FSY**
Money Supply - *FSM*, FSY*, MEI*, UNY, WTA**

Exchange Rates

Currency - *French Franc*
Cross Rates - *FTI, WSJ*
Forward Exchange Rate - *FTI*
Per ECU - *FTI*
Per SDR - *FSM*, FSY*, FTI*
Per U.S. Dollar - *BAR, DJN, DRF, FRB, FSM*, FSY*, MEI*, NYT, WSJ*

Government Finance

Debt - *FSM*, FSY*, GSY**
Deficit/Surplus - *FSM*, FSY*, GSY*, WDR, WTA**
Expenditure - *GSY*, WDR, WTA**
Revenue - *GSY*, WDR, WTA**

Interest Rates

Bank Rate - *N/A*
Discount Rate - *DRF, FRB, FSM*, FSY*, FS2*, MEI*, UNY*
Government Bonds - *BAR, DRF, FSM*, FSY*, FS1, FTI, UNY*
Money Market - *FSM*, FSY**
Treasury Bills - *FS1, DRF, UNY*
Pibor - *FS1, MEI**
Prime Rate - *DRF*

International Liquidity

Reserves Minus Gold - *FSM*, FSY*, MEI*, UNY, WTA**
Gold - *FSM*, FSY*, UNY, WTA**

International Transactions

Balance of Payments - *BOP*, FSM*, FSY*, MEI*, UNY, WDR*
Exports - *FSM*, FSY*, MEI*, UNN, UNY, WTA**
Imports - *FSM*, FSY*, MEI*, UNN, UNY, WTA**

National Accounts

Consumption
  Government - *FSM*, FSY*, UNN, WDR*
  Private - *FSM*, FSY*, UNN, WDR*
Gross Domestic Product - *FSM*, FSY*, GSY*, MEI*, UNN, UNY, WTA**
Gross National Product - *FSM*, FSY*, UNN, WDR, WTA**
National Income - *FSM*, FSY**

Prices, Production, Employment

Consumer Credit Outstanding - *FS2**
Consumer Prices - *ECI, FSM*, FSY*, FS1, GSY*, MEI*, WDR, WTA**
Earnings/Wages - *FSM*, FSY*, MEI*, UNY, WDR, WTA**
Employment - *FSM*, FSY*, MEI*, UNY, WTA**
Production
  Industrial - *ECI, FSM*, FSY*, MEI*, UNY, WTA**
  Manufacturing - *MEI*, UNN, UNY, WTA**
  Mining - *UNY*
Wholesale/Producer Prices - *FSY*, MEI*, UNY*

Securities Markets

Stock Exchange - *Paris Bourse*
Indexes
  CAC General
  CAC 40
Bonds
  Issue price - *FS2**
  Yield - *FS2**
Eurobonds
  Value of bonds issued - *FS1*
  Financial Futures - *FTI*
  Financial Options - *FTI*
Foreign Bonds
  Value of bonds issued - *FS1*
  Money Market Instruments Issued - *FS2**

Shares
Issue price - *FS2**
Price Index
CAC General - *BAR, DJN, DRI, FTI, FS1, FS2*, FSM*,*
FSY*, NYT, MEI*, UNY, WSJ
CAC 40 - *DRI*
Prices - Selected Issues - *BAR, FTI, NYT, WSJ*
Yield - *FS1, FS2**
Stock Exchange Capitalization - *FS2*

Frankfurt Stock Exchange - *see* **- Germany (Federal Republic) -
Securities Markets**

Frankfurter Allgemeine Zeitung Stock Index - *see* **- Germany
(Federal Republic) - Securities Markets**

Frankfurter Wertpapierböise (Frankfurt Stock Exchange) - *see* **-
Germany(Federal Republic) - Securities Markets**

French Franc - *see* **- France - Exchange Rates;** *see also* **-
Commodities**

FTSE Actuaries 350 Index - *see* **- United Kingdom - Securities
Markets**

FTSE All Share Index - *see* **- United Kingdom - Securities Markets**

FTSE Mid 250 Index - *see* **- United Kingdom - Securities markets**

FTSE 100 Index - *see* **- United Kingdom - Securities Markets;** *see
also* **- Commodities**

FTSE 30 Index - *see* **- United Kingdom - Securities Markets**

G

Gabon

Banking, Finance, and Money

Banking Institutions - Assets/Liabilities - *FSM**, *FSY**
Monetary Authorities - Assets/Liabilities - *FSM**, *FSY**
Money Supply - *UNY*

Exchange Rates

Currency - *CFA Franc*
Cross Rates - *N/A*
Forward Exchange Rate - *N/A*
Per ECU - *N/A*
Per SDR - *FSM**, *FSY**
Per U.S. Dollar - *FSM**, *FSY**, *UNY*

Government Finance

Debt - GSY*, WTA*
Deficit/Surplus - FSM*, FSY*, GSY*, WDR, WTA*
Expenditure - GSY*, WDR, WTA*
Revenue - GSY*, WDR, WTA*

Interest Rates

Discount Rate - *FSM**, *FSY**, *UNY*
Government Bonds - *FSM**, *FSY**, *UNY*
Money Market - *N/A*
Treasury Bills - *N/A*

International Liquidity

Reserves Minus Gold - *FSM**, *FSY**, *UNY*, *WTA**
Gold - *FSM**, *FSY**, *UNY*, *WTA**

International Transactions

Balance of Payments - *BOP*, FSM*, FSY*, UNY, WDR, WTA**
Exports - FSM*, FSY*, UNN, UNY, WTA*
Imports - FSM*, FSY*, UNN, UNY, WTA*

National Accounts

Consumption
Government - *FSY*, UNN, WTA**
Private - *FSY*, UNN, WTA**
Gross Domestic Product - *FSM*, FSY*, GSY*, UNN, WDR, WTA**
Gross National Product - *FSY*, UNN, WDR, WTA**
National Income - *FSY*, UNN, WTA**

Prices, Production, Employment

Consumer Credit Outstanding - *N/A*
Consumer Prices - *FSM*, FSY*, GSY*, UNY, WDR, WTA**
Earnings/Wages - *N/A*
Employment - *N/A*
Producction - *N/A*
Wholesale/Producer Prices - *FSM*, FSY**

Securities Markets - *N/A*

Gambia

Banking, Finance, and Money

Banking Institutions - Assets/Liabilities - *FSM*, FSY**
Monetary Authorities - Assets/Liabilities - *FSM*, FSY**
Money Supply - *FSM*, FSY*, UNY, WTA**

Exchange Rates

Currency - *Gambian Dalasi*
Cross Rates - *N/A*
Per ECU - *N/A*
Per SDR - *FSM*, FSY**
Per U.S. Dollar - *DRF, FSM*, FSY**

Government Finance

Debt - *FSY*, GSY**
Deficit/Surplus - *FSM*, FSY*, GSY*, WTA**
Expenditure - *GSY*, WTA**

Revenue - *GSY*, WTA**

Interest Rates

Bank Rate - *N/A*
Discount Rate - *FSM*, FSY*, UNY*
Government Bonds - *N/A*
Money Market - *N/A*
Treasury Bills - *N/A*

International Liquidity

Reserves Minus Gold - *FSM*, FSY*, UNY, WTA**
Gold - *N/A*

International Transactions

Balance of Payments - *BOP*, FSM*, FSY*, GSY*, UNY, WTA**
Exports - *FSM*, FSY*, UNN, UNY, WTA**
Imports - *FSM*, FSY*, UNN, UNY, WTA**

National Accounts

Consumption
  Government - *UNN*
Gross Domestic Product - *FSM*, FSY*, GSY*, UNN, WTA**
Gross National Product - *UNN, WTA**
National Income - *UNN, WTA**

Prices, Production, Employment

Consumer Credit Outstanding - *N/A*
Consumer Prices - *FSM*, FSY*, GSY*, WTA**
Earnings/Wages - *UNY, WTA**
Employment - *UNY, WTA**
Production
  Industrial - *WTA**
  Manufacturing - *UNN, WTA**

Securities Markets - *N/A*

Gambian Dalasi - *see* - **Gambia - Exchange Rates**

Gasoline - *see* - **Commodities**

General Share Price Index (IGPA) - *see* - **Chile - Securities Markets**

Germany (Federal Republic)

Banking, Finance, and Money

Banking Institutions - Assets/Liabilities - *FSM*, FSY**
Monetary Authorities - Assets/Liabilities - *FSM*, FSY**
Money Supply - *FSM*, FSY*, UNY, MEI*, WTA**

Exchange Rates

Currency - *Deutsche Mark*
Cross Rates - *FTI, WSJ*
Currency Futures - *BAR, NYT*
Currency Options - *BAR, NYT, WSJ*
Forward Exchange Rate - *FTI, MEI**
Per ECU - *FTI*
Per SDR - *FSM*, FSY*, FTI*
Per U.S. Dollar - *BAR, DJN, DRF, FRB, FSM*, FSY*, MEI*, NYT, UNY, WSJ*

Government Finance

Debt - *FSY*, GSY**
Deficit/Surplus - *FSY*, GSY*, WDR, WTA**
Expenditure - *GSY*, WDR, WTA**
Revenue - *GSY*, WDR, WTA**

Interest Rates

Bank Rate - *N/A*
Discount Rate - *DRF, FRB, FSM*, FSY*, FS1, FS2*, MEI*, UNY WDR*
Fibor - *FS1, MEI**
Government Bonds - *BAR, DRF, FSM*, FSY*, FTI, UNY*
Money Market - *FSM*, FSY**
Prime Rate - *BAR, WSJ*
Treasury Bills - *FSM*, FSY*, UNY*

International Liquidity

Reserves Minus Gold - *FSM*, FSY*, MEI*, UNY, WTA**
Gold - *FSM*, FSY*, UNY, WTA**

International Transactions

Balance of Payments - *BOP*, FSM*, FSY*, MEI*, UNY, WDR, WTA**
Exports - *FSM*, FSY*, MEI*, UNN, UNY*

Imports - *FSM*, FSY*, MEI*, UNN, UNY, WTA**

National Accounts

Consumption

Government - *FSM*, FSY*, UNN, WDR, WTA**

Private - *FSM*, FSY*, UNN, WDR, WTA**

Gross Domestic Product - *FSM*, FSY*, GSY*, MEI, UNN, WDR, WTA**

Gross National Product - *FSM*, FSY*, WDR, WTA**

National Income - *FSM*, FSY*, WTA**

Prices, Production, Employment

Consumer Credit Outstanding - *FS2**

Consumer Prices - *ECI, FSM*, FSY*, GSY*, MEI*, UNY, WDR, WTA**

Earnings/Wages - *FSM*, FSY*, MEI*, UNY, WDR, WTA**

Employment - *FSM*, FSY*, MEI*, UNY, WDR, WTA**

Production

Industrial - *ECI, FSM*, FSY*, MEI*, UNY, WTA**

Manufacturing - *MEI*, UNN, UNY, WTA**

Mining - *UNY*

Wholesale/Producer Prices - *FSM*, FSY*, MEI*, UNY*

Securities Markets

Stock Exchange - *Frankfurt Stock Exchange*

Indexes

Commerzbank

FAZ Aktien

DAX

Bonds

Issue price - *FS2*

Yield - *FS2*

Eurobonds

Value of bonds issued - *FS1*

Foreign Bonds

Value of bonds issued - *FS1*

Money Market Instruments Issued - *FS2**

Shares

Issue price - *FS2**

Price Indexes

Commerzbank - *BAR, DRI, FTI*

DAX - *BAR, DRI, DJN, FSM*, FSY*, FS1, FS2*, MEI*, UNY, WSJ*
FAZ Aktien - *BAR, FTI, DRI*
Prices - Selected Issues - *BAR, FTI, NYT, WSJ*
Total Gross - *FS2**
Yield - *FS1, FS2**
Stock Exchange Capitalization - *FS2**

Germany (German Democratic Republic)

Banking, Finance, and Money

Banking Institutions - Assets/Liabilities - *N/A*
Banking Institutions - Assets/Liabilities - *N/A*
Money Supply - *N/A*

Exchange Rates

Currency - *Mark*
Cross Rates - *N/A*
Forward Exchange Rate - *N/A*
Per ECU - *N/A*
Per SDR - *N/A*
Per U.S. Dollar - *UNY*

International Transactions

Balance of Payments
Exports - *UNN, UNY*
Imports - *UNN, UNY*

National Accounts

Consumption
  Government - *UNN*
  Private - *UNN*
Gross Domestic Product - *UNN, UNY*
Gross National Product - *N/A*
National Income - *N/A*

Prices, Production, Employment

Consumer Credit Outstanding - *N/A*
Consumer Prices - *UNY*
Earnings/Wages - *UNY*
Employment - *UNY*
Production

Industrial - *UNY*
Manufacturing - *UNY*
Mining - *UNY*
Wholesale/Producer Prices - *N/A*

Securities Markets - *N/A*

Ghana

Banking, Finance, and Money

Banking Institutions - Assets/Liabilities - *FSM*, FSY**
Monetary Authorities - Assets/Liabilities - *FSM*, FSY**
Money Supply - *FSM*, FSY*, UNY, WTA**

Exchange Rates

Currency - *Ghanaian Cedi*
Cross Rates - *N/A*
Forward Exchange Rate - *N/A*
Per ECU - *N/A*
Per SDR - *FSM*, FSY**
Per U.S. Dollar - *DRF, FSM*, FSY*, UNY*

Government Finance

Debt - *FSM*, GSY*, WTA**
Deficit/Surplus - *FSM*, FSY*, GSY*, WDR, WTA**
Expenditure - *GSY*, WDR, WTA**
Revenue - *GSY*, WDR, WTA**

Interest Rates

Bank Rate - *N/A*
Discount Rate - *FSM*, FSY*, UNY*
Government Bonds - *N/A*
Money Market - *N/A*
Treasury Bills - *FSM*, FSY*, UNY*

International Liquidity

Reserves Minus Gold - *FSM*, FSY*, UNY, WTA**
Gold - *FSM*, FSY*, UNY, WTA**

International Transactions

Balance of Payments - *BOP*, FSM*, FSY*, UNY, WDR, WTA**
Exports - *FSM*, FSY*, UNN, UNY, WTA**
Imports - *FSM*, FSY*, UNN, UNY, WTA**

National Accounts

Consumption
Government - *FSM*, FSY*, UNN, WDR*
Private - *FSM*, FSY*, UNN, WDR*
Gross Domestic Product - *FSM*, FSY*, GSY*, UNN, UNY, WDR, WTA**
Gross National Product - *FSM*, FSY*, UNN, WDR, WTA**
National Income - *FSM*, FSY*, UNN, WTA**

Prices, Production, Employment

Consumer Credit Outstanding - *N/A*
Consumer Prices - *FSM*, FSY*, GSY*, WDR, WTA**
Earnings/Wages - *UNY, WDR, WTA**
Employment - *UNY*
Production
Industrial - *UNY, WTA**
Manufacturing - *UNN, UNY, WTA**
Mining - *UNA, UNY*
Wholesale/Producer Prices - *FSM*, FSY**

Securities Markets - *N/A*

Ghanaian Cedi - *see* - Ghana - Exchange Rates

Gold - *see* - Commodities; Individual Countries - International Liquidity; *see also* - Commodities

Government Bonds - *see* - Individual Countries - Interest Rates

Great Britain - *see* - United Kingdom

Greece

Banking, Finance, and Money

Banking Institutions - Assets/Liabilities - *FSM*, FSY**
Monetary Authorities - Assets/Liabilities - *FSM*, FSY**
Money Supply - *FSM*, FSY*, MEI*, UNY, WDR, WTA**

Exchange Rates

Currency - *Greek Drachma*
Cross Rates - *N/A*
Forward Exchange Rate - *N/A*
Per ECU - *FTI*
Per SDR - *FSM*, FSY*, FTI*

Per U.S. Dollar - *DJN, DRF, FRB, FSM*, FSY*, FTI, MEI*, UNY, WSJ*

Government Finance

Debt - *GSY**
Deficit/Surplus - *FSM*, FSY*, GSY*, WDR, WTA**
Expenditure - *GSY*, WDR, WTA**
Revenue - *GSY*, WDR, WTA**

Interest Rates

Bank Rate - *N/A*
Discount Rate - *FSM*, FSY*, UNY*
Government Bonds - *N/A*
Money Market - *N/A*
Treasury Bills - *FSM*, FSY*, UNY*

International Liquidity

Reserves Minus Gold - *FSM*, FSY*, MEI*, UNY, WTA**
Gold - *FSM*, FSY*, UNY, WTA**

International Transactions

Balance of Payments - *BOP*, FSM*, FSY*, MEI*, UNY, WDR, WTA**
Exports - *FSM*, FSY*, MEI*, UNN, UNY, WTA**
Imports - *FSM*, FSY*, MEI*, UNN, UNY, WTA**

National Accounts

Consumption
Government - *FSM*, FSY*, UNN, WDR, WTA**
Private - *FSM*, FSY*, UNN, WDR, WTA**
Gross Domestic Product - *FSM*, FSY*, GSY*, UNN, UNY, WDR, WTA**
Gross National Product - *FSM*, FSY*, UNN, WDR, WTA**
National Income - *FSM*, FSY*, UNN, WTA**

Prices, Production, Employment

Consumer Credit Outstanding - *FS2**
Consumer Prices *FSM*, FSY*, GSY*, MEI*, UNY, WDR, WTA**
Earnings/Wages - *FSM*, FSY*, MEI*, UNY, WDR, WTA**
Employment - *FSM*, FSY*, UNY, MEI*, WTA**
Production

Industrial - *FSY*, MEI*, UNY, WTA**
Manufacturing - *FSM*, MEI*, UNN, UNY, WTA**
Mining - *UNY*
Wholesale/Producer Prices - *UNY*

Securities Markets

Stock Exchange - *Athens Stock Exchange (ASE)*
Index - *Athens Stock Exchange Share Price Index*
Eurobonds
  Value of bonds issued - *FS1*
Foreign Bonds
  Value of bonds issued - *FS1*
Shares
  Price Index - *BAR, MEI**
Stock Exchange Capitalization - *FS2**

Greek Drachma - *see* - Greece - Exchange Rates

Grenada

Banking, Finance, and Money

Banking Institutions - Assets/Liabilities - *FSM*, FSY**
Monetary Authorities - Assets/Liabilities - *FSM*, FSY**
Money Supply - *FSM*, FSY*, UNY, WTA**

Exchange Rates

Currency - *East Caribbean Dollar*
Cross Rates - *N/A*
Forward Exchange Rate - *N/A*
Per ECU - *N/A*
Per SDR - *FSM*, FSY**
Per U.S. Dollar - *DRF, FSM*, FSY*, UNY*

Government Finance

Debt - *WTA**
Deficit/Surplus - *FSY**
Expenditure - *N/A*
Revenue - *N/A*

Interest Rates

Bank Rate - *N/A*
Discount Rate - *N/A*
Government Bonds - *N/A*

Money Market - *N/A*
Treasury Bills - *FSM*, FSY*, UNY*

International Liquidity

Reserves Minus Gold - *FSM*, UNY, WTA**
Gold - *N/A*

International Transactions

Balance of Payments - *BOP*, FSM*, FSY*, UNY, WTA**
Exports - *FSM*, FSY*, UNN, UNY, WTA**
Imports - *FSM*, FSY*, UNN, UNY, WTA**

National Accounts

Consumption
  Government - *FSM*, FSY*, UNN*
  Private - *FSM*, FSY*, UNN*
Gross Domestic Product - *FSM*, FSY*, UNN, UNY, WTA**
Gross National Product - *UNN, WTA**
National Income - *N/A*

Prices, Production, Employment

Consumer Credit Outstanding - *N/A*
Consumer Prices - *FSM*, FSY*, UNY, WTA**
Earnings/Wages - *N/A*
Employment - *N/A*
Production
  Industrial - *WTA**
  Manufacturing - *WTA**
Wholesale/Producer Prices - *N/A*

Securities Markets - *N/A*

Gross Domestic Product - *see* **- Individual Countries - National Accounts**

Gross National Product - *see* **- Individual Countries - National Accounts**

Guadeloupe

Banking, Finance, and Money

Banking Institutions - Assets/Liabilities - *N/A*
Monetary Authorities - Assets/Liabilities - *N/A*
Money Supply - *N/A*

Exchange Rates

Currency - *Guadeloupe Franc*
Cross Rates - *N/A*
Forward Exchange Rate - *N/A*
Per ECU - *N/A*
Per SDR - *N/A*
Per U.S. Dollar - *DRF*

Government Finance

Debt - *N/A*
Deficit/Surplus - *N/A*
Expenditure - *N/A*
Revenue - *N/A*

Interest Rates

Bank Rate - *N/A*
Discount Rate - *N/A*
Government Bonds - *N/A*
Money Market - *N/A*
Treasury Bills - *N/A*

International Liquidity

Reserves Minus Gold - *N/A*
Gold - *N/A*

International Transactions

Balance of Payments - *N/A*
Exports - *UNN, UNY*
Imports - *UNN, UNY*

National Accounts

Consumption
  Government - *UNN*
  Private - *UNN*
Gross Domestic Product - *UNN, UNY*
Gross National Product - *UNN*
National Income - *N/A*

Prices, Production, Employment

Consumer Credit Outstanding - *N/A*
Consumer Prices - *UNY*
Earnings/Wages - *N/A*

Employment - *N/A*
Production - *N/A*
Wholesale/Producer Prices - *N/A*

Securities Markets - *N/A*

Guadeloupe Franc - *see -* **Guadeloupe - Exchange Rates**

Guarani - *see -* **Paraguay - Exchange Rates**

Guatemala

Banking, Finance, and Money

Banking Institutions - Assets/Liabilities - *FSM*, FSY**
Monetary Authorities - Assets/Liabilities - *FSM*, FSY**
Money Supply - *FSM*, FSY*, UNY, WTA**

Exchange Rates

Currency - *Guatemalan Quetzale*
Cross Rates - *N/A*
Forward Exchange Rate - *N/A*
Per ECU - *N/A*
Per SDR - *FSM*, FSY**
Per U.S. Dollar - *DRF, FSM*, FSY*, UNY*

Government Finance

Debt - *FSM*, FSY*, GSY*, WTA**
Deficit/Surplus - *FSM*, FSY*, GSY*, WDR, WTA**
Expenditure - *GSY*, WDR, WTA**
Revenue - *GSY*, WDR, WTA**

Interest Rates

Bank Rate - *N/A*
Discount Rate - *FSM*, FSY**
Government Bonds - *N/A*
Money Market - *N/A*
Treasury Bills - *N/A*

International Liquidity

Reserves Minus Gold - *FSM*, FSY*, UNY, WTA**
Gold - *FSM*, FSY*, UNY, WTA**

International Transactions

Balance of Payments - *BOP*, FSM*, FSY*, UNY, WDR, WTA**
Exports - *FSM*, FSY*, UNN, UNY, WTA**
Imports - *FSM*, FSY*, UNN, UNY, WTA**

National Accounts

Consumption
  Government - *FSM*, FSY*, UNN, WDR, WTA**
  Private - *FSM*, FSY*, UNN, WDR, WTA**
Gross Domestic Product - *FSM*, FSY*, GSY*, UNN, UNY, WDR, WTA**
Gross National Product - *FSM*, FSY*, UNN, WDR, WTA**
National Income - *UNN, WTA**

Prices, Production, Employment

Consumer Credit Outstanding - *N/A*
Consumer Prices - *FSM*, FSY*, GSY*, UNY, WDR, WTA**
Earnings/Wages - *UNY, WDR, WTA**
Employment - *UNY, WTA**
Production - *N/A*
Wholesale/Producer Prices - *FSY**

Securities Markets - *N/A*

Guatemalan Quetzal - *see* - **Guatemala - Exchange Rates**

Guilder - *see* - **Netherlands - Exchange Rates; Netherlands Antilles - Exchange Rates; Suriname - Exchange Rates**

Guinea - Bissau

Banking, Finance, and Money

Banking Institutions - Assets/Liabilities - *N/A*
Monetary Authorities - Assets/Liabilities - *N/A*
Money Supply - *WTA**

Exchange Rates

Currency - *Guinea Peso*
Cross Rates - *N/A*
Forward Exchange Rate - *N/A*
Per ECU - *N/A*
Per SDR - *N/A*

Per U.S. Dollar - *DRF, UNY*

Government Finance

Debt - *GSY*, WTA**
Deficit/Surplus - *GSY*, WDR, WTA**
Expenditure - *UNY, WDR, WTA**
Revenue - *UNY, WDR, WTA**

Interest Rates

Bank Rate - *N/A*
Discount Rate - *N/A*
Government Bonds - *N/A*
Money Market - *N/A*
Treasury Bills - *N/A*

International Liquidity

Reserves Minus Gold - *WTA**
Gold - *N/A*

International Transactions

Balance of Payments - *BOP*, UNY, WDR, WTA**
Exports - *UNN, UNY, WTA**
Imports - *UNN, UNY, WTA**

National Accounts

Consumption
  Government - *UNN, WTA**
  Private - *UNN, WTA**
Gross Domestic Product - *GSY*, WDR, WTA**
Gross National Product - *UNN, WDR, WTA**
National Income - *UNN, UNY, WTA**

Prices, Production, Employment

Consumer Credit Outstanding - *N/A*
Consumer Prices - *UNY, WTA**
Earnings/Wages - *N/A*
Employment - *N/A*
Production
  Industrial - *WTA**
  Manufacturing - *WTA**
Wholesale/Producer Prices - *N/A*

Securities Markets - *N/A*

Guinea Peso - *see* **- Guinea-Bissau - Exchange Rates**

Guyana

Banking, Finance, and Money

Banking Institutions - Assets/Liabilities - *FSM*, FSY**
Monetary Authorities - Assets/Liabilities - *FSM*, FSY**
Money Supply - *FSM*, FSY*, UNY, WTA**

Exchange Rates

Currency - *Guyana Dollar*
Cross Rates - *N/A*
Forward Exchange Rate - *N/A*
Per ECU - *N/A*
Per SDR - *FSM*, FSY**
Per U.S. Dollar - *DRF, FSM*, FSY*, UNN*

Government Finance

Debt - *FSM*, FSY*, GSY*, WTA**
Deficit/Surplus - *FSM*, FSY*, GSY*, WTA**
Expenditure - *GSY*, WTA**
Revenue - *GSY*, WTA**

Interest Rates

Bank Rate - *N/A*
Discount Rate - *FSM*, FSY*, UNY*
Government Bonds - *N/A*
Money Market - *N/A*
Treasury Bills - *FSM*, FSY*, UNY*

International Liquidity

Reserves Minus Gold - *FSM*, FSY*, UNN, WTA**
Gold - *N/A*

International Transactions

Balance of Payments - *BOP*, FSY*, WTA**
Exports - *FSM*, FSY*, UNN, UNY, WTA**
Imports - *FSM*, FSY*, UNN, UNY, WTA**

National Accounts

Consumption
Government - FSM*, FSY*, UNN, WTA*
Private - FSM*, FSY*, UNN, WTA*

Gross Domestic Product - *FSM*, FSY*, GSY*, UNN, UNY,
WTA**
Gross National Product - *FSM*, FSY*, UNN, WTA**
National Income - *FSM*, FSY*, UNN, WTA**

Prices, Production, Employment

Consumer Credit Outstanding - *N/A*
Consumer Prices - *FSM*, FSY*, GSY*, UNY, WTA**
Earnings/Wages - *N/A*
Employment - *N/A*
Production
   Industrial - *WTA**
   Manufacturing - *WTA**
Wholesale/Producer Prices - *N/A*

Securities Markets - *N/A*

Guyana Dollar - *see* - Guyana - Exchange Rates

H

Haiti

Banking, Finance, and Money

Banking Institutions - Assets/Liabilities - *FSM*, FSY**
Monetary Authorities - Assets/Liabilities - *FSM*, FSY**
Money Supply - *FSM*, FSY*, UNY, WTA**

Exchange Rates

Currency - *Haitian Gourde*
Cross Rates - *N/A*
Forward Exchange Rate - *N/A*
Per ECU - *N/A*
Per SDR - *FSM*, FSY**
Per U.S. Dollar - *DRF, FSM*, FSY*, UNY*

Government Finance

Debt - *WTA**
Deficit/Surplus - *FSY*, GSY*, WTA**
Expenditure - *GSY*, WDR, WTA**
Revenue - *GSY*, WTA**

Interest Rates

Bank Rate - *N/A*
Discount Rate - *N/A*
Government Bonds - *N/A*
Money Market - *N/A*
Treasury Bills - *N/A*

International Liquidity

Reserves Minus Gold - *FSM*, FSY*, UNY, WTA**
Gold - *FSM*, FSY*, UNY, WTA**

International Transactions

Balance of Payments - *BOP*, FSM*, FSY*, UNY, WDR, WTA**

Exports - *FSM*, FSY*, UNN, UNY, WTA**

Imports - *FSM*, FSY*, UNN, UNY, WTA**

National Accounts

Consumption
  Government - *UNA, WDR, WTA**
  Private - *FSM*, FSY*, WDR, WTA**
  Gross Domestic Product - *FSM*, FSY*, GSY*, UNN, UNY, WDR, WTA**
  Gross National Product - *FSM*, FSY*, UNN, WDR, WTA**
  National Income - *FSM*, FSY*, UNN, WTA**

Prices, Production, Employment

Consumer Credit Outstanding - *N/A*
Consumer Prices - *FSM*, FSY*, GSY*, UNN, WDR, WTA**
Earnings/Wages - *WDR*
Employment - *UNY, WTA**
Production - *N/A*
Wholesale/Producer Prices - *N/A*

Securities Markets - *N/A*

Haitian Gourde - *see* - Haiti - Exchange Rates

Hang Seng Index - *see* - Hong Kong - Securities Markets; *see also* - Commodities

Hang Seng Bank Index - *see* - Hong Kong - Securities Markets

Heating Oil - *see* - Commodities

Helibor - *see* - Finland - Interest Rates

Helsinki Stock Exchange - *see* - Finland - Securities Markets

Hex General - *see* - Finland - Securities Markets

Hogs - *see* - Commodities

Honduran Lempira - *see* - Honduras - Exchange Rates

Honduras

Banking, Finance, and Money

Banking Institutions - Assets/Liabilities - *FSM**, *FSY**
Monetary Authorities - Assets/Liabilities - *FSM**, *FSY**
Money Supply - *FSM**, *FSY**, *UNY*, *WTA**

Exchange Rates

Currency - *Honduran Lempira*
Cross Rates - *N/A*
Forward Exchange Rate - *N/A*
Per ECU - *N/A*
Per SDR - *FSM**, *FSY**
Per U.S. Dollar - DRF, FSM*, FSY*, UNY

Government Finance

Debt - *FSM**, *FSY**, *WTA**
Deficit/Surplus - *FSM**, *FSY**, *WDR*, *WTA**
Expenditure - *WDR*, *WTA**
Revenue - *WDR*, *WTA**

Interest Rates

Bank Rate - *N/A*
Discount Rate - *FSM**, *FSY**, *UNY*
Government Bonds - *FSM**, *FSY**
Money Market - *N/A*
Treasury Bills - *N/A*

International Liquidity

Reserves Minus Gold - *FSM**, *FSY**, *UNY*, *WTA**
Gold - *FSM**, *FSY**, *UNY*, *WTA**

International Transactions

Balance of Payments - *BOP**, *FSM**, *FSY**, *UNY*, *WDR*, *WTA**
Exports - *FSM**, *FSY**, *UNN*, *UNY*, *WTA**
Imports - *FSM**, *FSY**, *UNN*, *UNY*, *WTA**

National Accounts

Consumption
Government - *FSM**, *FSY**, *UNN*, *WDR*, *WTA**
Private - *FSM**, *FSY**, *UNN*, *WDR*, *WTA**

Gross Domestic Product - *FSM*, FSY*, UNN, UNY, WDR, WTA**

Gross National Product - *FSM*, FSY*, UNN, WDR, WTA**

National Income - *FSM*, FSY*, UNN, WTA**

Prices, Production, Employment

Consumer Credit Outstanding - *N/A*

Consumer Prices - *FSM*, FSY*, UNY, WDR, WTA**

Earnings/Wages - *UNY, WDR, WTA**

Employment - *UNY*

Production

  Industrial - *UNY, WTA**

  Manufacturing - *UNY, WTA**

  Mining - *UNY*

Wholesale/Producer Prices - *UNY*

Securities Markets - *N/A*

Hong Kong

Banking, Finance, and Money

Banking Institutions - Assets/Liabilities - *N/A*

Monetary Authorities - Assets/Liabilities - *N/A*

Money Supply - *N/A*

Exchange Rates

Currency - *Hong Kong Dollar*

Cross Rates - *N/A*

Forward Exchange Rate - *N/A*

Per ECU - *N/A*

Per SDR - *N/A*

Per U.S. Dollar - *BAR, DJN, DRF, FRB, FTI, NYT, UNY, WSJ*

Government Finance

Debt - *N/A*

Deficit/Surplus - *WDR*

Expenditure - *WDR*

Revenue - *WDR*

Interest Rates

Bank Rate - *N/A*

Discount Rate - *N/A*

Government Bonds - *N/A*

Money Market - *N/A*
Treasury Bills - *N/A*

International Liquidity

Reserves Minus Gold - *N/A*
Gold - *N/A*

International Transactions

Balance of Payments - *WDR, WTA**
Exports - *UNN, UNY, WTA**
Imports - *UNN, UNY, WTA**

National Accounts

Consumption
  Government - *UNN, WDR, WTA**
  Private - *UNN, WDR, WTA**
Gross Domestic Product - *UNN, UNY, WDR, WTA**
Gross National Product - *WDR, WTA**
National Income - *WTA**

Prices, Production, Employment

Consumer Credit Outstanding - *N/A*
Consumer Prices - *UNY, WDR, WTA**
Earnings/Wages - *WDR*
Employment - *UNY*
Production - *UNY*
Wholesale/Producer Prices - *N/A*

Securities Markets

Stock Exchange - *The Stock Exchange of Hong Kong Limited*
Indexes
  Hang Seng Index
  Hang Seng Bank Index
  Hong Kong Stock Index
Foreign Bonds
  Value of bonds issued - *FS1*
Shares
  Price Indexes
    Hang Seng Bank Index - *DRI, FTI*
    Hang Seng Stock Index - *BAR, DJN, DRI, NYT, WSJ*
    Hong Kong Stock Index - *DRI*
  Prices - Selected Issues - *BAR, FTI, NYT, WSJ*

Hong Kong Dollar - *see* - **Hong Kong - Exchange Rates**

Hong Kong Stock Index - *see* - **Hong Kong - Securities Markets;** *see also* - **Commodities**

Hungarian Florint - *see* - **Hungary - Exchange Rates**

Hungary

Banking, Finance, and Money

Banking Institutions - Assets/Liabilities - *FSM*, FSY**
Monetary Authorities - Assets/Liabilities - *FSM*, FSY**
Money Supply - *FSM*, FSY*, UNN, WTA**

Exchange Rates

Currency - *Hungarian Florint*
Cross Rates - *N/A*
Forward Exchange Rate - *N/A*
Per ECU - *N/A*
Per SDR - *FSM*, FSY**
Per U.S. Dollar - *BAR, DJN, DRF, FSM*, FSY*, NYT, UNY, WSJ*

Government Finance

Debt - *GSY*, WTA**
Deficit/Surplus - *FSM*, FSY*, GSY*, WTA**
Expenditure - *GSY*, WDR, WTA**
Revenue - *GSY*, WDR, WTA**

Interest Rates

Bank Rate - *N/A*
Discount Rate - *FSM*, FSY*, UNY*
Government Bonds - *N/A*
Money Market - *N/A*
Treasury Bills - *N/A*

International Liquidity

Reserves Minus Gold - *FSM*, FSY*, UNY, WTA**
Gold - *FSM*, FSY*, UNY, WTA**

International Transactions

Balance of Payments - BOP*, FSM*, FSY*, UNY, WDR, WTA*
Exports - FSM*, FSY*, UNN, UNY, WTA*

Imports - FSM*, FSY*, UNN, UNY, WTA*

National Accounts

Consumption
Government - FSM*, FSY*, UNN, WDR, WTA*
Private - FSM*, FSY*, UNN, WDR, WTA*
Gross Domestic Product - *FSM*, FSY*, GSY*, UNN, UNY, WDR, WTA**
Gross National Product - *WDR, WTA**
National Income - *FSM*, FSY*, WTA**

Prices, Production, Employment

Consumer Credit Outstanding - *N/A*
Consumer Prices - *FSM*, FSY*, GSY*, UNY, WDR, WTA**
Earnings/Wages - *FSM*, FSY*, UNY, WTA**
Employment - *FSM*, FSY*, UNY, WDR, WTA**
Production
Industrial - *UNN, UNY, WTA**
Manufacturing - *UNN, UNY*
Mining - *UNY*
Wholesale/Producer Prices - *FSM*, FSY**

Securities Markets

Stock Exchange - *Budapesti Ertekpapir Tozsde (Budapest Stock Exchange)*
Foreign Bonds
Value of bonds issued - *FS1*

I

Iceland

Banking, Finance, and Money

Banking Institutions - Assets/Liabilities - *FSM*, FSY**
Monetary Authorities - Assets/Liabilities - *FSM*, FSY**
Money Supply - *FSM*, FSY*, UNY, WDR, WTA**

Exchange Rates

Currency - *Icelandic Krona*
Cross Rates - *N/A*
Forward Exchange Rate - *N/A*
Per ECU - *N/A*
Per SDR - *FSM*, FSY**
Per U.S. Dollar - *DJN, DRF, FSM*, FSY*, MEI*, UNY*

Government Finance

Debt - *FSM*, FSY*, GSY*, WTA**
Deficit/Surplus - *FSM*, FSY*, GSY**
Expenditure - *GSY*, WTA**
Revenue - *GSY*, WTA**

Interest Rates

Bank Rate - *N/A*
Discount Rate - *FSM*, FSY*, UNY*
Government Bonds - *N/A*
Money Market - *N/A*
Treasury Bills - *N/A*

International Liquidity

Reserves Minus Gold - *FSM*, FSY*, MEI*, UNY, WTA**
Gold - *FSM*, FSY*, UNY, WTA**

International Transactions

Balance of Payments - *BOP*, FSM*, FSY*, UNY, WTA**
Exports - *FSM*, FSY*, MEI*, UNN, UNY, WTA**
Imports - *FSM*, FSY*, UNN, UNY, MEI*, WTA**

National Accounts

Consumption
  Government - *FSM*, FSY*, UNN, WTA**
  Private - *FSM*, FSY*, UNN, WTA**
Gross Domestic Product - *FSM*, FSY*, GSY*, UNN, UNY, WTA**
Gross National Product - *FSM*, FSY*, UNN, WTA**
National Income - *FSM*, FSY*, UNN, WTA**

Prices, Production, Employment

Consumer Credit Outstanding - *N/A*
Consumer Prices - *FSM*, FSY*, GSY*, UNY, WDR, WTA**
Earnings/Wages - *FSM*, FSY*, WTA**
Employment - *FSY*, UNY, WTA**
Production
  Fish Catch - *FSY*, MEI**
  Industrial - *UNN*
  Manufacturing - *UNN*
Wholesale/Producer Prices - *N/A*

Securities Markets - *N/A*

Icelandic Krona - *see* - Iceland - Exchange Rates

IGPA (General Share Price Index) - *see* - Chile - Securities Markets

Imports - *see* - Individual Countries - International Transactions

India

Banking, Finance, and Money

Banking Institutions - Assets/Liabilities - *N/A*
Monetary Authorities - Assets/Liabilities - *FSM*, FSY**
Money Supply - *FSM*, FSY*, UNY, WTA**

Exchange Rates

Currency - *Indian Rupee*
Cross Rates - *N/A*

Forward Exchange Rate - *N/A*
Per ECU - *N/A*
Per SDR - *FSM*, FSY**
Per U.S. Dollar - *BAR, DJN, DRF, FRB, FSM*, FSY*, NYT, UNY, WSJ*

Government Finance

Debt - *FSM*, FSY*, GSY*, WTA**
Deficit/Surplus - *FSM*, FSY*, GSY*, WDR, WTA**
Expenditure - *GSY*, WDR, WTA**
Revenue - *GSY*, WDR, WTA**

Interest Rates

Bank Rate - *FSM*, FSY**
Discount Rate - *GSY**
Government Bonds - *FSY**
Money Market - *FSM*, FSY**
Treasury Bills - *N/A*

International Liquidity

Reserves Minus Gold - *FSM*, FSY*, UNY, WTA**
Gold - *FSM*, FSY*, UNY, WTA**

International Transactions

Balance of Payments - *BOP*, FSM*, FSY*, UNY, WDR, WTA**
Exports - *FSM*, FSY*, UNN, UNY, WTA**
Imports - *FSM*, FSY*, UNN, UNY, WTA**

National Accounts

Consumption
Government - *FSM*, FSY*, UNN, WDR, WTA**
Private - *FSM*, FSY*, UNN, WDR, WTA**
Gross Domestic Product - *FSM*, FSY*, GSY*, UNN, WDR, WTA**
Gross National Product - *FSM*, FSY*, UNN, WDR, WTA**
National Income - *FSM*, FSY*, UNN, WTA**

Prices, Production, Employment

Consumer Credit Outstanding - *N/A*
Consumer Prices - *FSM*, FSY*, GSY*, UNY, WDR, WTA**
Earnings/Wages - *UNY, WDR, WTA**

Employment - *UNY, WTA**
Production
   Industrial - *FSM*, FSY*, UNN, UNY, WTA**
   Manufacturing - *UNN, UNY, WTA**
   Wholesale/Producer Prices - *FSM*, FSY*, UNY*

Securities Markets

Stock Exchange - *The Bombay Stock Exchange*
Index - *Economic Times Index of Ordinary Shares*
Bonds
   Issue price *N/A*
   Yield - *N/A*
Eurobonds
   Value of bonds issued - *N/A*
Foreign Bonds
   Value of bonds issued - *N/A*
Shares
   Dividend yield - *N/A*
   Issue price - *N/A*
   Last day of month - *N/A*
   Price/Earnings Ratio - *N/A*
   Price Index - *BAR, UNY*
   Prices - Selected Issues - *N/A*
   Total Gross - *N/A*
   Yield - *N/A*
Stock Exchange Capitalization - *N/A*
Stock Exchange Turnover - *N/A*

Indian Rupee - *see* - **India** - **Exchange Rates**

Indonesia

Banking, Finance, and Money

Banking Institutions - Assets/Liabilities - *FSM*, FSY**
Monetary Authorities - Assets/Liabilities - *FSM*, FSY**
Money Supply - *FSM*, FSY*, UNY, WTA**

Exchange Rates

Currency - *Indonesian Rupiah*
Cross Rates - *N/A*
Forward Exchange Rate - *N/A*
Per ECU - *N/A*

Per SDR - *FSM*, FSY**
Per U.S. Dollar - *BAR, DJN, DRF, FSM*, FSY*, NYT, UNY, WSJ*

Government Finance

Debt - *FSM*, FSY*, GSY*, WTA**
Deficit/Surplus - *FSM*, FSY*, GSY*, WDR, WTA**
Expenditure - *GSY*, WDR, WTA**
Revenue - *GSY*, WDR, WTA**

Interest Rates

Bank Rate - *N/A*
Discount Rate - *N/A*
Government Bonds - *N/A*
Money Market - *FSM*, FSY**
Treasury Bills - *N/A*

International Liquidity

Reserves Minus Gold - *FSM*, FSY*, UNY, WTA**
Gold - *FSM*, FSY*, UNY, WTA**

International Transactions

Balance of Payments - *BOP*, FSM*, FSY*, UNY, WDR, WTA**
Exports - *FSM*, FSY*, UNN, UNY, WTA**
Imports - *FSM*, FSY*, UNN, UNY, WTA**

National Accounts

Consumption
Government - *FSM*, FSY*, UNN, WDR, WTA**
Private - *FSM*, FSY*, UNN, WDR, WTA**
Gross Domestic Product - *FSM*, FSY*, GSY*, UNN, WDR, WTA**
Gross National Product - *FSM*, FSY*, UNN, WDR, WTA**
National Income - *FSM*, FSY*, UNN, WTA**

Prices, Production, Employment

Consumer Credit Outstanding - *N/A*
Consumer Prices - *FSM*, FSY*, GSY*, UNN, WDR, WTA**
Earnings/Wages - *WDR*
Employment - *UNY*
Production

    Crude Petroleum - *FSY**
    Industrial - *WTA**
    Manufacturing - *UNY, WTA**
    Wholesale/Producer Prices - *FSM*, FSY*, UNY*

Securities Markets

    Stock Exchange - *Bursa Efek Indonesia (The Jakarta Stock Exchange)*
    Index - *The Jakarta Stock Exchange Share Price Index*
    Bonds
        Issue price - *N/A*
        Yield - *N/A*
    Eurobonds
        Value of bonds issued - *N/A*
    Foreign Bonds
        Value of bonds issued - *FS1*
    Shares
        Dividend yield - *N/A*
        Issue price - *N/A*
        Last day of month - *N/A*
        Price/Earnings Ratio - *N/A*
        Price Index - *BAR, DRF*
        Prices - Selected Issues - *N/A*
        Total Gross - *N/A*
        Yield - *N/A*
    Stock Exchange Capitalization - *N/A*
    Stock Exchange Turnover - *N/A*

Indonesian Rupiah - *see* - **Indonesia - Exchange Rates**

Inti - *see* - **Peru - Exchange Rates**

Iran

Banking, Finance, and Money

    Banking Institutions - Assets/Liabilities - *FSM*, FSY**
    Monetary Authorities - Assets/Liabilities - *FSM*, FSY**
    Money Supply - *FSM*, FSY*, UNY, WTA**

Exchange Rates

    Currency - *Iranian Rial*
    Cross Rates - *N/A*
    Forward Exchange Rate - *N/A*

Per ECU - *N/A*
Per SDR - *FSM*, FSY**
Per U.S. Dollar - *DJN, DRF, FSM*, FSY*, FTI, UNY*

Government Finance

Debt - *FSY*, GSY**
Deficit/Surplus - *FSM*, FSY*, GSY*, WDR, WTA**
Expenditure - *GSY*, WDR, WTA**
Revenue - *GSY*, WDR, WTA**

Interest Rates

Bank Rate - *N/A*
Discount Rate - *FSY**
Government Bonds - *N/A*
Money Market - *N/A*
Treasury Bills - *N/A*

International Liquidity

Reserves Minus Gold - *FSM*, FSY*, UNY, WTA**
Gold - *FSM*, FSY*, UNY, WTA**

International Transactions

Balance of Payments - *FSM*, FSY*, UNY, WDR, WTA**
Exports - *FSM*, FSY*, UNN, UNY, WTA**
Imports - *FSM*, FSY*, UNN, UNY, WTA**

National Accounts

Consumption
  Government - *FSM*, FSY*, UNN, WDR, WTA**
  Private - *FSM*, FSY*, UNN, WDR, WTA**
Gross Domestic Product - *FSM*, FSY*, GSY*, UNN, UNY, WDR, WTA**
Gross National Product - *FSM*, FSY*, UNN, WDR, WTA**
National Income - *UNN, WTA**

Prices, Production, Employment

Consumer Credit Outstanding - *N/A*
Consumer Prices - *FSM*, FSY*, GSY*, UNY, WDR, WTA**
Earnings/Wages - *FSM*, FSY*, WDR, WTA**
Production
  Crude Petroleum - *FSM*, FSY**
  Industrial - *WTA**

Manufacturing - *UNY*
Wholesale/Producer Prices - *FSM**, *FSY**

Securities Markets - *N/A*

Iranian Rial - *see* **- Iran - Exchange Rates**

Iraq

Banking, Finance, and Money

Banking Institutions - Assets/Liabilities - *FSY**
Monetary Authorities - Assets/Liabilities - *FSY**
Money Supply - *FSY**

Exchange Rates

Currency - *Iraqi Dinar*
Cross Rates - *N/A*
Per ECU - *N/A*
Per SDR - *FSM**, *FSY**
Per U.S. Dollar - *DRF, FSM**, *FSY**, *UNY*

International Liquidity

Reserves Minus Gold - *FSY**, *UNY*
Gold - *FSY**

International Transactions

Balance of Payments - *FSY**, *WDR*
Exports - *FSY**, *UNN, UNY*
Imports - *FSY**, *UNN, UNY*

National Accounts

Consumption
  Government - *FSY**
  Private - *FSY**
Gross Domestic Product - *FSY**, *UNY, WDR*
Gross National Product - *FSY**
National Income - *FSY**

Prices, Production, Employment

Consumer Credit Outstanding - *N/A*
Consumer Prices - *FSY**, *UNY, WDR*
Earnings/Wages - *N/A*
Employment - *N/A*
Production

Crude Petroleum - *FSM*, FSY**
Wholesale/Producer Prices - *FSY**

Securities Markets - *N/A*

Iraqi Dinar - *see* - Iraq - Exchange Rates

Ireland

Banking, Finance, and Money

Banking Institutions - Assets/Liabilities - *FSM*, FSY**
Monetary Authorities - Assets/Liabilities - *FSM*, FSY**
Money Supply - *FSM*, FSY*, MEI*, WTA**

Exchange Rates

Currency - *Irish Pound*
Cross Rates - *N/A*
Forward Exchange Rate - *N/A*
Per ECU - *N/A*
Per SDR - *FSM*, FSY**
Per U.S. Dollar - *BAR, DRF, FRB, FSM*, FSY*, MEI*, UNY*
Currency - *Punt*
Cross Rates - *N/A*
Forward Exchange Rate - *FTI*
Per ECU - *FTI*
Per SDR - *FTI*
Per U.S. Dollar - *BAR, DJN, NYT, WSJ*

Government Finance

Debt - *FSY**
Deficit/Surplus - *FSM*, FSY*, GSY*, WDR, WTA**
Expenditure - *GSY*, WDR, WTA**
Revenue - *GSY*, WDR, WTA**

Interest Rates

Bank Rate - *N/A*
Discount Rate - *FSM*, FSY*, UNY*
Government Bonds - *FSM*, FSY*, FS1, UNY, WDR*
Money Market - *FSM*, FSY**
Treasury Bills - *FSM*, FSY*, UNY, WDR*

International Liquidity

Reserves Minus Gold - *FSM*, FSY*, WDR, WTA**
Gold - *FSM*, FSY*, WTA**

International Transactions

Balance of Payments - *FSM*, FSY*, MEI*, WDR, WTA**
Exports - *FSM*, FSY*, MEI*, UNN, WTA**
Imports - *FSM*, FSY*, MEI*, UNN, WTA**

National Accounts

Consumption
  Government - *FSM*, FSY*, UNN, WDR, WTA**
  Private - *FSM*, FSY*, UNN, WDR, WTA**
Gross Domestic Product - *FSM*, FSY*, GSY*, UNN, UNY, WDR, WTA**
Gross National Product - *FSM*, FSY*, UNN, WDR, WTA**
National Income - *FSM*, FSY*, UNN, WTA**

Prices, Production, Employment

Consumer Credit Outstanding - *N/A*
Consumer Prices - *FSM*, FSY*, GSY*, MEI*, UNY, WDR, WTA**
Earnings/Wages - *FSM*, FSY*, MEI*, UNY, WDR, WTA**
Employment - *FSM*, FSY*, MEI*, UNY, WTA**
Production
  Industrial - *FSM*, FSY*, MEI*, UNY*
  Manufacturing - *MEI*, UNY*
  Mining - *UNY*
Wholesale/Producer Prices - *FSM*, FSY*, MEI*, UNY*

Securities Markets

Stock Exchange - *The Irish Stock Exchange*
Index - ISEQ Overall
Bonds
  Issue price - *N/A*
  Yield - *N/A*
Eurobonds
  Value of bonds issued - *FS1*
Foreign Bonds
  Value of bonds issued - *FS1*
Shares
  Dividend yield - *N/A*
  Issue price - *N/A*
  Price/Earnings Ratio - *N/A*
  Price Index - *BAR, FSM*, FSY*, FTI, MEI*, UNY*

Prices - *FSM*, FSY*, MEI*, UNY*
Prices - Selected Issues - *N/A*
Yield - *N/A*
Stock Exchange Capitalization - *N/A*
Stock Exchange Turnover - *N/A*

Irish Pound - *see* **- Ireland - Exchange Rates**

ISEQ Overall - *see* **- Ireland - Securities Markets**

Israel

Banking, Finance, and Money

Banking Institutions - Assets/Liabilities - *FSM*, FSY**
Monetary Authorities - Assets/Liabilities - *FSM*, FSY**
Money Supply - *FSM*, FSY*, UNY, WTA**

Exchange Rates

Currency - *Israel New Sheqalim*
Cross Rates - *N/A*
Forward Exchange Rate - *N/A*
Per ECU - *N/A*
Per SDR - *FSM*, FSY**
Per U.S. Dollar - *DJN, DRF, FSM*, FSY*, UNY*
Currency - *Shekel*
Cross Rates - *N/A*
Forward Exchange Rate - *N/A*
Per ECU - *N/A*
Per SDR - *N/A*
Per U.S. Dollar - *BAR, NYT, WSJ*

Government Finance

Debt - *FSY*, GSY**
Deficit/Surplus - *FSM*, GSY*, WDR, WTA**
Expenditure - *GSY*, WDR, WTA**
Revenue - *GSY*, WDR, WTA**

Interest Rates

Bank Rate - *N/A*
Discount Rate - *FSM*, FSY*, UNY*
Government Bonds - *N/A*
Money Market - *N/A*
Treasury Bills - *FSM*, FSY*, UNY*

International Liquidity

Reserves Minus Gold - *FSM*, FSY*, UNY, WTA**
Gold - *FSM*, FSY*, UNY, WTA**

International Transactions

Balance of Payments - *BOP*, FSM*, FSY*, UNY, WDR, WTA**
Exports - *FSM*, FSY*, UNN, UNY, WTA**
Imports - *FSM*, FSY*, UNN, UNY, WTA**

National Accounts

Consumption
  Government - *FSM*, FSY*, UNN, WDR, WTA**
  Private - *FSM*, FSY*, UNN, WDR, WTA**
Gross Domestic Product - *FSM*, FSY*, GSY*, UNN, UNY, WDR, WTA**
Gross National Product - *FSM*, FSY*, UNN, WDR, WTA**
National Income - *FSY*, UNN, WTA**

Prices, Production, Employment

Consumer Credit Outstanding - *N/A*
Consumer Prices - *FSM*, FSY*, GSY*, UNY, WDR, WTA**
Earnings/Wages - *FSM*, FSY*, UNY, WTA**
Employment - *FSM*, FSY*, UNY, WDR, WTA**
Production
  Industrial - *FSM*, FSY*, UNY*
  Manufacturing - *UNY*
  Mining - *UNY*
Wholesale/Producer Prices - *FSM*, FSY*, UNY, WTA**

Securities Markets

Stock Exchange - *Tel Aviv Stock Exchange*
Index
  TASE General Share Index
Foreign Bonds
  Value of bonds issued - *FS1*
Shares
  Price Index - *FSM*, FSY*, UNY*
  Prices - Selected Issues - *N/A*
  Share Prices - *FSM*, FSY*, UNY*

Israel New Sheqalim - *see* **- Israel - Exchange Rates**

Istanbul Menkulklymetler Borsasi (Istanbul Stock Exchange) - *see*
- Turkey - Securities Markets

Istanbul Stock Exchange - *see* **- Turkey - Securities Markets**

Italian Lira - *see* **- Italy - Exchange Rates**

Italy

Banking, Finance, and Money

Banking Institutions - Assets/Liabilities - *FSM*, FSY**
Monetary Authorities - Assets/Liabilities - *FSM*, FSY**
Money Supply - *FSM*, FSY*, MEI*, UNY, WTA**

Exchange Rates

Currency - *Italian Lira*
Cross Rates - *FTI, WSJ*
Forward Exchange Rate - *FTI*
Per ECU - *FTI*
Per SDR - *FSM*, FSY*, FTI, UNY*
Per U.S. Dollar - *BAR, DJN, DRF, FRB, FSM*, FSY*, GSY*,
MEI*, NYT, WSJ*

Government Finance

Debt - *FSM*, FSY*, GSY**
Deficit/Surplus - *FRB, FSM*, FSY*, FS1, FS2, UNY, WDR*
Expenditure - *GSY*, WDR, WTA**
Revenue - *GSY*, WDR, WTA**

Interest Rates

Bank Rate - *N/A*
Discount Rate - *DRF, FRB, FSM*, FSY*, FS1, FS2*, UNY,
WDR*
Government Bonds - *BAR, DRF, FSM*, FSY*, FTI, MEI*,
UNY*
Money Market - *FSM*, FSY**
Prime Rate - *DRF*
Treasury Bills - *FSM*, FSY*, FS1, UNY*

International Liquidity

Reserves Minus Gold - *FSM*, FSY*, UNY, WDR, WTA**
Gold - *FSM*, FSY*, UNY, WTA**

International Transactions

Balance of Payments - *BAR, FSM*, FSY*, MEI*, UNY, WDR, WTA**
Exports - *FSM*, FSY*, MEI*, UNN, UNY, WTA**
Imports - *FSM*, FSY*, MEI*, UNN, UNY, WTA**

National Accounts

Consumption
Government - *FSM*, FSY*, UNN, WDR, WTA**
Private - *FSM*, FSY*, UNN, WDR, WTA**
Gross Domestic Product - *FSM*, FSY*, GSY*, MEI*, UNN, UNY, WDR, WTA**
Gross National Product - *FSM*, FSY*, UNN, WDR, WTA**
National Income - *FSM*, FSY*, UNN, WTA**

Prices, Production, Employment

Consumer Credit Outstanding - *FS2**
Consumer Prices - *ECI, FSM*, FSY*, FS1, GSY*, MEI*, UNY, WDR, WTA**
Earnings/Wages - *FSM*, FSY*, MEI*, UNY, WDR, WTA**
Employment - *FSM*, FSY*, MEI*, UNY, WTA**
Production
Industrial - *ECI, FSM*, FSY*, MEI*, UNY, WTA**
Manufacturing - *MEI*, UNY, WTA**
Mining - *UNY*
Wholesale/Producer Prices - *FSM*, FSY*, MEI*, UNY*

Securities Markets

Stock Exchange - *Borsa Valori di Milano (Milan Stock Exchange)*
Indexes
BCI (Banca Commerciale Italiana)
MIB (Milano Indice Borsa)
Bonds
Issue price - *FS2**
Yield - *FS2**

Eurobonds
Value of bonds issued - *FS1*
Foreign Bonds
Value of bonds issued - *FS1*
Money Market Instruments Issued - *FS2**
Shares
Issue price - *FS2*
Price/Earnings Ratio - *FS1, FS2*
Price Indexes
BCI - *DRF, FTI*
MIB - *BAR, FTI, FS1, FS2*, FSM*, FSY*, DJN, DRI, NYT, UNY, WSJ*
Prices - FSM*, FSY*, FS1, FS2*, UNY
Prices - Selected Issues - BAR, FTI, NYT, WSJ
Total Gross - FS2*
Yield - FS1, FS2*
Stock Exchange Capitalization - *FS2**
Stock Exchange Turnover - *FS2**
Stock Market Instruments Issued - *FS2**

Ivory Coast - *see* - **Côte D'Ivoire**

J

Jakarta Stock Exchange (Bursa Efek Indonesia) - *see* - Indonesia - Securities Markets

Jakarta Stock Exchange Share Price Index - *see* - Indsonesia - Securities Markets

Jamaica

Banking, Finance, and Money

Banking Institutions - Assets/Liabilities - *FSM*, FSY**
Monetary Authorities - Assets/Liabilities - *FSM*, FSY**
Money Supply - *FSM*, FSY*, UNY, WTA**

Exchange Rates

Currency - *Jamaica Dollar*
Cross Rates - *N/A*
Forward Exchange Rate - *N/A*
Per ECU - *N/A*
Per SDR - *FSM*, FSY**
Per U.S. Dollar - *DJN, DRF, FSM*, FSY*, UNY*

Government Finance

Debt - *FSM*, GSY*, WTA**
Deficit/Surplus - *FSY*, GSY*, WTA**
Expenditure - *GSY*, WTA**
Revenue - *GSY*, WTA**

Interest Rates

Bank Rate - *FSY**
Discount Rate - *UNY*
Government Bonds - *FSY*, UNY*

Money Market - *FSY**
Treasury Bills - *FSY**, *UNY*

International Liquidity

Reserves Minus Gold - *FSY**, *UNY*, *WTA**
Gold - *FSY**, *WTA**

International Transactions

Balance of Payments - *BOP**, *FSM**, *UNY*, *WDR*, *WTA**
Exports - *FSY**, *UNN*, *UNY*, *WTA**
Imports - *FSY**, *UNN*, *UNY*, *WTA**

National Accounts

Consumption
  Government - *FSM**, *FSY**, *UNN*, *WDR*, *WTA**
  Private - *FSM**, *FSY**, *UNN*, *WDR*, *WTA**
  Gross Domestic Product - *FSM**, *FSY**, *GSY**, *UNN*, *UNY*, *WDR*, *WTA**
  Gross National Product - *FSM**, *FSY**, *UNN*, *WDR*, *WTA**
  National Income - *UNN*, *WTA**

Prices, Production, Employment

Consumer Credit Outstanding - *N/A*
Consumer Prices - *FSM**, *FSY**, *GSY**, *UNY*, *WDR*, *WTA**
Earnings/Wages - *UNY*, *WDR*, *WTA**
Employment - *UNY*
Production
  Industrial - *WTA**
  Manufacturing - *UNN*, *WTA**
  Wholesale/Producer Prices - *N/A*

Securities Markets - *N/A*

Jamaica Dollar - *see* - Jamaica - Exchange Rates

Japan

Banking, Finance, and Money

Banking Institutions - Assets/Liabilities - *FSM**, *FSY**
Monetary Authorities - Assets/Liabilities - *FSM**, *FSY**
Money Supply - *FSM**, *FSY**, *MEI**, *WDR*, *WTA**

Exchange Rates

Currency - *Japanese Yen*

Cross Rates - *FTI, WSJ*
Currency Futures - *BAR, NYT, WSJ*
Currency Options - *BAR, NYT, WSJ*
Forward Exchange Rate - *FTI*
Per ECU - *FTI*
Per SDR - *FSM*, FSY*, FTI*
Per U.S. Dollar - *BAR, DJN, DRF, FRB, FSM*, FSY*, MEI*, NYT, UNY, WSJ*

Government Finance

Debt - *FSM*, FSY**
Deficit/Surplus - *FSM*, FSY*, GSY*, WDR, WTA**
Expenditure - *GSY*, WDR, WTA**
Revenue - *GSY*, WDR, WTA**

Interest Rates

Bank Rate - *N/A*
Discount Rate - *FRB, FSM*, FSY*, FS1, FS2, FTI, MEI, UNY*
Government Bonds - *BAR, DRF, FSM*, FSY*, FS1, MEI, UNY*
Money Market - *FSM*, FSY**
Prime Rate - *BAR, DJN, DRF, FS1, WSJ*
Treasury Bills - *DRF, UNY*

International Liquidity

Reserves Minus Gold - *FSM*, FSY*, MEI*, UNY, WTA**
Gold - *FSM*, FSY*, UNY, WTA**

International Transactions

Balance of Payments - *BOP*, FSM*, FSY*, MEI*, UNY, WDR, WTA**
Exports - *FSM*, FSY*, MEI*, UNN, UNY, WTA**
Imports - *FSM*, FSY*, MEI*, UNN, UNY, WTA**

National Accounts

Consumption
Government - FSM*, FSY*, UNN, WDR, WTA*
Private - FSM*, FSY*, GSY*, UNN, WDR, WTA*
Gross Domestic Product - *FSM*, FSY*, GSY*, UNN, UNY, WDR, WTA**
Gross National Product - *FSM*, FSY*, MEI*, UNN, WDR, WTA**
National Income - *FSM*, FSY*, UNN, WTA**

Prices, Production, Employment

Consumer Credit Outstanding - *FS2**

Consumer Prices - *ECI, FSM***, FSY***, FS1, GSY***, MEI***, UNY, WDR, WTA**

Earnings/Wages - *FSM***, FSY***, MEI***, UNY, WDR, WTA**

Employment - *FSM***, FSY***, MEI***, UNY, WTA**

Production

  Industrial - *ECI, FSM***, FSY***, MEI***, UNY, WTA**

  Manufacturing - *MEI***, UNY, WTA**

  Mining - *UNY*

Wholesale/Producer Prices - *FSY***, MEI***, UNY*

Securities Markets

Stock Exchange - *Tokyo Stock Exchange (TSE)*

Indexes

  Tokyo Stock Exchange Stock Price Index (TOPIX)

  Nikkei Index

Bonds

  Issue price - *FS2**

  Yield - *FS2**

Eurobonds

  Value of bonds issued - *FS1*

Foreign Bonds

  Value of bonds issued - *FS1*

Money Market Instruments Issued - *FS2**

Shares

  Dividend yield - *N/A*

  Issue price - *FS2**

  Most Active Stocks - *FTI*

  Price/Earnings Ratio - *FS1, FS2**

  Price Indexes

    TOPIX - *FTI, NYT, FSM***, FSY***, FS1, MEI***, DJN, DRI, UNY*

    Nikkei Index - *NYT, WSJ, FTI, BAR, DJN, DRF*

  Prices - FSM*, FSY*, FS1, MEI*, UNY

  Prices - Selected Issues - BAR, FTI, WSJ, NYT

  Total Gross - FS2*

  Yield - FS1, FS2

Stock Exchange Capitalization - *FS2**

Stock Exchange Turnover - *FS2**

Japanese Yen - *see* - **Japan** - **Exchange Rates;** *see also* - **Commodities**

Johannesburg Stock Exchange (JSE) - *see* - **South Africa** - **Securities Markets**

Jordan

Banking, Finance, and Money

Banking Institutions - Assets/Liabilities - *FSM*, FSY**
Monetary Authorities - Assets/Liabilities - *FSM*, FSY**
Money Supply - *FSM*, FSY*, UNY, WTA**

Exchange Rates

Currency - *Jordan Dinar*
Cross Rates - *N/A*
Forward Exchange Rate - *N/A*
Per ECU - *N/A*
Per SDR - *FSM*, FSY**
Per U.S. Dollar - *BAR, DJN, DRF, FSM*, FSY*, NYT, UNY, WSJ*

Government Finance

Debt - *FSY*, GSY*, WTA**
Deficit/Surplus - *FSY*, GSY*, WDR, WTA**
Expenditure - *GSY*, WDR, WTA**
Revenue - *GSY*, WDR, WTA**

Interest Rates

Bank Rate - *N/A*
Discount Rate - *FSY*, UNY*
Government Bonds - *FSY**
Money Market - *FSY**
Treasury Bills - *N/A*

International Liquidity

Reserves Minus Gold - *FSM*, FSY*, UNY, WTA**
Gold - *FSM*, FSY*, UNY, WTA**

International Transactions

Balance of Payments - *BOP*, FSM*, FSY*, UNY, WDR, WTA**
Exports - *FSM*, FSY*, UNN, UNY, WTA**

Imports - *FSM*, FSY*, UNN, UNY, WTA**

National Accounts

Consumption
  Government - *FSM*, FSY*, UNN, WTA**
  Private - *FSM*, FSY*, UNN, WTA**
  Gross Domestic Product - *FSM*, FSY*, GSY*, UNN, UNY, WDR, WTA**
  Gross National Product - *FSM*, FSY*, UNN, WDR, WTA**
  National Income - *FSM*, FSY*, UNN, WTA**

Prices, Production, Employment

Consumer Credit Outstanding - *N/A*
Consumer Prices - *FSM*, FSY*, GSY*, UNY, WTA**
Earnings/Wages - *UNY, WDR, WTA**
Employment - *UNY, WTA**
Production
  Industrial - *FSM*, FSY*, UNY, WTA**
  Manufacturing - *UNN, WTA**
  Wholesale/Producer Prices - *UNY*

Securities Markets - *N/A*

Jordan Dinar - *see* - Jordan - Exchange Rates

JSE (Johannesburg Stock Exchange) - *see* - South Africa - Securities Markets

JSE Gold Index - *see* - South Africa - Securities Markets

JSE Industrial Index - *see* - South Africa - Securities Markets

K

KCSPI (Korean Composite Stock Price Index) - *see* - **Korea (South)** - **Securities Markets**

Kenya

Banking, Finance, and Money

Banking Institutions - Assets/Liabilities - *FSM*, FSY**
Monetary Authorities - Assets/Liabilities - *FSM*, FSY**
Money Supply - *FSM*, FSY*, UNY, WTA**

Exchange Rates

Currency - *Kenya Shilling*
Cross Rates - *N/A*
Forward Exchange Rate - *N/A*
Per ECU - *N/A*
Per SDR - *FSM*, FSY**
Per U.S. Dollar - *DJN, DRF, FSM*, FSY*, UNY*

Government Finance

Debt - *GSY*, WTA**
Deficit/Surplus - *FSM*, FSY*, GSY*, WDR, WTA**
Expenditure - *GSY*, WDR, WTA**
Revenue - *GSY*, WDR, WTA**

Interest Rates

Bank Rate - *N/A*
Discount Rate - *FSM*, FSY*, UNY*
Money Market - *N/A*
Treasury Bills - *FSY*, UNY*

International Liquidity

Reserves Minus Gold - *FSM*, FSY*, UNY, WTA**
Gold - *FSM*, FSY*, UNY, WTA**

International Transactions

Balance of Payments - *BOP*, FSM*, FSY*, UNY, WDR, WTA**
Exports - *FSM*, FSY*, UNN, UNY, WTA**
Imports - *FSM*, FSY*, UNN, UNY, WTA**

National Accounts

Consumption
Government - *FSM*, FSY*, UNN, WDR, WTA**
Private - *FSM*, FSY*, UNN, WDR, WTA**
Gross Domestic Product - *FSM*, FSY*, GSY*, UNN, WDR, WTA**
Gross National Product - *FSM*, FSY*, UNN, WDR, WTA**
National Income - *UNN, WTA**

Prices, Production, Employment

Consumer Credit Outstanding - *N/A*
Consumer Prices - *FSM*, FSY*, GSY*, UNY, WDR, WTA**
Earnings/Wages - *UNY, WDR, WTA**
Employment - *UNY, WTA**
Production
Industrial - *FSM*, FSY*, WTA**
Manufacturing - *UNY, WTA**
Mining - *UNY*
Wholesale/Producer Prices - *N/A*

Securities Markets - *N/A*

Kenya Shilling - *see* **- Kenya - Exchange Rates**

Kina - *see* **- Papua New Guinea - Exchange Rates**

Kip - *see* **- Lao - Exchange Rates**

KLSE (Kuala Lumpur Stock Exchange) - *see* **- Malaysia - Securities Markets**

KLSE Composite (Kuala Lumpur Stock Exchange Composite Index) - *see* **- Malaysia - Securities Markets**

København Føndsbørs Stock Exchange (Copenhagen Stock Exchange) - *see* - **Denmark** - **Securities Markets**

Korea (South)

Banking, Finance, and Money

Banking Institutions - Assets/Liabilities - *FSM*, FSY**
Monetary Authorities - Assets/Liabilities - *FSM*, FSY**
Money Supply - *FSM*, FSY*, UNY, WTA**

Exchange Rates

Currency - *Korean Won*
Cross Rates - *N/A*
Forward Exchange Rate - *N/A*
Per ECU - *N/A*
Per SDR - *FSM*, FSY**
Per U.S. Dollar - *BAR, DJN, DRF, FRB, FSM*, FSY*, FTI, NYT, UNY, WSJ*

Government Finance

Debt - *FSM*, FSY*, GSY*, WTA**
Deficit/Surplus - *FSM*, FSY*, GSY*, WDR, WTA**
Expenditure - *GSY*, WDR, WTA**
Revenue - *GSY*, WDR, WTA**

Interest Rates

Bank Rate - *N/A*
Discount Rate - *FSM*, FSY*, UNY*
Government Bonds - *FSM*, FSY*, UNY*
Money Market - *FSM*, FSY**
Treasury Bills - *N/A*

International Liquidity

Reserves Minus Gold - *FSM*, FSY*, UNY, WTA**
Gold - *FSM*, FSY*, UNY, WTA**

International Transactions

Balance of Payments - *BOP*, FSM*, FSY*, UNY, WDR, WTA**
Exports - *FSM*, FSY*, UNN, UNY, WTA**
Imports - *FSM*, FSY*, UNN, UNY, WTA**

National Accounts

Consumption
Government - *FSM*, FSY*, UNN, WDR, WTA**
Private - *FSM*, FSY*, UNN, WDR, WTA**
Gross Domestic Product - *FSM*, FSY*, GSY*, UNN, UNY, WDR, WTA**
Gross National Product - *FSM*, FSY*, UNN, WTA**
National Income - *FSM*, FSY*, UNN, WTA**

Prices, Production, Employment

Consumer Credit Outstanding - *N/A*
Consumer Prices - *FSM*, FSY*, GSY*, UNY, WDR, WTA**
Earnings/Wages - *FSM*, FSY*, UNY, WDR, WTA**
Employment - *FSM*, FSY*, UNY, WTA**
Production
Industrial - *FSM*, FSY*, UNN, UNY, WTA**
Manufacturing - *UNN, UNY, WTA**
Mining - *UNY*
Wholesale/Producer Prices - *FSM*, FSY*, UNY*

Securities Markets

Stock Exchange - *Korea Stock Exchange (KSE)*
Index - *Korean Composite Stock Price Index (KCSPI)*
Bonds
Issue price - *N/A*
Yield - *N/A*
Eurobonds
Value of bonds issued - *N/A*
Foreign Bonds
Value of bonds issued - *FS1*
Shares
Dividend yield - *N/A*
Issue price - *N/A*
Last day of month - *N/A*
Price/Earnings Ratio - *N/A*
Price Index - *BAR, DRI, FTI, UNY*
Prices - *UNY*
Prices - Selected Issues - *N/A*
Yield - *N/A*

Stock Exchange Capitalization - *N/A*
Stock Exchange Turnover - *N/A*

Korean Composite Stock Price Index (KCSPI) - *see* - **Korea (South) - Securities Markets**

Korean Stock Exchange - *see* - **Korea (South) - Securities Markets**

Korean Won - *see* - **Korea (South) - Exchange Rates**

Koruna - *see* - **Czechoslovakia - Exchange Rates**

KSE (Korean Stock Exchange) - *see* - **Korea (South) - Securities Markets**

Kuala Lumpur Stock Exchange (KLSE) - *see* - **Malaysia - Securities Markets**

Kuala Lumpur Stock Exchange Composite Index (KLSE Composite) - *see* - **Malaysia - Securities Markets**

Kuwait

Banking, Finance, and Money

Banking Institutions - Assets/Liabilities - *FSM*, FSY**
Monetary Authorities - Assets/Liabilities - *FSM*, FSY**
Money Supply - *FSM*, FSY*, WTA**

Exchange Rates

Currency - *Kuwati Dinar*
Cross Rates - *N/A*
Forward Exchange Rate - *N/A*
Per ECU - *N/A*
Per SDR - *FSM*, FSY**
Per U.S. Dollar - *BAR, DJN, DRF, FSM*, FSY*, FTI, NYT, UNY, WSJ*

Government Finance

Debt - *GSY**
Deficit/Surplus - *FSM*, FSY*, UNY, WDR, WTA**
Expenditure - *GSY*, WDR, WTA**
Revenue - *GSY*, WDR, WTA**

Interest Rates

Bank Rate - *N/A*

Discount Rate - *FSM*, FSY*, UNY*
Government Bonds - *N/A*
Money Market - *FSM*, FSY*, UNY*
Treasury Bills - *FSM*, FSY**

International Liquidity

Reserves Minus Gold - *FSM*, FSY*, UNY, WTA**
Gold - *FSM*, FSY*, UNY, WTA**

International Transactions

Balance of Payments - *BOP*, FSM*, FSY*, UNY, WDR, WTA**
Exports - *FSM*, FSY*, UNN, UNY, WTA**
Imports - *FSM*, FSY*, UNN, UNY, WTA**

National Accounts

Consumption
  Government - *FSM*, FSY*, UNN, WDR, WTA**
  Private - *FSM*, FSY*, UNN, WDR, WTA**
Gross Domestic Product - *FSM*, FSY*, GSY*, UNN, UNY, WDR, WTA**
Gross National Product - *FSM*, FSY*, UNN, WDR, WTA**
National Income - *FSM*, FSY*, UNN, WTA**

Prices, Production, Employment

Consumer Credit Outstanding - *N/A*
Consumer Prices - *FSM*, FSY*, GSY*, UNY, WDR, WTA**
Earnings/Wages - *WDR, WTA**
Production
  Crude Petroleum - *FSM*, FSY**
  Industrial - *WTA**
  Manufacturing - *UNN, WTA**
Wholesale/Producer Prices - *FSM*, FSY*, UNY*

Securities Markets - *N/A*

Kuwati Dinar - *see* - **Kuwait - Exchange Rates**

Kwacha - *see* - **Malawi - Exchange Rates; Zambia - Exchange Rates**

Kwanza - *see* - **Angola - Exchange Rates**

Kyat - *see* - **Myanmar - Exchange Rates**

L

Lahore Stock Exchange - *see* - **Pakistan** - **Securities Markets**

Lahore Stock Exchange Price Index - *see* - **Pakistan** - **Securities Markets**

Laos

Banking, Finance, and Money

    Banking Institutions - Assets/Liabilities - *N/A*
    Monetary Authorities - Assets/Liabilities - *N/A*
    Money Supply - *N/A*

Exchange Rates

    Currency - *New Kip*
    Cross Rates - *N/A*
    Forward Exchange Rate - *N/A*
    Per ECU - *N/A*
    Per SDR - *N/A*
    Per U.S. Dollar - *DRF, UNY*

Government Finance

    Debt - *N/A*
    Deficit/Surplus - *N/A*
    Expenditure - *WDR*
    Revenue - *WDR*

International Transactions

    Balance of Payments - *BOP, MEI*, UNY*
    Exports - *UNY*
    Imports - *UNY*

National Accounts

Consumption
  Government - *N/A*
  Private - *N/A*
Gross Domestic Product - *WDR*
Gross National Product - *WDR*
National Income - *N/A*

Prices, Production, Employment

Consumer Credit Outstanding - *N/A*
Consumer Prices - *N/A*
Earnings/Wages - *N/A*
Employment - *N/A*
Production - *N/A*
Wholesale/Producer Prices - *N/A*

Securities Markets - *N/A*

Lead - *see* - Commodities

Lebanese Pound - *see* - Lebanon - Exchange Rates

Lebanon

Banking, Finance, and Money

Banking Institutions - Assets/Liabilities - *FSM*, FSY**
Monetary Authorities - Assets/Liabilities - *FSM*, FSY**
Money Supply - *FSM*, FSY*, UNY*

Exchange Rates

Currency - *Lebanese Pound*
Cross Rates - *N/A*
Forward Exchange Rate - *N/A*
Per ECU - *N/A*
Per SDR - *FSM*, FSY**
Per U.S. Dollar - *BAR, DJN, DRF, FSM*, FSY*, NYT, UNY, WSJ*

Interest Rates

Bank Rate - *N/A*
Discount Rate - *FSM*, FSY*, UNY*
Government Bonds - *N/A*
Money Market - *N/A*

Treasury Bills - *FSM*, FSM*, UNY*

International Liquidity

Reserves Minus Gold - *FSM*, FSY*, UNY*
Gold - *FSM*, FSY*, UNY*

International Transactions

Balance of Payments - *BOP**
Exports - *FSM*, FSY*, UNN, UNY*
Imports - *FSM*, FSY*, UNN, UNY*

National Accounts

Consumption
  Government - *UNN*
  Private - *UNN*
Gross Domestic Product - *UNN, UNY, WDR*
Gross National Product - *UNN*
National Income - *FSM*, UNN*

Prices, Production, Employment

Consumer Credit Outstanding - *N/A*
Consumer Prices - *WDR*
Earnings/Wages - *N/A*
Employment - *N/A*
Production - *N/A*
Wholesale/Producer Prices - *N/A*

Securities Markets - *N/A*

Lek - *see* **- Albania - Exchange Rates**

Lempira - *see* **- Honduras - Exchange Rates**

Leone - *see* **- Sierra Leone - Exchange Rates**

Lesotho

Banking, Finance, and Money

Banking Institutions - Assets/Liabilities - *FSM*, FSY**
Monetary Authorities - Assets/Liabilities - *FSM*, FSY**
Money Supply - *FSM*, FSY*, UNY, WTA**

Exchange Rates

Currency - *Lesotho Loti*
Cross Rates - *N/A*

Forward Exchange Rate - *N/A*
Per ECU - *N/A*
Per SDR - *FSM*, FSY**
Per U.S. Dollar - *DRF, FSM*, FSY*, UNY*

Government Finance

Debt - *FSM*, FSY*, GSY*, WTA**
Deficit/Surplus - *FSM*, FSY*, GSY*, WDR, WTA**
Expenditure - *GSY*, WDR, WTA**
Revenue - *GSY*, WDR, WTA**

Interest Rates

Bank Rate - *N/A*
Discount Rate - *FSM*, FSY*, UNY*
Government Bonds - *N/A*
Money Market - *N/A*
Treasury Bills - *FSM*, FSY*, UNY*

International Liquidity

Reserves Minus Gold - *FSM*, FSY*, UNY, WTA**
Gold - *N/A*

International Transactions

Balance of Payments - *BOP*, FSM*, FSY*, UNY, WDR, WTA**
Exports - *FSM*, FSY*, UNN, WTA**
Imports - *FSM*, FSY*, UNN, WTA**

National Accounts

Consumption
  Government - *FSM*, FSY*, UNN, WDR, WTA**
  Private - *FSM*, FSY*, UNN, WDR, WTA**
Gross Domestic Product - F*SM*, FSY*, GSY*, UNN, UNY, WDR, WTA**
Gross National Product - *FSY*, UNN, WDR, WTA**
National Income - *FSM*, FSY*, UNN, WTA**

Prices, Production, Employment

Consumer Credit Outstanding - *N/A*
Consumer Prices - *FSM*, FSY*, GSY*, UNY, WDR, WTA**
Earnings/Wages - *WTA**
Production

Industrial - *WTA**
Manufacturing - *WTA**
Wholesale/Producer Prices - *FSY**

Securities Markets - *N/A*

Lesotho Loti - *see* - Lesotho - Exchange Rates

Leu - *see* - Romania - Exchange Rates

Leva - *see* - Bulgaria - Exchange Rates

Liberia

Banking, Finance, and Money

Banking Institutions - Assets/Liabilities - *FSM*, FSY**
Monetary Authorities - Assets/Liabilities - *FSM*, FSY**
Money Supply - *FSM*, FSY*, UNY, WTA**

Exchange Rates

Currency - *Liberian Dollar*
Cross Rates - *N/A*
Forward Exchange Rate - *N/A*
Per ECU - *N/A*
Per SDR - *FSM*, FSY**
Per U.S. Dollar - *DJN, DRF, FSM*, FSY*, UNY*

Government Finance

Debt - *FSM*, FSY*, GSY*, WTA**
Deficit/Surplus - *FSM*, FSY*, GSY*, WDR, WTA**
Expenditure - *GSY*, WDR, WTA**
Revenue - *GSY*, WDR, WTA**

International Liquidity

Reserves Minus Gold - *FSY*, UNY, WTA**
Gold - *N/A*

International Transactions

Balance of Payments - *BOP*, FSM*, FSY*, UNY, WDR, WTA**
Exports - *FSM*, FSY*, UNN, UNY, WTA**
Imports - *FSM*, FSY*, UNN, UNY, WTA**

National Accounts

Consumption
Government - *FSM*, FSY*, UNN, WDR, WTA**
Private - *FSM*, FSY*, UNN, WDR, WTA**
Gross Domestic Product - *FSM*, FSY*, GSY*, UNN, UNY, WDR, WTA**
Gross National Product - *FSM*, FSY*, UNN, WTA**
National Income - *UNN, WTA**

Prices, Production, Employment

Consumer Credit Outstanding - *N/A*
Consumer Prices - *FSM*, FSY*, GSY*, UNY, WDR, WTA**
Earnings/Wages - *WDR*
Employment - *N/A*
Production
Industrial - *WTA**
Manufacturing - *WTA**
Wholesale/Producer Prices - *N/A*

Securities Markets - *N/A*

Liberian Dollar - *see* - Liberia - Exchange Rates

Libor - *see* - United Kingdom - Interest Rates

Libor Rate - *see* - Commodities

Libya

Banking, Finance, and Money

Banking Institutions - Assets/Liabilities - *FSM*, FSY**
Monetary Authorities - Assets/Liabilities - *FSM*, FSY**
Money Supply - *FSM*, FSY*, UNY, WTA**

Exchange Rates

Currency - *Libyan Dinar*
Cross Rates - *N/A*
Forward Exchange Rate - *N/A*
Per ECU - *N/A*
Per SDR - *FSM*, FSY**
Per U.S. Dollar - *DRF, FSM*, FSY*, UNY*

Government Finance

Debt - *N/A*

    Deficit/Surplus - *N/A*
    Expenditure - *N/A*
    Revenue - *N/A*

Interest Rates

    Bank Rate - *N/A*
    Discount Rate - *FSM*, FSY*, UNY*
    Government Bonds - *N/A*
    Money Market - *FSM*, FSY**
    Treasury Bills - *N/A*

International Liquidity

    Reserves Minus Gold - *FSM*, FSY*, UNY, WTA**
    Gold - *FSM*, FSY*, UNY, WTA**

International Transactions

    Balance of Payments - *BOP*, FSM*, FSY*, UNY, WDR, WTA**
    Exports - *FSM*, FSY*, UNN, UNY, WTA**
    Imports - *FSM*, FSY*, UNN, UNY, WTA**

National Accounts

    Consumption
      Government - *FSY*, UNN, WDR, WTA**
      Private - *FSY*, UNN, WDR, WTA**
    Gross Domestic Product - *FSM*, FSY*, UNN, UNY, WDR, WTA**
    Gross National Product - *FSM*, UNN, WDR, WTA**
    National Income - *FSY*, UNN, WTA**

Prices, Production, Employment

    Consumer Credit Outstanding - *N/A*
    Consumer Prices - *FSY*, WDR, WTA**
    Earnings/Wages - *WTA**
    Production
      Industrial - *WTA**
      Manufacturing - *UNN, WTA**
      Crude Petroleum - *FSM*, FSY**
    Wholesale/Producer Prices - *N/A*

Securities Markets - *N/A*

Libyan Dinar - *see* **- Libya - Exchange Rates**

Lira - *see* **- Italy   Exchange Rates; Malta - Exchange Rates; Turkey - Exchange Rates**

Lisbon BVL - *see* **- Portugal - Securities Markets**

Lisbon Stock Exchange - *see* **- Portugal - Securities Markets**

London Gold Mines Index - *see* **- United Kingdom - Securities Markets**

London Stock Exchange - *see* **- United Kingdom - Securities Markets**

Loti - *see* **- Lesotho - Exchange Rates**

Luxembourg

Banking, Finance, and Money
Banking Institutions - Assets/Liabilities - *FSY**
Monetary Authorities - Assets/Liabilities - *N/A*
Money Supply - *N/A*

Exchange Rates
Currency - *Luxembourg Franc*
Cross Rates - *N/A*
Forward Exchange Rate - *N/A*
Per ECU - *N/A*
Per SDR - *FSM*, FSY**
Per U.S. Dollar - *DJN, DRF, FSM*, FSY*, UNY, WTA**

Government Finance
Debt - *FSM*, FSY**
Deficit/Surplus - *FSM*, FSY*, GSY*, WTA**
Expenditure - *GSY*, WTA**
Revenue - *GSY*, WTA**

Interest Rates
Bank Rate - *N/A*
Discount Rate - *N/A*
Government Bonds - *FSY*, UNY*
Money Market - *N/A*
Treasury Bills - *N/A*

International Liquidity
Reserves Minus Gold - *UNY*

Gold - *FSY*, UNY, WTA**

International Transactions

Balance of Payments - *BOP**
Exports - *FSM*, FSY*, UNN*
Imports - *FSM*, FSY*, UNN*

National Accounts

Consumption
Government - *FSM*, FSY*, UNN, WTA**
Private - *FSM*, FSY*, UNN, WTA**
Gross Domestic Product - F*SM*, FSY*, GSY*, UNN, UNY, WTA**
Gross National Product - *FSM*, FSY*, UNN, WTA**
National Income - *FSM*, FSY*, UNN, WTA**

Prices, Production, Employment

Consumer Credit Outstanding - *N/A*
Consumer Prices - *FSM*, GSY*, MEI, UNY, WTA**
Earnings/Wages - *UNY*
Employment - *UNY*
Production
Industrial - *FSM*, FSY*, MEI*, UNY, WTA**
Manufacturing - *MEI*, UNY, WTA**
Mining - *UNY*
Steel - *FSM*, FSY**
Wholesale/Producer Prices - *FSM*, MEI*, UNY*

Securities Markets

Stock Exchange - *Bourse de Luxembourg SA*
Index - *Luxembourg Shares Index*
Bonds
Issue price - *FS2**
Foreign Bonds
Value of bonds issued - *FS1*
Shares
Issue price - *FS2**
Price Index - *UNY*
Total Gross - *FS2**
Stock Exchange Capitalization - *FS2**

Luxembourg Franc - *see* - **Luxembourg - Exchange Rates**

Luxembourg Shares Index - *see* - **Luxembourg - Securities Markets**

M

Madagascar

Banking, Finance, and Money

Banking Institutions - Assets/Liabilities - *FSM*, FSY**
Monetary Authorities - Assets/Liabilities - *FSM*, FSY**
Money Supply - *FSM*, FSY*, UNY, WTA**

Exchange Rates

Currency - *Madagasy Franc*
Cross Rates - *N/A*
Forward Exchange Rate - *N/A*
Per ECU - *N/A*
Per SDR - *FSM*, FSY**
Per U.S. Dollar - *DJN, DRF, FSM*, FSY*, UNY*

Government Finance

Debt - *FSM*, WTA**
Deficit/Surplus - *FSM*, FSY*, WDR, WTA**
Expenditure - *WDR, WTA**
Revenue - *WDR, WTA**

Interest Rates

Bank Rate - *N/A*
Discount Rate - *FSY*, UNY*
Government Bonds - *N/A*
Money Market - *N/A*
Treasury Bills - *N/A*

International Liquidity

Reserves Minus Gold - *FSM*, FSY*, UNY, WTA**
Gold - *N/A*

International Transactions

Balance of Payments - *FSM*, FSY*, UNY, WDR, WTA**
Exports - *FSM*, FSY*, UNN, UNY, WTA**
Imports - *FSM*, FSY*, UNN, UNY, WTA**

National Accounts

Consumption
  Government - *FSY*, UNN, WDR, WTA**
  Private - *FSY*, UNN, WDR, WTA**
Gross Domestic Product - *FSM*, FSY*, UNN, UNY, WDR, WTA**
Gross National Product - *FSY*, UNN, WDR, WTA**
National Income - *WTA**

Prices, Production, Employment

Consumer Credit Outstanding - *N/A*
Consumer Prices - *FSM*, FSY*, UNY, WDR, WTA**
Earnings/Wages - *WDR, WTA**
Production
  Industrial - *WTA**
  Manufacturing - *WTA**
Wholesale/Producer Prices - *N/A*

Securities Markets - *N/A*

Madagasy Franc - *see* - **Madagascar - Exchange Rates**

Madrid Stock Exchange - *see* - **Spain - Securities Markets**

Madrid Stock Exchange General Index - *see* - **Spain - Securities Markets**

Makati Stock Exchange - *see* - **Philippines - Securities Markets**

Malawi

Banking, Finance, and Money

Banking Institutions - Assets/Liabilities - *FSM*, FSY**
Monetary Authorities - Assets/Liabilities - *FSM*, FSY**
Money Supply - *FSM*, FSY*, UNY, WTA**

Exchange Rates

Currency - *Malawi Kwacha*
Cross Rates - *N/A*

Forward Exchange Rate - *N/A*
Per ECU - *N/A*
Per SDR - *FSM*, FSY**
Per U.S. Dollar - *DRF, FSM*, FSY*, UNY*

Government Finance

Debt - *FSM*, FSY*, GSY*, WTA**
Deficit/Surplus - *FSM*, FSY*, GSY*, WDR, WTA**
Expenditure - *GSY*, WDR, WTA**
Revenue - *GSY*, WDR, WTA**

Interest Rates

Bank Rate - *N/A*
Discount Rate - *FSM*, FSY*, UNY*
Government Bonds - *FSM*, FSY*, UNY*
Money Market - *N/A*
Treasury Bills - *FSM*, FSY*, UNY*

International Liquidity

Reserves Minus Gold - *FSM*, FSY*, UNY, WTA**
Gold - *FSM*, FSY*, UNY, WTA**

International Transactions

Balance of Payments - *FSM*, FSY*, MEI*, UNY, WTA**
Exports - *FSM*, FSY*, UNN, UNY, WTA**
Imports - *FSM*, FSY*, UNN, UNY, WTA**

National Accounts

Consumption
  Government - *FSM*, FSY*, UNN, WDR, WTA**
  Private - *FSM*, FSY*, UNN, WDR, WTA**
Gross Domestic Product - *FSM*, FSY*, GSY*, UNN, UNY, WDR, WTA**
Gross National Product - *FSM*, FSY*, UNN, WDR, WTA**
National Income - *WTA**

Prices, Production, Employment

Consumer Credit Outstanding - *N/A*
Consumer Prices - *FSM*, FSY*, GSY*, UNY, WDR, WTA**
Earnings/Wages - *UNY, WDR*
Employment - *UNY*

Production
  Industrial - *FSM*, FSY*, UNY, WTA**
  Manufacturing - *UNY, WTA**
  Wholesale/Producer Prices - *N/A*

Securities Markets - *N/A*

Malawi Kwacha - *see* - Malawi - Exchange Rates

Malaysia

Banking, Finance, and Money

Banking Institutions - Assets/Liabilities - *FSM*, FSY**
Monetary Authorities - Assets/Liabilities - *FSM*, FSY**
Money Supply - *FSM*, FSY*, UNY, WTA**

Exchange Rates

Currency - *Malaysian Ringgit*
Cross Rates - *N/A*
Forward Exchange Rate - *N/A*
Per ECU - *N/A*
Per SDR - *FSM*, FSY**
Per U.S. Dollar - *BAR, DJN, DRF, FRB, FSM*, FSY*, FTI, NYT, UNY, WSJ*

Government Finance

Debt - *FSM*, FSY*, GSY*, WTA**
Deficit/Surplus - *FSM*, FSY*, GSY*, WDR, WTA**
Expenditure - *GSY*, WDR, WTA**
Revenue - *GSY*, WDR, WTA**

Interest Rates

Bank Rate - *N/A*
Discount Rate - *FSM*, FSY*, UNY*
Government Bonds - *N/A*
Money Market - *FSM*, FSY**
Treasury Bills - *N/A*

International Liquidity

Reserves Minus Gold - *FSM*, FSY*, UNY, WTA**
Gold - *FSM*, FSY*, UNY, WTA**

International Transactions

Balance of Payments - *BOP*, FSM*, FSY*, UNY, WDR, WTA**

Exports - *FSM*, FSY*, UNN, UNY, WTA**

Imports - *FSM*, FSY*, UNN, UNY, WTA**

National Accounts

Consumption

Government - *FSM*, FSY*, UNN, WDR, WTA**

Private - *FSM*, FSY*, UNN, WDR, WTA**

Gross Domestic Product - *FSM*, FSY*, GSY*, UNN, UNY, WDR, WTA**

Gross National Product - *FSM*, UNN, WDR, WTA**

National Income - *UNN, WTA**

Prices, Production, Employment

Consumer Credit Outstanding - *N/A*

Consumer Prices - *FSM*, FSY*, GSY*, UNY, WDR, WTA**

Earnings/Wages - *WDR, WTA**

Employment - *UNY, WTA**

Production

Industrial - *FSM*, FSY*, UNY, WTA**

Manufacturing - *UNY, WTA**

Mining - *UNY*

Wholesale/Producer Prices - *FSM**

Securities Markets

Stock Exchange - *Kuala Lumpur Stock Exchange (KLSE)*

Index - *Kuala Lumpur Stock Exchange Composite Index (KLSE Composite)*

Shares

Price Index - *BAR, DRI, FTI*

Prices - Selected Issues - *BAR, FTI*

Malaysian Ringgit - *see* **- Malaysia - Exchange Rates**

Maldives

Banking, Finance, and Money

Banking Institutions - Assets/Liabilities - *FSM*, FSY**

Monetary Authorities - Assets/Liabilities - *FSM*, FSY**

Money Supply - *FSM*, FSY*, UNY*

Exchange Rates

Currency - *Rufiyaa*
Cross Rates - *N/A*
Forward Exchange Rate - *N/A*
Per ECU - *N/A*
Per SDR - *FSM*, FSY**
Per U.S. Dollar - *DRF, FSM*, FSY*, UNY*

Government Finance

Debt - *FSM*, FSY*, GSY**
Deficit/Surplus - *FSM*, FSY*, GSY**
Expenditure - *GSY**
Revenue - *GSY**

Interest Rates

Bank Rate - *N/A*
Discount Rate - *N/A*
Government Bonds - *N/A*
Money Market - *FSM*, FSY**
Treasury Bills - *N/A*

International Liquidity

Reserves Minus Gold - *FSM*, FSY*, UNY*
Gold - *FSM*, FSY**

International Transactions

Balance of Payments - *BOP*, FSM*, FSY*, UNY*
Exports - *FSM*, FSY*, UNN, UNY*
Imports - *FSM*, FSY*, UNN, UNY*

National Accounts

Consumption
   Government - *UNN*
   Private - *UNN*
Gross Domestic Product - *FSM*, FSY*, GSY*, UNN, UNY*

Prices, Production, Employment

Consumer Credit Outstanding - *N/A*
Consumer Prices - *GSY**
Earnings/Wages - *N/A*
Employment - *N/A*
Production - *N/A*

Wholesale/Producer Prices - *N/A*

Securities Markets - *N/A*

Mali

Banking, Finance, and Money

Banking Institutions - Assets/Liabilities - *FSM*, FSY**
Monetary Authorities - Assets/Liabilities - *FSM*, FSM**
Money Supply - *FSM*, FSY**

Exchange Rates

Currency - *CFA Franc*
Cross Rates - *N/A*
Forward Exchange Rate - *N/A*
Per ECU - *N/A*
Per SDR - *FSM*, FSY**
Per U.S. Dollar - *DRF, FSM*, FSY*, UNY*

Government Finance

Debt - *FSM*, FSY*, GSY**
Deficit/Surplus - *FSM*, FSY*, GSY*, WDR, WTA**
Expenditure - *GSY*, WDR, WTA**
Revenue - *GSY*, WDR, WTA**

Interest Rates

Bank Rate - *N/A*
Discount Rate - *FSM*, FSY*, UNY*
Government Bonds - *FSM**
Money Market - *FSM*, FSY**
Treasury Bills - *FSM**

International Liquidity

Reserves Minus Gold - *FSM*, FSY*, UNY, WTA**
Gold - *FSM*, FSY*, UNY, WTA**

International Transactions

Balance of Payments - *BOP*, FSM*, FSY*, UNY, WDR, WTA**
Exports - *FSM*, FSY*, UNN, UNY, WTA**
Imports - *FSM*, FSY*, UNN, UNY, WTA**

National Accounts

Consumption
  Government - *UNN, WDR*
  Private - *UNN, WDR, WTA**
  Gross Domestic Product - *GSY*, UNN, UNY, WDR, WTA**
  Gross National Product - *UNN, WDR, WTA**
  National Income - *UNN, WTA**

Prices, Production, Employment

Consumer Credit Outstanding - *N/A*
Consumer Prices - *FSM*, FSY*, UNY, WDR, WTA**
Earnings/Wages - *WTA**
Employment - *N/A*
Production
  Industrial - *WTA**
  Manufacturing - *WTA**
Wholesale/Producer Prices - *N/A*

Securities Markets - *N/A*

Malta

Banking, Finance, and Money

Banking Institutions - Assets/Liabilities - *FSM*, FSY**
Monetary Authorities - Assets/Liabilities - *FSM*, FSY**
Money Supply - *FSM*, FSY*, UNY, WTA**

Exchange Rates

Currency - *Maltese Lira*
Cross Rates - *N/A*
Forward Exchange Rate - *N/A*
Per ECU - *N/A*
Per SDR - *FSM*, FSY**
Per U.S. Dollar - *BAR, DJN, DRF, FSM*, FSY*, UNY, WSJ*

Government Finance

Debt - *FSM*, FSY*, GSY, WTA**
Deficit/Surplus - *FSM*, FSY*, GSY*, WTA**
Expenditure - *GSY*, WTA**
Revenue - *GSY*, WTA**

Interest Rates

Bank Rate - *N/A*

Discount Rate - *FSM*, FSY*, UNY*
Government Bonds - *N/A*
Money Market - *N/A*
Treasury Bills - *UNY*

International Liquidity

Reserves Minus Gold - *FSM*, FSY*, UNY, WTA**
Gold - *FSM*, FSY*, UNY, WTA**

International Transactions

Balance of Payments - *BOP*, FSM*, FSY*, UNY, WTA**
Exports - *FSM*, FSY*, UNY, WTA**
Imports - *FSM*, FSY*, UNY, WTA**

National Accounts

Consumption
  Government - *FSM*, FSY*, UNN, WTA**
  Private - *FSM*, FSY*, UNN, WTA**
  Gross Domestic Product - FSM*, FSY*, GSY*, UNN, UNY, WTA*
  Gross National Product - FSM*, FSY*, UNN, WTA*
  National Income - FSM*, FSY*, UNN, WTA*

Prices, Production, Employment

Consumer Credit Outstanding - *N/A*
Consumer Prices - *FSM*, FSY*, GSY*, UNY, WTA**
Earnings/Wages - *WTA**
Employment - *UNY, WTA**
Production
  Industrial - *FSM*, FSY*, UNY, WTA**
  Manufacturing - *UNN, UNY, WTA**
  Mining - *UNY*
Wholesale/Producer Prices - *N/A*

Securities Markets - *N/A*

Maltese Lira - *see* - **Malta - Exchange Rates**

Manila Composite Index - *see* - **Philippines - Securities Markets**

Mark - *see* - **Germany (German Democratic Republic) - Exchange Rates**

Markka - *see* - **Finland - Exchange Rates**

Mauritania

Banking, Finance, and Money

Banking Institutions - Assets/Liabilities - *FSM*, FSY**
Monetary Authorities - Assets/Liabilities - *FSM*, FSY**
Money Supply - *FSM*, FSY*, WTA**

Exchange Rates

Currency - *Mauritanian Ougviya*
Cross Rates - *N/A*
Forward Exchange Rate - *N/A*
Per ECU - *N/A*
Per SDR - *FSM*, FSY**
Per U.S. Dollar - *DRF, FSM*, FSY*, UNY*

Government Finance

Debt - *FSY*, WTA**
Deficit/Surplus - *FSY*, WDR, WTA**
Expenditure - *WDR, WTA**
Revenue - *WDR, WTA**

Interest Rates

Bank Rate - *N/A*
Discount Rate - *FSM*, FSY**
Government Bonds - *N/A*
Money Market - *N/A*
Treasury Bills - *N/A*

International Liquidity

Reserves Minus Gold - *FSM*, FSY*, UNY, WTA**
Gold - *FSM*, FSY*, UNY, WTA**

International Transactions

Balance of Payments - *BOP*, FSM*, FSY*, UNY, WDR, WTA**
Exports - *FSM*, FSY*, UNN, UNY, WTA**
Imports - *FSM*, FSY*, UNN, UNY, WTA**

National Accounts

Consumption
    Government - *FSY*, UNN, WDR, WTA**
    Private - *FSY*, UNN, WDR, WTA**

Gross Domestic Product - *FSM*, FSY*, UNN, UNY, WDR, WTA**
Gross National Product - *UNN, WDR, WTA**
National Income - *UNN, WTA**

Prices, Production, Employment

Consumer Credit Outstanding - *N/A*
Consumer Prices - *FSM*, FSY*, WDR, WTA**
Earnings/Wages - *N/A*
Employment - *N/A*
Production
  Industrial - *WTA**
Wholesale/Producer Prices - *FSY**

Securities Markets - *N/A*

Mauritanian Ougviya - *see* **- Mauritania - Exchange Rates**

Mauritian Rupee - *see* **- Mauritius - Exchange Rates**

Mauritius

Banking, Finance, and Money

Banking Institutions - Assets/Liabilities - *FSM*, FSY**
Monetary Authorities - Assets/Liabilities - *FSM*, FSY**
Money Supply - *FSM*, FSY*, UNY, WTA**

Exchange Rates

Currency - *Mauritian Rupee*
Cross Rates - *N/A*
Forward Exchange Rate - *N/A*
Per ECU - *N/A*
Per SDR - *FSM*, FSY**
Per U.S. Dollar - *DJN, FSM*, FSY*, UNY*

Government Finance

Debt - *FSM*, FSY*, GSY*, WTA**
Deficit/Surplus - *FSM*, FSY*, GSY*, WDR, WTA**
Expenditure - *GSY*, WDR, WTA**
Revenue - *GSY*, WDR, WTA**

Interest Rates

Bank Rate - *N/A*
Discount Rate - *FSM*, FSY*, UNY*

Government Bonds - *N/A*
Money Market - *FSM*, FSY**
Treasury Bills - *N/A*

International Liquidity

Reserves Minus Gold - *FSM*, FSY*, UNY, WTA**
Gold - *FSM*, FSY*, UNY, WTA**

International Transactions

Balance of Payments - *BOP*, FSM*, FSY*, UNY, WDR, WTA**
Exports - *FSM*, FSY*, UNN, UNY, WTA**
Imports - *FSM*, FSY*, UNN, UNY, WTA**

National Accounts

Consumption
  Government - *FSM*, FSY*, UNN, WDR, WTA**
  Private - *FSM*, FSY*, UNN, WDR, WTA**
Gross Domestic Product - *FSM*, FSY*, GSY*, UNN, UNY, WDR, WTA**
Gross National Product - *FSM*, FSY*, UNN, WDR, WTA**
National Income - *UNN, WTA**

Prices, Production, Employment

Consumer Credit Outstanding - *N/A*
Consumer Prices - *FSM*, FSY*, GSY*, UNY, WDR, WTA**
Earnings/Wages - *UNY, WDR, WTA**
Employment - *UNY, WTA**
Production
  Industrial - *WTA**
  Manufacturing - *UNN, WTA**
Wholesale/Producer Prices - *FSY**

Securities Markets - *N/A*

Metical - *see* - **Mozambique - Exchange Rates**

Mexican Peso - *see* - **Mexico - Exchange Rates**

Mexican Stock Exchange - *see* - **Mexico - Securities Markets**

Mexico

Banking, Finance, and Money

Banking Institutions - Assets/Liabilities - *FSM*, FSY**

Monetary Authorities - Assets/Liabilities - *FSM*, FSY**
Money Supply - *FSM*, FSY*, UNY, WTA**

Exchange Rates

Currency - *Mexican Peso*
Cross Rates - *N/A*
Forward Exchange Rate - *N/A*
Per ECU - *N/A*
Per SDR - *FSM*, FSY**
Per U.S. Dollar - *BAR, DJN, DRF, FSM*, FSY*, FTI, NYT, UNY, WSJ*

Government Finance

Debt - *FSY*, GSY*, WTA**
Deficit/Surplus - *FSM*, FSY*, GSY*, WDR, WTA**
Expenditure - *GSY*, WDR, WTA**
Revenue - *FSY*, WDR, WTA**

Interest Rates

Bank Rate - *N/A*
Discount Rate - *N/A*
Government Bonds - *N/A*
Money Market - *FSM*, FSY**
Treasury Bills - *FSM*, FSY*, UNY*

International Liquidity

Reserves Minus Gold - *FSM*, FSY*, UNY, WTA**
Gold - *FSM*, FSY*, UNY, WTA**

International Transactions

Balance of Payments - *BOP*, FSM*, FSY*, UNY, WDR, WTA**
Exports - *FSM*, FSY*, UNN, UNY, WTA**
Imports - *FSM*, FSY*, UNN, UNY, WTA**

National Accounts

Consumption
    Government - *FSM*, FSY*, GSY*, UNN, WDR, WTA**
    Private - *FSM*, FSY*, UNN, WDR, WTA**
Gross Domestic Product - *FSM*, FSY*, GSY*, UNN, UNY, WDR, WTA**
Gross National Product - *FSM*, FSY*, UNN, WDR, WTA**

National Income - *UNN, WTA**

Prices, Production, Employment

Consumer Credit Outstanding - *N/A*
Consumer Prices - *FSM*, FSY*, GSY*, UNY, WDR, WTA**
Earnings/Wages - *FSM*, FSY*, UNY, WDR, WTA**
Employment - *FSY*, WTA**
Production
  Crude Petroleum - *FSM*, FSY**
  Industrial - *UNY, WTA**
  Manufacturing - *UNN, UNY, WTA**
  Mining - *FSM*, FSY*, UNN, UNY*
Wholesale/Producer Prices - *FSM*, FSY*, UNY*

Securities Markets

Stock Exchange - *Bolsa Mexicana de Valores (The Mexican Stock Exchange)*
Index - *BMV Index*
Foreign Bonds
  Value of bonds issued - *FS1*
Shares
  Price Index - *BAR, FSM, FSY*, FTI, UNY, WSJ*
  Prices - *FSM, FSY, UNY*
  Prices - Selected Issues - *BAR, WSJ*

MIB (Milano Indice Borsa) - *see* **- Italy - Securities Markets**

Midwest Stock Exchange - *see-* **United States - Securities Markets**

Milan Stock Exchange - *see -* **Italy - Securities Markets**

Milano Indice Borsa (MIB) - *see* **- Italy - Securities Markets**

Monetary Authorities - Assets/Liabilities - *see* **- Individual Countries - Banking, Finance, and Money**

Money Market - *see* **- Individual Countries - Banking, Finance, and Money**

Money Supply - *see* **- Individual Countries - Banking, Finance, and Money**

Montreal Stock Exchange - *see* **- Bourse de Montréal**

Moroccan Dirham - *see -* **Morocco - Exchange Rates**

Morocco

Banking, Finance, and Money

Banking Institutions - Assets/Liabilities - *FSM**, *FSY**
Monetary Authorities - Assets/Liabilities - *FSM**, *FSY**
Money Supply - *FSM**, *FSY**, *UNY, WTA**

Exchange Rates

Currency - *Moroccan Dirham*
Cross Rates - *N/A*
Forward Exchange Rate - *N/A*
Per ECU - *N/A*
Per SDR - *FSM**, *FSY**
Per U.S. Dollar - *DJN, DRF, FSM**, *FSY**, *UNY*

Government Finance

Debt - *FSY**, *GSY**, *WTA**
Deficit/Surplus - *FSM**, *FSY**, *GSY**, *WDR, WTA**
Expenditure - *GSY**, *WDR, WTA**
Revenue - *GSY**, *WDR, WTA**

Interest Rates

Bank Rate - *N/A*
Discount Rate - *FSM**, *FSY**
Government Bonds - *N/A*
Money Market - *FSM**, *FSY**
Treasury Bills - *FSM**, *FSY**

International Liquidity

Reserves Minus Gold - *FSM**, *FSY**, *UNY, WTA**
Gold - *FSM**, *FSY**, *UNY, WTA**

International Transactions

Balance of Payments - *BOP**, *FSM**, *FSY**, *UNY, WDR,
WTA*
Exports - *FSM**, *FSY**, *UNN, UNY, WTA**
Imports - *FSM**, *FSY**, *UNN, UNY, WTA**

National Accounts

Consumption
  Government - *FSM**, *FSY**, *UNN, WDR, WTA**
  Private - *FSM**, *FSY**, *UNN, WTA**

Gross Domestic Product - *FSM*, FSY*, GSY*, UNN, UNY, WDR, WTA**
Gross National Product - *FSM*, FSY*, UNN, WDR, WTA**
National Income - *FSY*, UNN, WTA**

Prices, Production, Employment

Consumer Credit Outstanding - *N/A*
Consumer Prices - *FSM*, FSY*, GSY*, UNY, WDR, WTA**
Earnings/Wages - *WDR, WTA**
Employment - *WTA**
Production
  Industrial - *UNY, WTA**
  Manufacturing - *FSM*, FSY*, UNY, WTA**
  Mining - *FSM*, FSY*, UNY*
Wholesale/Producer Prices - *FSM*, FSY**

Securities Markets - *N/A*

Mozambique

Banking, Finance, and Money

Banking Institutions - Assets/Liabilities - *N/A*
Monetary Authorities - *N/A*
Money Supply - *N/A*

Exchange Rates

Currency - *Mozambique Metical*
Cross Rates - *N/A*
Forward Exchange Rate - *N/A*
Per ECU - *N/A*
Per SDR - *N/A*
Per U.S. Dollar - *DRF*

International Transactions

Balance of Payments - *BOP*, UNY, WDR, WTA**
Exports - *UNN, UNY, WTA**
Imports - *UNY, WTA**

National Accounts

Consumption
  Government - *UNN, WDR, WTA**
  Private - *UNN, WDR, WTA**
Gross Domestic Product - *UNN, UNY, WDR, WTA**

Gross National Product - *UNN, WDR, WTA**
National Income - *UNN, WTA**

Prices, Production, Employment

Consumer Credit Outstanding - *N/A*
Consumer Prices - *UNY, WDR*
Earnings/Wages - *N/A*
Employment - *UNY*
Production
  Industrial - *WTA**
Wholesale/Producer Prices - *N/A*

Securities Markets - *N/A*

Myanmar

Banking, Finance, and Money

Banking Institutions - Assets/Liabilities - *FSM*, FSY**
Monetary Authorities - Assets/Liabilities - *FSM*, FSY**
Money Supply - *FSM*, FSY*, UNY*

Exchange Rates

Currency - *Myanmarese Kyat*
Cross Rates - *N/A*
Forward Exchange Rate - *N/A*
Per ECU - *N/A*
Per SDR - *FSM*, FSY**
Per U.S. Dollar - *DRF, FSM*, FSY*, UNY*

Government Finance

Debt - *FSY*, GSY**
Deficit/Surplus - *FSM*, FSY*, GSY**
Expenditure - *GSY*, WDR*
Revenue - *GSY**

International Liquidity

Reserves Minus Gold - *FSM*, FSY*, UNY*
Gold - *FSM*, FSY*, UNY*

International Transactions

Balance of Payments - *BOP*, FSM*, FSY*, UNY, WDR*
Exports - *FSM*, FSY*, UNN, UNY*
Imports - *FSM*, FSY*, UNN, UNY*

National Accounts

Consumption
    Government - *FSY*, UNN*
    Private - *FSM*, FSY**
Gross Domestic Product - *FSM*, FSY*, GSY*, UNN, UNY*
Gross National Product - *UNN*
National Income - *UNN*

Prices, Production, Employment

Consumer Credit Outstanding - *N/A*
Consumer Prices - *FSM*, FSY*, GSY*, UNY*
Earnings/Wages - *UNY*
Employment - *UNY*
Production
    Manufacturing - *UNN*
Wholesale/Producer Prices - *N/A*

Securities Markets - *N/A*

Myanmarese Kyat - *see* - **Myanmar - Exchange Rates**

N

Naria, Nigerian - *see* - Nigeria - Exchange Rates

NASDAQ (National Association of Securities Dealers Automated Quotation System) - *see* - United States - Securities Markets

National Association of Securities Dealers Automated Quotation System (NASDAQ) - *see* - United States - Securities Markets

National Income - *see* - Individual Countries - National Accounts

Natural Gas - *see* - Commodities

Nepal

Banking, Finance, and Money

Banking Institutions - Assets/Liabilities - *FSM*, FSY**
Monetary Authorities - Assets/Liabilities - *FSM*, FSY**
Money Supply - *FSM*, FSY*, UNY, WTA**

Exchange Rates

Currency - *Nepalese Rupee*
Cross Rates - *N/A*
Forward Exchange Rate - *N/A*
Per ECU - *N/A*
Per SDR - *FSM*, FSY**
Per U.S. Dollar - *FSM*, FSY*, UNY*

Government Finance

Debt - *FSM*, FSY*, GSY*, WTA**
Deficit/Surplus - *FSM*, FSY*, GSY*, WDR, WTA**
Expenditure - *GSY*, WDR, WTA**
Revenue - *GSY*, WDR, WTA**

Interest Rates

Bank Rate - *N/A*
Discount Rate - *FSM*, FSY*, UNY*
Government Bonds - *FSM*, FSY*, UNY*
Money Market - *N/A*
Treasury Bills - *FSM*, FSY*, UNY*

International Liquidity

Reserves Minus Gold - *FSM*, FSY*, UNY, WTA**
Gold - *FSM*, FSY*, UNY, WTA**

International Transactions

Balance of Payments - *BOP*, FSM*, FSY*, UNY, WDR, WTA**
Exports - *FSM*, FSY*, UNN, UNY, WTA**
Imports - *FSM*, FSY*, UNN, UNY, WTA**

National Accounts

Consumption
  Government - *FSM*, FSY*, UNN*
  Private - *FSM*, FSY*, UNN*
Gross Domestic Product - *FSM*, FSY*, UNN, UNY, WDR, WTA**
Gross National Product - *FSM*, FSY*, GSY*, UNN, WDR, WTA**
National Income - *FSY*, UNN, WTA**

Prices, Production, Employment

Consumer Credit Outstanding - *N/A*
Consumer Prices - *FSM*, FSY*, GSY*, UNY, WDR, WTA**
Earnings/Wages - *WTA**
Employment - *WTA**
Production - *N/A*
Wholesale/Producer Prices - *N/A*

Securities Markets - *N/A*

Nepalese Rupee - *see* - Nepal - Exchange Rates

Netherlands

Banking, Finance, and Money

Banking Institutions - Assets/Liabilities - *FSM*, FSY**
Monetary Authorities - Assets/Liabilities - *FSM*, FSY**
Money Supply - *FSM*, FSY*, MEI*, WTA**

Exchange Rates

Currency - *Netherlands Guilder*
Cross Rates - *FTI, WSJ*
Forward Exchange Rate - *FTI*
Per ECU - *FTI*
Per SDR - *FSM*, FSY*, FTI*
Per U.S. Dollar - *BAR, DJN, DRF, FRB, FSM*, FSY*, MEI*,
  NYT, UNY, WSJ*

Government Finance

Debt - *FSM*, FSY*, GSY**
Deficit/Surplus - *FSM*, FSY*, GSY*, WDR, WTA**
Expenditure - *GSY*, WDR, WTA**
Revenue - *GSY*, WDR, WTA**

Interest Rates

Aibor - *FS1, MEI**
Bank Rate - *N/A*
Discount Rate - *DRF, FRB, FSM*, FSY*, FS1, FS2, MEI*,
  UNY*
Government Bonds - *BAR, DRF, FSM*, FSY*, FS1, FTI, MEI*,
  UNY*
Money Market - *FSM*, FSY**
Treasury Bills - *FSY*, UNY*

International Liquidity

Reserves Minus Gold - *FSM*, FSY*, MEI*, UNY, WTA**
Gold - *FSM*, FSY*, UNY, WTA**

International Transactions

Balance of Payments - *BOP*, FSM*, FSY*, MEI*, UNY,
  WDR, WTA**
Exports - *FSM*, FSY*, MEI*, UNN, UNY, WTA**
Imports - *FSM*, FSY*, MEI*, UNN, UNY, WTA**

National Accounts

Consumption
   Government - *FSM*, FSY*, UNN, WDR, WTA**
   Private - *FSM*, FSY*, UNN, WDR, WTA**
   Gross Domestic Product - *FSM*, FSY*, GSY*, UNN, UNY, WDR, WTA**
   Gross National Product - *FSM*, FSY*, UNN, WDR, WTA**
   National Income - *FSM*, FSY*, UNN, WTA**

Prices, Production, Employment

Consumer Credit Outstanding - *FS2**
Consumer Prices - *FSM*, FSY, FS1, GSY*, MEI*, UNY, WDR, WTA**
Earnings/Wages - *FSM*, FSY*, MEI*, UNY, WDR, WTA**
Employment - *FSM*, FSY*, MEI*, UNY, WTA**
Production
   Industrial - *FSM*, FSY*, MEI*, UNY, WTA**
   Manufacturing - *MEI*, UNN, UNY*
   Mining - *UNY*
Wholesale/Producer Prices - *MEI*, UNY*

Securities Markets

Stock Exchange - *Amsterdam Stock Exchange*
Indexes
   ANP-CBS General Index
   CBS All Share Index
   CBS Stock Trend Index
Bonds
   Issue price - *FS2**
   Yield - *FS2**
Eurobonds
   Value of bonds issued - *FS1*
Foreign Bonds
   Value of bonds issued - *FS1*
Shares
   Issue price - *FS2**
   Price/Earnings Ratio - *FS1, FS2**
   Price Indexes
      ANP-CBS - *BAR, DJN, DRI, FSM*, FSY*, MEI*, NYT, UNY, WSJ*

CBX Allshare - *FTI*
Prices - FSM*, FSY*, FS1, MEI*, UNY
Prices - Selected Issues - *BAR, FTI, NYT, WSJ*
Total Gross - *FS2**
Yield - *FS1, FS2**
Stock Exchange Capitalization - *FS2**
Stock Market Instruments Issued - *FS2**

Netherlands Antilles

Banking, Finance, and Money

Banking Institutions - Assets/Liabilities - *FSM*, FSY**
Monetary Authorities - Assets/Liabilities - *FSM*, FSY**
Money Supply - *FSM*, FSY*, UNY*

Exchange Rates

Currency - *Netherlands Antilles Guilder*
Cross Rates - *N/A*
Forward Exchange Rate - *N/A*
Per ECU - *N/A*
Per SDR - *FSM*, FSY**
Per U.S. Dollar - *DJN, DRF, FSM*, FSY*, UNY*

Government Finance

Debt - *FSM*, FSY*, GSY**
Deficit/Surplus - *FSM*, FSY*, GSY**
Expenditure - *GSY**
Revenue - *GSY**

Interest Rates

Bank Rate - *N/A*
Discount Rate - *FSM*, FSY*, UNY*
Government Bonds - *FSM*, FSY*, UNY*
Money Market - *N/A*
Treasury Bills - *FSM*, FSY*, UNY*

International Liquidity

Reserves Minus Gold - *FSM*, FSY*, UNY*
Gold - *FSM*, FSY*, UNY*

International Transactions

Balance of Payments - *BOP*, FSM*, FSY*, UNY*
Exports - *FSM*, FSY*, UNN, UNY*

Imports - *FSM*, FSY*, UNN, UNY*

National Accounts

Consumption
  Government - *UNN*
  Private - *UNN*
Gross Domestic Product - *UNN, UNY*
Gross National Product - *UNN*
National Income - *UNN*

Prices, Production, Employment

Consumer Credit Outstanding - *N/A*
Consumer Prices - *FSM*, FSY*, GSY*, UNY*
Earnings/Wages - *UNY*
Employment - *UNY*
Production
  Refined Petroleum - *FSM*, FSY**
Wholesale/Producer Prices - *N/A*

Securities Markets - *N/A*

Netherlands Antilles Guilder - *see* - **Netherlands Antilles - Exchange Rates**

Netherlands Guilder - *see* - **Netherlands - Exchange Rates**

New Riel - *see* - **Cambodia**

New York Stock Exchange (NYSE) - *see* - **United States - Securities Markets**

New Zealand

Banking, Finance, and Money

Banking Institutions - Assets/Liabilities - *FSM*, FSY**
Monetary Authorities - Assets/Liabilities - *FSM*, FSY**
Money Supply - *FSM*, FSY*, MEI*, UNY, WTA**

Exchange Rates

Currency - *New Zealand Dollar*
Cross Rates - *N/A*
Forward Exchange Rate - *N/A*
Per ECU - *N/A*
Per SDR - *FSM*, FSY**

Per U.S. Dollar - *BAR, DJN, DRF, FRB, FSM*, FSY*, MEI*, NYT, UNY, WSJ*

Government Finance

Debt - *FSM*, FSY*, GSY**
Deficit/Surplus - *FSM*, FSY*, GSY*, WDR, WTA**
Expenditure - *GSY*, WDR, WTA**
Revenue - *GSY*, WDR, WTA**

Interest Rates

Bank Rate - *N/A*
Discount Rate - *FSM*, FSY*, UNY*
Government Bonds - *FSM*, FSY*, FS1, MEI*, UNY*
Money Market - *N/A*
Treasury Bills - *FSM*, FSY*, UNY*

International Liquidity

Reserves Minus Gold - *FSM*, FSY*, MEI*, UNY, WTA**
Gold - *FSM*, FSY*, UNY, WTA**

International Transactions

Balance of Payments - *BOP*, FSM*, FSY*, MEI*, UNY, WDR, WTA**
Exports - *FSM*, FSY*, MEI*, UNN, UNY, WTA**
Imports - *FSM*, FSY*, MEI*, UNN, UNY, WTA**

National Accounts

Consumption
  Government - *FSM*, FSY*, UNN, WDR, WTA**
  Private - *FSM*, FSY*, UNN, WDR, WTA**
Gross Domestic Product - *FSM*, FSY*, GSY*, UNN, WDR, WTA**
Gross National Product - *FSM*, FSY*, UNN, WDR, WTA**
National Income - *FSM*, FSY*, UNN, WTA**

Prices, Production, Employment

Consumer Credit Outstanding - *N/A*
Consumer Prices - *FSM*, FSY*, GSY*, MEI*, UNY, WDR, WTA**
Earnings/Wages - *FSM*, FSY*, MEI*, UNY, WTA**
Employment - *FSM*, FSY*, MEI*, UNY, WTA**

Production
  Industrial - *WTA**
  Manufacturing - *FSM*, UNN, WTA**
  Wholesale/Producer Prices - *FSY*, MEI*, UNY*

Securities Markets

Stock Exchange - *New Zealand Stock Exchange (NZSE)*
Index - *Wellington Barclays Stock Index (NZSE 40 Cap Stock Index)*
Eurobonds
  Value of bonds issued - *FS1*
Shares
  Prices last day of month - *MEI**
  Price Index - *BAR, FTI, DRI, FSM*, FSY*, MEI*, UNY, WTA**
  Prices - *FSM*, FSY*, MEI*, UNY, WTA**
  Prices - Selected Issues - *BAR*

New Zealand Dollar - *see* - **New Zealand - Exchange Rate**

New Zealand Stock Exchange (NZSE) - *see* - **New Zealand - Securities Markets**

Ngultrum - *see* - **Bhutan - Exchange Rates**

Nibor - *see* - **Norway - Interest Rates**

Nicaragua

Banking, Finance, and Money

Banking Institutions - Assets/Liabilities - *FSM*, FSY**
Monetary Authorities - Assets/Liabilities - *FSM*, FSY**
Money Supply - *FSM*, FSY*, UNY, WTA**

Exchange Rates

Currency - *Nicaraguan New Cordoba*
Cross Rates - *N/A*
Forward Exchange Rate - *N/A*
Per ECU - *N/A*
Per SDR - *FSM*, FSY**
Per U.S. Dollar - *DRF, FSM*, FSY*, UNY*

Government Finance

Debt - *FSM*, FSY*, GSY*, WTA**

Deficit/Surplus - *FSM*, FSY*, GSY*, WTA**
Expenditure - *GSY*, WDR, WTA**
Revenue - *GSY*, WDR, WTA**

International Liquidity

Reserves Minus Gold - *FSM*, FSY*, WTA**
Gold - *FSM*, FSY*, UNY, WTA**

International Transactions

Balance of Payments - *BOP*, FSM*, FSY*, UNY, WDR, WTA**
Exports - *FSM*, FSY*, UNN, UNY, WTA**
Imports - *FSM*, FSY*, UNN, UNY, WTA**

National Accounts

Consumption
  Government - *FSM*, FSY*, UNN, WDR, WTA**
  Private - *FSM*, FSY*, UNN, WDR, WTA**
Gross Domestic Product - *FSM*, FSY*, GSY*, UNN, UNY, WDR, WTA**
Gross National Product - *FSM*, UNN, WDR, WTA**
National Income - *FSY*, UNN, WTA**

Prices, Production, Employment

Consumer Credit Outstanding - *N/A*
Consumer Prices - *FSM*, FSY*, GSY*, UNY, WDR, WTA**
Earnings/Wages - *WDR, WTA**
Employment - *UNY*
Production
  Industrial - *WTA**
  Manufacturing - *WTA**
Wholesale/Producer Prices - *N/A*

Securities Markets - *N/A*

Nicaraguan New Cordoba - *see* - Nicaragua - Exchange Rates

Nickel - *see* - Commodities

Niger

Banking, Finance, and Money

Banking Institutions - Assets/Liabilities - *FSM*, FSY**

Monetary Authorities - Assets/Liabilities - *FSM*, FSY**
Money Supply - *FSM*, FSY*, UNY, WTA**

Exchange Rates

Currency - *CFA Franc*
Cross Rates - *N/A*
Forward Exchange Rate - *N/A*
Per ECU - *N/A*
Per SDR - *FSM*, FSY**
Per U.S. Dollar - *DRF, FSM*, FSY*, UNY*

Government Finance

Debt - *WTA**
Deficit/Surplus - *FSY**
Expenditure - *WDR*
Revenue - *WDR*

Interest Rates

Bank Rate - *N/A*
Discount Rate - *FSM*, FSY*, UNY*
Government Bonds - *N/A*
Money Market - *FSM*, FSY**
Treasury Bills - *N/A*

International Liquidity

Reserves Minus Gold - *FSM*, FSY*, UNY, WTA**
Gold - *FSM*, FSY*, UNY, WTA**

International Transactions

Balance of Payments - *BOP*, FSM*, FSY*, UNY, WDR, WTA**
Exports - *FSM*, FSY*, UNN, UNY, WTA**
Imports - *FSM*, FSY*, UNN, UNY, WTA**

National Accounts

Consumption
  Government - *FSM*, FSY*, UNN, WDR, WTA**
  Private - *FSM*, FSY*, UNN, WDR, WTA**
Gross Domestic Product - *FSM*, FSY*, UNN, WDR, WTA**
Gross National Product - *UNN, WDR, WTA**
National Income - *FSY*, UNN, WTA**

Prices, Production, Employment

Consumer Credit Outstanding - *N/A*
Consumer Prices - *FSM*, FSY*, UNY, WDR, WTA**
Earnings/Wages - *WDR, WTA**
Employment - *UNY, WTA**
Production
  Industrial - *WTA**
Wholesale/Producer Prices - *N/A*

Securities Markets - *N/A*

Nigeria

Banking, Finance, and Money

Banking Institutions - Assets/Liabilities - *FSM*, FSY**
Monetary Authorities - Assets/Liabilities - *FSM*, FSY**
Money Supply - *FSM*, FSY*, UNY, WTA**

Exchange Rates

Currency - *Nigerian Naira*
Cross Rates - *N/A*
Forward Exchange Rate - *N/A*
Per ECU - *N/A*
Per SDR - *FSM*, FSY**
Per U.S. Dollar - *DJN, DRF, FSM*, FSY*, UNY*

Government Finance

Debt - *FSM*, FSY*, GSY*, WTA**
Deficit/Surplus - *FSM*, FSY*, GSY*, WDR, WTA**
Expenditure - *GSY*, WDR, WTA**
Revenue - *GSY*, WDR, WTA**

Interest Rates

Bank Rate - *N/A*
Discount Rate - *FSM*, FSY**
Government Bonds - *N/A*
Money Market - *N/A*
Treasury Bills - *N/A*

International Liquidity

Reserves Minus Gold - *FSM*, FSY*, UNY, WTA**
Gold - *FSM*, FSY*, UNY, WTA**

International Transactions

Balance of Payments - *BOP*, FSM*, FSY*, UNY, WDR, WTA**
Exports - *FSM*, FSY*, UNN, UNY, WTA**
Imports - *FSM*, FSY*, UNN, UNY, WTA**

National Accounts

Consumption
  Government - *FSM*, FSY*, UNN, WDR, WTA**
  Private - *FSM*, FSY*, UNN, WDR, WTA**
Gross Domestic Product - *FSM*, FSY*, GSY*, UNN, UNY, WDR, WTA**
Gross National Product - *FSM*, FSY*, UNN, WDR, WTA**
National Income - *UNN, WTA**

Prices, Production, Employment

Consumer Credit Outstanding - *N/A*
Consumer Prices - *FSM*, FSY*, GSY*, UNY, WDR, WTA**
Earnings/Wages - *UNN*
Employment - *UNN*
Production
  Crude Petroleum - *FSM*, FSY**
  Industrial - *FSM*, FSY*, WTA**
  Manufacturing - *FSM*, FSY*, WTA**
Wholesale/Producer Prices - *N/A*

Securities Markets - *N/A*

Nigerian Naira - *see* - **Nigeria - Exchange Rates**

Nikkei Index - *see* - **Japan - Securities Markets;** *see also* - **Commodities**

Norway

Banking, Finance, and Money

Banking Institutions - Assets/Liabilities - *FSM*, FSY**
Monetary Authorities - Assets/Liabilities - *FSM*, FSY**
Money Supply - *FSM*, FSY*, MEI*, UNY, WTA**

Exchange Rates

Currency - *Norwegian Krone*
Cross Rates - *N/A*
Forward Exchange Rate - *FTI*
Per ECU - *FTI*

Per SDR - *FSM*, FSY*, FTI*
Per U.S. Dollar - *BAR, DJN, DRF, FRB, FSM*, FSY*, MEI*, NYT, WSJ*

Government Finance

Debt - *FSM*, FSY*, GSY**
Deficit/Surplus - *FSM*, FSY*, GSY*, WDR, WTA**
Expenditure - *GSY*, WDR, WTA**
Revenue - *GSY*, WDR, WTA**

Interest Rates

Bank Rate - *N/A*
Discount Rate - *FRB, FSM*, FSY*, FS2*, UNY*
Government Bonds - *FSM*, FSY*, FS1, MEI*, UNY*
Money Market - *FSY**
Nibor - *FS1, MEI**
Treasury Bills - *FS1, UNY*

International Liquidity

Reserves Minus Gold - *FSM*, FSY*, MEI*, UNY, WTA**
Gold - *FSM*, FSY*, UNY, WTA**

International Transactions

Balance of Payments - *BOP*, FSM*, FSY*, MEI*, UNY, WDR, WTA**
Exports - *FSM*, FSY*, MEI*, UNN, UNY, WTA**
Imports - *FSM*, FSY*, MEI*, UNN, UNY, WTA**

National Accounts

Consumption
    Government - *FSM*, FSY*, UNN, WDR, WTA**
    Private - *FSM*, FSY*, UNN, WDR, WTA**
Gross Domestic Product - *FSM*, FSY*, GSY*, UNN, UNY, WTA**
Gross National Product - *FSM*, FSY*, UNN, WDR, WTA**
National Income - *FSM*, FSY*, UNN, WTA**

Prices, Production, Employment

Consumer Credit Outstanding - *FS2*
Consumer Prices - *FSM*, FSY*, FS1, GSY*, MEI*, UNY, WDR, WTA**
Earnings/Wages - *FSM*, FSY*, MEI*, UNY, WDR, WTA**

Employment - *FSM*, FSY*, MEI*, UNY, WTA**
Production
   Crude Petroleum - *FSM*, FSY*, UNN, UNY*
   Industrial - *FSM*, FSY*, UNY, WTA**
   Manufacturing - *MEI*, UNN, UNY, WTA**
   Mining - *UNY*
Wholesale/Producer Prices - *MEI*, UNY*

Securities Markets

Stock Exchange - *Øslø Børs (Oslo Stock Exchange)*
Index - *Oslo Stock Exchange Composite Index*
Bonds
   Issue price - *FS2**
   Yield - *FS2**
Eurobonds
   Value of bonds issued - *FS1*
Foreign Bonds
   Value of bonds issued - *FS1*
Money Market Instruments Issued - *FS2**
Shares
   Issue price - *FS2**
   Price last day of month - *MEI**
   Price/Earnings Ratio - *FS1, FS2**
   Price Index - *BAR, DRI, FSM*, FSY*, FS1, FS2*, FTI, MEI*, UNY*
   Prices - *FSM, FSY, FS1, MEI, UNY*
   Prices - Selected Issues - *FTI*
   Total Gross - *FS2**
Stock Exchange Capitalization - *FS2**
Stock Market Instruments Issued - *FS2**

Norwegian Krone - *see* - **Norway - Exchange Rates**

NYSE (New York Stock Exchange) - *see* - **United States - Securities Markets**

NZSE (New Zealand Stock Exchange) - *see* - **New Zealand - Securities Markets**

NZSE 40 Cap Stock Index - *see* - **New Zealand - Securities Markets**

O

Oats - *see* **- Commodities**

Oman

Banking, Finance, and Money

Banking Institutions - Assets/Liabilities - *FSM*, FSY**
Monetary Authorities - Assets/Liabilities - *FSM*, FSY**
Money Supply - *FSM*, FSY*, UNY, WTA**

Exchange Rates

Currency - *Omani Rial*
Cross Rates - *N/A*
Forward Exchange Rate - *N/A*
Per ECU - *N/A*
Per SDR - *FSM*, FSY**
Per U.S. Dollar - *DRF, FSM*, FSY*, UNY*

Government Finance

Debt - *FSM*, FSY*, GSY*, WTA**
Deficit/Surplus - *FSM*, FSY*, GSY*, WDR, WTA**
Expenditure - *GSY*, WDR, WTA**
Revenue - *GSY*, WDR, WTA**

Interest Rates

Bank Rate - *N/A*
Discount Rate - *N/A*
Government Bonds - *N/A*
Money Market - *N/A*
Treasury Bills - *N/A*

International Liquidity

Reserves Minus Gold - *FSM*, FSY*, UNY, WTA**
Gold *FSM*, FSY*, UNN, UNY, WTA**

International Transactions

Balance of Payments - *BOP*, FSM*, FSY*, UNY, WDR, WTA**
Exports - *FSM*, FSY*, UNN, UNY, WTA**
Imports - *FSM*, FSY*, UNN, UNY, WTA**

National Accounts

Consumption
  Government - *FSM*, FSY*, UNN*
  Private - *FSM*, FSY*, UNN*
Gross Domestic Product - *FSM*, FSY*, GSY*, UNN, UNY, WDR, WTA**
Gross National Product - *FSM*, UNN, WDR, WTA**
National Income - *WTA**

Prices, Production, Employment

Consumer Credit Outstanding - *N/A*
Consumer Prices - *UNY, WDR*
Earnings/Wages - *N/A*
Employment - *N/A*
Production - *N/A*
Wholesale/Producer Prices - *N/A*

Securities Markets - *N/A*

Omani Rial - *see* - **Oman - Securities Markets**

Orange Juice - *see* - **Commodities**

Øslø Børs (Oslo Stock Exchange) - *see* - **Norway - Securities Markets**

Oslo Stock Exchange - *see* - **Norway - Securities Markets**

Oslo Stock Exchange Composite Index - *see* - **Norway - Securities Markets**

OTC (Over the Counter) Market - *see* - **United States - Securities Markets**

Ougvivyas - *see* - **Mauritania - Exchange Rates**

Over the Counter Market (OTC Market) - *see* - **United States -
Securities Markets**

P

Pa'anga - *see* - **Tonga - Exchange Rates**

Pacific Stock Exchange (PSE) - *see* - **United States - Securities Markets**

Pakistan

Banking, Finance, and Money

Banking Institutions - Assets/Liabilities - *FSM*, FSY**
Monetary Authorities - Assets/Liabilities - *FSM**
Money Supply - *FSM*, UNY, WTA**

Exchange Rates

Currency - *Pakistan Rupee*
Cross Rates - *N/A*
Forward Exchange Rate - *N/A*
Per ECU - *N/A*
Per SDR - *FSM*, FSY**
Per U.S. Dollar - *BAR, DJN, DRF, FSM*, FSY*, NYT, UNY, WSJ*

Government Finance

Debt - *FSM*, GSY*, WTA**
Deficit/Surplus - *FSM*, GSY*, WDR, WTA**
Expenditure - *GSY*, WDR, WTA**
Revenue - *GSY*, WDR, WTA**

Interest Rates

Bank Rate - *FSM**
Discount Rate - *UNY*
Government Bonds - *FSM*, UNY*

Money Market - *FSM**
Treasury Bills - *N/A*

International Liquidity

Reserves Minus Gold - *FSM*, UNY, WTA**
Gold - *FSM*, UNY, WTA**

International Transactions

Balance of Payments - *BOP*, FSM*, UNY, WDR, WTA**
Exports - *FSM*, UNN, UNY, WTA**
Imports - *FSM*, UNN, UNY, WTA**

National Accounts

Consumption
  Government - *FSM*, UNN, WDR, WTA**
  Private - *FSM*, UNN, WDR, WTA**
Gross Domestic Product - *FSM*, GSY*, UNN, UNY, WDR, WTA**
Gross National Product - *FSM*, UNN, WDR, WTA**
National Income - *FSM*, UNN, WTA**

Prices, Production, Employment

Consumer Credit Outstanding - *N/A*
Consumer Prices - *FSM*, GSY*, WDR, WTA**
Earnings/Wages - *UNY, WDR, WTA**
Employment - *UNY*
Production
  Industrial - *UNY, WTA**
  Manufacturing - *FSM*, UNY, WTA**
  Mining - *UNY*
Wholesale/Producer Prices - *FSM*, UNY*

Securities Markets

Stock Exchange - *Lahore Stock Exchange*
Index - *Lahore Stock Exchange Price Index*
Shares
  Price Index - *BAR, FSM*, FTI, UNY*
  Prices - *FSM*, UNY*

Pakistan Rupee - *see* **- Pakistan - Exchange Rates**

Palladium - *see* **- Commodities**

Panama

Banking, Finance, and Money

Banking Institutions - Assets/Liabilities - *FSM*, FSY**
Monetary Authorities - Assets/Liabilities - *FSM*, FSY**
Money Supply - *FSM*, FSY*, UNY, WTA**

Exchange Rates

Currency - *Panamanian Balboa*
Cross Rates - *N/A*
Forward Exchange Rate - *N/A*
Per ECU - *N/A*
Per SDR - *FSM*, FSY**
Per U.S. Dollar - *DJN, DRF, FSM*, FSY*, UNY*

Government Finance

Debt - *FSM*, FSY*, GSY*, WTA**
Deficit/Surplus - *FSM*, FSY*, GSY*, WDR, WTA**
Expenditure - *GSY*, WDR, WTA**
Revenue - *GSY*, WDR, WTA**

International Liquidity

Reserves Minus Gold - *FSM*, FSY*, UNY, WTA**
Gold - *FSM*, FSY**

International Transactions

Balance of Payments - *BOP*, FSM*, FSY*, UNY, WDR, WTA**
Exports - *FSM*, FSY*, UNN, UNY, WTA**
Imports - *FSM*, FSY*, UNN, UNY, WTA**

National Accounts

Consumption
  Government - *FSM*, FSY*, UNN, WDR, WTA**
  Private - *FSM*, FSY*, UNN, WDR, WTA**
Gross Domestic Product - *FSM*, FSY*, GSY*, UNN, UNY, WDR, WTA**
Gross National Product - *FSM*, FSY*, UNN, WDR, WTA**
National Income - *FSM*, FSY*, UNN, WTA**

Prices, Production, Employment

Consumer Credit Outstanding - *N/A*
Consumer Prices - *FSM*, FSY*, GSY*, UNY, WDR, WTA**

Earnings/Wages - *UNY, WDR, WTA**
Employment - *UNY, WTA**
Production
  Industrial - *WTA**
  Manufacturing - *UNN, UNY, WTA**
  Wholesale/Producer Prices - *FSM*, FSY*, UNY*

Securities Markets - *N/A*

Panamanian Balboa - *see* - Panama - Exchange Rates

Papua New Guinea

Banking, Finance, and Money

Banking Institutions - Assets/Liabilities - *FSM*, FSY**
Monetary Authorities - Assets/Liabilities - *FSM*, FSY**
Money Supply - *FSM*, FSY*, UNY, WTA**

Exchange Rates

Currency - *Papua New Guinea Kina*
Cross Rates - *N/A*
Forward Exchange Rate - *N/A*
Per ECU - *N/A*
Per SDR - *FSM*, FSY**
Per U.S. Dollar - *DJN, DRF, FSM*, FSY*, UNY*

Government Finance

Debt - *FSM*, FSY*, GSY*, WTA**
Deficit/Surplus - *FSM*, FSY*, GSY*, WDR, WTA**
Expenditure - *GSY*, WDR, WTA**
Revenue - *GSY*, WDR, WTA**

Interest Rates

Bank Rate - *N/A*
Discount Rate - *FSM*, FSY*, UNY*
Government Bonds - *N/A*
Money Market - *N/A*
Treasury Bills - *FSM*, FSY*, UNY*

International Liquidity

Reserves Minus Gold - *FSM*, FSY*, UNY, WTA**
Gold - *FSM*, FSY*, UNY, WTA**

International Transactions

Balance of Payments - *BOP*, FSM*, FSY*, UNY, WDR, WTA**

Exports - *FSM*, FSY*, UNN, UNY, WTA**

Imports - *FSM*, FSY*, UNN, UNY, WTA**

National Accounts

Consumption

Government - *FSM*, FSY*, UNN, WDR, WTA**

Private - *FSM*, FSY*, UNN, WDR, WTA**

Gross Domestic Product - FSM*, FSY*, GSY*, UNN, UNY, WDR, WTA*

Gross National Product - FSM*, FSY*, UNN, WDR, WTA*

National Income - FSM*, FSY*, UNN, WDR, WTA*

Prices, Production, Employment

Consumer Credit Outstanding - *N/A*

Consumer Prices - *FSM*, FSY*, GSY*, UNY, WTA**

Earnings/Wages - *WDR, WTA**

Production

Industrial - *WTA**

Manufacturing - *WTA**

Wholesale/Producer Prices - *N/A*

Securities Markets - *N/A*

Papua New Guinea Kina - *see* - Papua New Guinea - Exchange Rates

Paraguay

Banking, Finance, and Money

Banking Institutions - Assets/Liabilities - *FSM*, FSY**

Monetary Authorities - Assets/Liabilities - *FSM*, FSY**

Money Supply - *FSM*, FSY*, UNY, WTA**

Exchange Rates

Currency - *Paraguayan Guarani*

Cross Rates - *N/A*

Forward Exchange Rate - *N/A*

Per ECU - *N/A*

Per SDR - *FSM**

Per U.S. Dollar - *DRF, FSM*, FSY*, UNY*

Government Finance

Debt - *FSM*, FSY*, GSY*, WTA**
Deficit/Surplus - *FSM*, FSY*, GSY*, WDR, WTA**
Expenditure - *GSY*, WDR, WTA**
Revenue - *GSY*, WDR, WTA**

International Liquidity

Reserves Minus Gold - *FSM*, FSY*, UNY, WTA**
Gold - *FSM*, FSY*, UNY, WTA**

International Transactions

Balance of Payments - *BOP*, FSM*, FSY*, UNY, WDR, WTA**
Exports - *FSM*, FSY*, UNN, UNY, WTA**
Imports - *FSM*, FSY*, UNN, UNY, WTA**

National Accounts

Consumption
Government - *FSM*, FSY*, UNN, WDR, WTA**
Private - *FSM*, FSY*, UNN, WDR, WTA**
Gross Domestic Product - *FSM*, FSY*, GSY*, UNN, UNY, WDR, WTA**
Gross National Product - *FSM*, FSY*, UNN, WDR, WTA**
National Income - *FSM*, FSY*, UNN, WTA**

Prices, Production, Employment

Consumer Credit Outstanding - *N/A*
Consumer Prices - *FSM*, FSY*, GSY*, UNY, WDR, WTA**
Earnings/Wages - *UNY*
Employment - *UNY*
Production
Industrial - *UNY, WTA**
Manufacturing - *UNN, UNY, WTA**
Wholesale/Producer Prices - *FSM*, FSY**

Securities Markets - *N/A*

Paraguayan Guarani - *see* - Paraguay - Exchange Rates

Paris Bourse - *see* - France - Securities Markets

People's Bank Dollar - *see* - China (People's Republic) - Exchange Rates - Chinese Yuan

People's Democratic Republic of Yemen - *see* - **Yemen (People's Democratic Republic)**

Peru

Banking, Finance, and Money

Banking Institutions - Assets/Liabilities - *FSM*, FSY**
Monetary Authorities - Assets/Liabilities - *FSM*, FSY**
Money Supply - *FSM*, FSY*, WTA**

Exchange Rates

Currency - *Peruvian Inti*
Cross Rates - *N/A*
Forward Exchange Rate - *N/A*
Per ECU - *N/A*
Per SDR - *FSY**
Per U.S. Dollar - DJN, DRF, *FSY**, NYT, WSJ
Currency - *Sol*
Cross Rates - *N/A*
Forward Exchange Rate - *N/A*
Per ECU - *N/A*
Per SDR - *N/A*
Per U.S. Dollar - *BAR, FSM*, UNY*

Government Finance

Debt - *GSY*, WTA**
Deficit/Surplus - *FSM*, FSY*, GSY*, WDR, WTA**
Expenditure - *GSY*, UNN, WTA**
Revenue - *GSY*, UNN, WTA**

Interest Rates

Bank Rate - *N/A*
Discount Rate - *FSM*, FSY*, UNY*
Government Bonds - *N/A*
Money Market - *N/A*
Treasury Bills - *N/A*

International Liquidity

Reserves Minus Gold - *FSM*, FSY*, UNY, WTA**
Gold - *FSM*, FSY*, UNY, WTA**

International Transactions

Balance of Payments - *BOP*, FSM*, FSY*, UNY, WDR, WTA**

Exports - *FSM*, FSY*, UNN, UNY, WTA**

Imports - *FSM*, FSY*, UNN, UNY, WTA**

National Accounts

Consumption

Government - *FSM*, FSY*, UNN, WDR, WTA**

Private - *FSM*, FSY*, UNN, WDR, WTA**

Gross Domestic Product - *FSM*, FSY*, GSY*, UNN, UNY, WDR, WTA**

Gross National Product - *FSY*, UNN, WDR, WTA**

National Income - *FSM*, UNN, WTA**

Prices, Production, Employment

Consumer Credit Outstanding - *N/A*

Consumer Prices - *FSM*, FSY*, GSY*, UNY, WDR, WTA**

Earnings/Wages - *UNN, UNY, WTA**

Employment - *FSM*, UNY, WTA**

Production

Industrial - *WTA**

Manufacturing - *FSM*, FSY*, UNN, UNY, WTA**

Wholesale/Producer Prices - *UNY*

Securities Markets - *N/A*

Peruvian Inti - *see* **- Peru - Exchange Rates**

Peseta - *see* **- Spain - Exchange Rates**

Peso - *see* **- Argentina - Exchange Rates; Chile - Exchange Rates; Colombia - Exchange Rates; Dominican Republic - Exchange Rates; Guinea-Bissau - Exchange Rates; Mexico - Exchange Rates; Philippines - Exchange Rates; Uruguay - Exchange Rates**

Philadelphia Stock Exchange (PHLX) - *see* **- United States - Securities Markets**

Philippine Peso - *see* **- Philippines - Exchange Rates**

Philippines

Banking, Finance, and Money

Banking Institutions - Assets/Liabilities - *FSM**
Monetary Authorities - Assets/Liabilities - *FSM**
Money Supply - *FSM*, FSY*, UNY, WTA**

Exchange Rates

Currency - *Philippine Peso*
Cross Rates - *N/A*
Forward Exchange Rate - *N/A*
Per ECU - *N/A*
Per SDR - *FSM*, FSY**
Per U.S. Dollar - *BAR, DJN, DRF, FSM*, FSY*, NYT, UNY, WSJ*

Government Finance

Debt - *FSM*, FSY*, GSY*, WTA**
Deficit/Surplus - *FSM*, FSY*, GSY*, WDR, WTA**
Expenditure - *GSY*, WDR, WTA**
Revenue - *GSY*, WDR, WTA**

Interest Rates

Bank Rate - *N/A*
Discount Rate - *FSM*, FSY*, UNY*
Government Bonds - *N/A*
Money Market - *N/A*
Treasury Bills - *FSM*, FSY*, UNY*

International Liquidity

Reserves Minus Gold - *FSM*, UNY, WTA**
Gold - *FSY*, UNY, WTA**

International Transactions

Balance of Payments - *BOP*, FSM*, FSY*, UNY, WDR, WTA**
Exports - *FSM*, FSY*, UNN, UNY, WTA**
Imports - *FSM*, FSY*, UNN, UNY, WTA**

National Accounts

Consumption
Government - *FSM*, FSY*, UNN, WDR, WTA**
Private - *FSM*, FSY*, UNN, WDR, WTA**

Gross Domestic Product - *FSM*, FSY*, GSY*, UNN, UNY, WDR, WTA**
Gross National Product - *FSM*, FSY*, UNN, WDR, WTA**
National Income - *FSM*, FSY*, UNN*

Prices, Production, Employment

Consumer Credit Outstanding - *N/A*
Consumer Prices - *FSM*, FSY*, GSY*, UNY, WDR, WTA**
Earnings/Wages - *UNY, WDR, WTA**
Employment - *FSM*, UNY, WTA**
Production
  Industrial - *UNY, WTA**
  Manufacturing - *UNN, UNY, WTA**
Wholesale/Producer Prices - *FSM, FSY, UNY*

Securities Markets

Stock Exchange - *Makati Stock Exchange Inc.*
Index - *Manilla Composite Index*
Shares
  Price Index - *BAR, DRI, FSM*, FSY*, FTI*
  Prices - *FSM*, FSY**
  Prices - Selected Issues - *BAR*

PHLX (Philadelphia Stock Exchange) - *see* - United States - Securities Markets

Pibor - *see* - France - Interest Rates; *see also* - Commodities

Platinum - *see* - Commodities

Poland

Banking, Finance, and Money

Banking Institutions - Assets/Liabilities - *FSM*, FSY**
Monetary Authorities - Assets/Liabilities - *FSM*, FSY**
Money Supply - *FSM*, FSY*, UNY, WTA**

Exchange Rates

Currency - *Polish Zloty*
Cross Rates - *N/A*
Forward Exchange Rate - *N/A*
Per ECU - *N/A*
Per SDR - *N/A*

Per U.S. Dollar - *BAR, FSM*, FSY*, NYT, UNY, WSJ*

Government Finance

Debt - *GSY*, WTA**
Deficit/Surplus - *FSM*, GSY*, WDR, WTA**
Expenditure - *GSY*, WDR, WTA**
Revenue - *GSY*, WDR, WTA**

Interest Rates

Bank Rate - *N/A*
Discount Rate - *FSY**
Government Bonds - *N/A*
Money Market - *N/A*
Rediscount Rate - *FSM*, FSY***
Refinancing - *FSM*, FSY**
Treasury Bills - *N/A*

International Liquidity

Reserves Minus Gold - *FSM*, FSY*, UNY, WTA**
Gold - *FSM*, FSY*, UNY, WTA**

International Transactions

Balance of Payments - *BOP*, FSM*, FSY*, UNY, WDR, WTA**
Exports - *FSM*, FSY*, UNN, UNY, WTA**
Imports - *FSM*, FSY*, UNN, UNY, WTA**

National Accounts

Consumption
  Government - *FSM*, FSY*, WDR, WTA**
  Private - *FSM*, FSY*, UNN, WDR, WTA**
Gross Domestic Product - *FSM*, FSY*, GSY*, UNN, UNY, WDR, WTA**
Gross National Product - *WDR, WTA**
National Income - *WTA**

Prices, Production, Employment

Consumer Credit Outstanding - *N/A*
Consumer Prices - *FSM*, FSY*, GSY*, UNY, WDR, WTA**
Earnings/Wages - *FSM*, FSY*, UNY, WTA**
Employment - *FSM*, FSY*, UNY, WTA**

Production
Industrial - *FSM*, FSY*, UNY*
Manufacturing - *UNY*
Mining - *UNY*
Wholesale/Producer Prices - *FSM**

Securities Markets -*N/A*

Polish Zloty - *see* - **Poland** - **Exchange Rates**

Pork Bellies - *see* - **Commodities**

Portugal

Banking, Finance, and Money

Banking Institutions - Assets/Liabilities - *FSM*, FSY**
Monetary Authorities - Assets/Liabilities - *FSM*, FSY**
Money Supply - *FSM*, FSY*, MEI*, UNY, WTA**

Exchange Rates

Currency - *Portugese Escudo*
Cross Rates - *N/A*
Forward Exchange Rate - *FTI*
Per ECU - *N/A*
Per SDR - *FSM*, FSY**
Per U.S. Dollar - *BAR, DJN, DRF, FRB, FSM*, FSY*, MEI*, NYT, WSJ*

Government Finance

Debt - *FSY*, GSY*, WTA**
Deficit/Surplus - *FSM*, FSY*, GSY*, WDR, WTA**
Expenditure - *GSY*, WDR, WTA**
Revenue - *GSY*, WDR, WTA**

Interest Rates

Bank Rate - *N/A*
Discount Rate - *FSM*, FSY*, UNY*
Government Bonds - *FSM*, FSY**
Money Market - *FSM*, FSY*, UNY*
Treasury Bills - *FSM*, FSY*, UNY*

International Liquidity

Reserves Minus Gold - *FSM*, FSY*, MEI*, UNY, WTA**
Gold - *FSM*, FSY*, UNY, WTA**

International Transactions

Balance of Payments - *BOP*, FSM*, FSY*, MEI*, UNY, WDR, WTA**
Exports - *FSM*, FSY*, MEI*, UNN, UNY, WTA**
Imports - *FSM*, FSY*, MEI*, UNN, UNY, WTA**

National Accounts

Consumption
  Government - *FSM*, FSY*, UNN, WDR, WTA**
  Private - *FSM*, FSY*, GSY*, MEI*, UNN, WDR, WTA**
  Gross Domestic Product - *FSM*, FSY*, GSY*, MEI*, UNN, UNY, WDR, WTA**
  Gross National Product - *FSM*, FSY*, UNN, WDR, WTA**
  National Income - *FSM*, FSY*, UNN, WTA**

Prices, Production, Employment

Consumer Credit Outstanding - *FS2*
Consumer Prices - *FSM*, FSY*, GSY*, MEI*, UNY, WDR, WTA**
Earnings/Wages - *FSM*, FSY*, UNY, WDR, WTA**
Employment - *MEI*, UNY, WTA**
Production
  Industrial - *FSM*, FSY*, MEI*, UNY, WTA**
  Manufacturing - *MEI*, UNN, UNY*
  Mining - *UNY*
Wholesale/Producer Prices - *N/A*

Securities Markets

Stock Exchange - *Lisbon Stock Exchange*
Index - *Lisbon BVL*
Eurobonds
  Value of bonds issued - *FS1*
Shares
  Prices last day of month - *MEI**
  Prices - *MEI*, UNY*
  Price Index - *BAR, FTI, MEI*, UNY*
Stock Exchange Turnover - *FS2**

Portugese Escudo - *see* **- Portugal - Exchange Rates**

Pound - *see* **- Cyprus - Exchange Rates; Egypt - Exchange Rates; Ireland - Exchange Rates; Lebanon - Exchange Rates; Sudan -**

Q

Qatar

Banking, Finance, and Money

Banking Institutions - Assets/Liabilities - *FSM*, FSY**
Monetary Authorities - Assets/Liabilities - *FSM*, FSY**
Money Supply - *FSM*, FSY**

Exchange Rates

Currency - *Rial*
Cross Rates - *N/A*
Forward Exchange Rate - *N/A*
Per ECU - *N/A*
Per SDR - *FSM*, FSY**
Per U.S. Dollar - *DJN, DRF, FSM*, FSY*, UNY*

Government Finance

Debt - *N/A*
Deficit/Surplus - *FSY**
Expenditure - *N/A*
Revenue - *N/A*

International Liquidity

Reserves Minus Gold - *FSM*, FSY*, UNY*
Gold - *FSM*, FSY*, UNY*

International Transactions

Balance of Payments - *N/A*
Exports - *FSM*, FSY*, UNN, UNY*
Imports - *FSM*, FSY*, UNN, UNY*

National Accounts

Consumption
    Government - *UNN*
    Private - *UNN*
    Gross Domestic Product - *UNN, UNY*
    Gross National Product - *N/A*
    National Income - *N/A*

Prices, Production, Employment

Consumer Credit Outstanding - *N/A*
Consumer Prices - *FSM*, FSY**
Earnings/Wages - *N/A*
Employment - *N/A*
Production - *N/A*
Wholesale/Producer Prices - *N/A*

Securities Markets - *N/A*

Quetzal - *see* **- Guatemala - Exchange Rates**

R

Rand - *see* - South Africa - Exchange Rates

Renminbiao - *see* - China (People's Republic) - Exchange Rates - Chinese Yuan

Reserves Minus Gold - *see* - Individual Countries - International Liquidity

Revenue - *see* - Individual Countries - Government Finance

Rial - *see* - Iran - Exchange Rates; Oman - Exchange Rates; Qatar - Exchange Rates; Yemen Arab Republic - Exchange Rates

Ringgit - *see* - Malaysia - Exchange Rates

Riyal - *see* - Saudi Arabia - Exchange Rates

Romania

    Banking, Finance, and Money

        Banking Institutions - Assets/Liabilities - *FSM*, FSY**
        Monetary Authorities - Assets/Liabilities - *FSM*, FSY**
        Money Supply - *FSM*, FSY**

    Exchange Rates

        Currency - *Romanian Leu*
        Cross Rates - *N/A*
        Forward Exchange Rate - *N/A*
        Per ECU - *N/A*
        Per SDR - *FSM*, FSY**
        Per U.S. Dollar - *DJN, DRF, FSM*, FSY**

Government Finance

Debt - *FSM**
Deficit/Surplus - *FSM*, FSY*, GSY*, WDR*
Expenditure - *GSY*, WDR*
Revenue - *GSY*, WDR*

International Liquidity

Reserves Minus Gold - *FSM*, FSY**
Gold - *FSM*, FSY**

International Transactions

Balance of Payments - *FSM*, FSY*, WDR*
Exports - *FSM*, FSY*, UNN*
Imports - *FSM*, FSY**

National Accounts

Consumption
  Government - *FSM*, FSY*, UNN*
  Private - *FSM*, FSY*, UNN*
Gross Domestic Product - *FSM*, UNN, WDR*
Gross National Product - *FSY*, GSY*, WDR*
National Income - *FSY**

Prices, Production, Employment

Consumer Credit Outstanding - *FSM*, FSY*, GSY*, WDR*
Consumer Prices - *FSM*, FSY**
Earnings/Wages - *FSM*, FSY**
Employment - *FSM*, FSY**
Production
  Industrial - *FSM*, FSY**
Wholesale/Producer Prices - *N/A*

Securities Markets - *N/A*

Romanian Leu - *see* - **Romania - Exchange Rates**

Ruble - *see* - **Union of Soviet Socialist Republics - Exchange Rates**

Rufiyaa - *see* - **Maldives - Exchange Rates**

Rupee - *see* - **India - Exchange Rates; Mauritius - Exchange Rates; Nepal - Exchange Rates; Pakistan - Exchange Rates; Seychelles - Exchange Rates; Sri Lanka - Exchange Rates**

Rupiah - *see* **- Indonesia - Exchange Rates**

Rwanda

Banking, Finance, and Money

Banking Institutions - Assets/Liabilities - *FSM**, *FSY**
Monetary Authorities - Assets/Liabilities - *FSM**, *FSY**
Money Supply - *FSM**, *FSY**, *WTA**

Exchange Rates

Currency - *Rwanda Franc*
Cross Rates - *N/A*
Forward Exchange Rate - *N/A*
Per ECU - *N/A*
Per SDR - *FSM**, *FSY**
Per U.S. Dollar - *DRF, FSM**, *FSY**

Government Finance

Debt - *FSY**, *WTA**
Deficit/Surplus - *FSY**, *WDR, WTA**
Expenditure - WDR, WTA*
Revenue - WDR, WTA*

Interest Rates

Bank Rate - *N/A*
Discount Rate - *FSM**, *FSY**
Government Bonds - *N/A*
Money Market - *N/A*
Treasury Bills - *N/A*

International Liquidity

Reserves Minus Gold - *FSM**, *FSY**, *WTA**
Gold - *N/A*

International Transactions

Balance of Payments - *FSM**, *FSY**, *WDR, WTA**
Exports - *FSM**, *FSY**, *UNN, WTA**
Imports - *FSM**, *FSY**, *UNN, WTA**

National Accounts

Consumption
Government - *FSM**, *FSY**, *UNN, WDR, WTA**
Private - *FSM**, *FSY**, *UNN, WDR, WTA**

Gross Domestic Product - *FSM*, FSY*, UNN, WDR, WTA**
Gross National Product - *UNN, WDR, WTA**
National Income - *UNN, WTA**

Prices, Production, Employment

Consumer Credit Outstanding - *N/A*
Consumer Prices - *FSM*, FSY*, WDR, WTA**
Earnings/Wages - *WTA**
Production
  Industrial - *WTA**
  Manufacturing - *UNN*
Wholesale/Producer Prices - *N/A*

Rwanda Franc - *see* **- Rwanda - Exchange Rates**

S

S & P 500 - *see* - **United States - Securities Markets**

S & P 400 - *see* - **United States - Securities Markets**

St. Kitts and Nevis

  Banking, Finance, and Money

   Banking Institutions - Assets/Liabilities - *FSM*, FSY**
   Monetary Authorities - Assets/Liabilities - *FSM*, FSY**
   Money Supply - *FSM*, FSY*, UNY, WTA**

  Exchange Rates

   Currency - *East Caribbean Dollar*
   Cross Rates - *N/A*
   Forward Exchange Rate - *N/A*
   Per ECU - *N/A*
   Per SDR - *FSM*, FSY**
   Per U.S. Dollar - *FSM*, FSY*, UNY*

  Government Finance

   Debt - *N/A*
   Deficit/Surplus - *FSM*, FSY*, GSY*, WTA**
   Expenditure - *GSY*, UNY, WTA**
   Revenue - *GSY*, UNY, WTA**

  Interest Rates

   Bank Rate - *N/A*
   Discount Rate - *N/A*
   Government Bonds - *N/A*
   Money Market - *N/A*
   Treasury Bills - *FSM*, UNY*

International Liquidity

Reserves Minus Gold - *FSM*, FSY*, UNY, WTA**
Gold - *N/A*

International Transactions

Balance of Payments - *BOP*, FSM*, FSY*, UNY, WTA**
Exports - *FSY*, UNN, UNY, WTA**
Imports - *UNN, UNY, WTA**

National Accounts

Consumption
    Government - *UNN*
    Private - *UNN*
Gross Domestic Product - *FSM*, FSY*, GSY*, UNN, UNY,
    WTA**
Gross National Product - *UNN, WTA**
National Income - *N/A*

Prices, Production, Employment

Consumer Credit Outstanding - *N/A*
Consumer Prices - *FSM*, FSY*, GSY*, UNY, WTA**
Earnings/Wages - *N/A*
Employment - *N/A*
Production
    Industrial - *WTA**
Wholesale/Producer Prices - *N/A*

Securities Markets - *N/A*

St. Lucia

Banking, Finance, and Money

Banking Institutions - Assets/Liabilities - *FSM*, FSY**
Monetary Authorities - Assets/Liabilities - *FSM*, FSY**
Money Supply - *FSM*, FSY*, WTA**

Exchange Rates

Currency - *East Caribbean Dollar*
Cross Rates - *N/A*
Forward Exchange Rate - *N/A*
Per ECU - *N/A*
Per SDR - *FSM*, FSY**
Per U.S. Dollar - *FSM*, FSY*, UNY*

Government Finance

Debt - *GSY**
Deficit/Surplus - *FSM*, FSY*, GSY*, WTA**
Expenditure - *GSY*, WTA**
Revenue - *GSY*, WTA**

Interest Rates

Bank Rate - *N/A*
Discount Rate - *N/A*
Government Bonds - *N/A*
Money Market - *N/A*
Treasury Bills - *FSM*, FSY*, UNY*

International Liquidity

Reserves Minus Gold - *FSM*, FSY*, UNY, WTA**
Gold - *N/A*

International Transactions

Balance of Payments - *BOP*, FSM*, FSY*, UNY, WTA**
Exports - *FSM*, FSY*, UNN, UNY, WTA**
Imports - *FSM*, FSY*, UNN, UNY, WTA**

National Accounts

Consumption
  Government - *FSY*, UNN*
  Private - *FSY*, UNN*
Gross Domestic Product - *FSM*, FSY*, GSY*, UNN, UNY, WTA**
Gross National Product - *WTA**
National Income - *N/A*

Prices, Production, Employment

Consumer Credit Outstanding - *N/A*
Consumer Prices - *FSM*, FSY*, GSY*, UNY, WTA**
Earnings/Wages - *UNY*
Employment - *N/A*
Production
  Industrial - *WTA**
  Manufacturing - *WTA**
Wholesale/Producer Prices - *N/A*

Securities Markets - *N/A*

St. Vincent

Banking, Finance, and Money

Banking Institutions - Assets/Liabilities - *FSM*, FSY**
Monetary Authorities - Assets/Liabilities - *FSM*, FSY**
Money Supply - *FSM*, FSY*, UNY, WTA**

Exchange Rates

Currency - *East Caribbean Dollar*
Cross Rates - *N/A*
Forward Exchange Rate - *N/A*
Per ECU - *N/A*
Per SDR - *FSM*, FSY**
Per U.S. Dollar - *DRF, FSM*, FSY*, UNY*

Government Finance

Debt - *FSM*, FSY*, GSY*, WTA**
Deficit/Surplus - *FSM*, FSY*, GSY*, WTA**
Expenditure - *GSY*, WTA**
Revenue - *GSY*, WTA**

Interest Rates

Bank Rate - *N/A*
Discount Rate - *N/A*
Government Bonds - *N/A*
Money Market - *N/A*
Treasury Bills - *FSM*, FSY*, UNY*

International Liquidity

Reserves Minus Gold - *FSM*, FSY*, UNY, WTA**
Gold - *N/A*

International Transactions

Balance of Payments - *BOP*, FSM*, FSY*, UNY, WTA**
Exports - *FSM*, FSY*, UNN, UNY, WTA**
Imports - *FSM*, FSY*, UNN, UNY, WTA**

National Accounts

Consumption
　Government - *FSM*, FSY*, UNN*
　Private - *FSM*, FSY*, UNN*
　Gross Domestic Product - *FSM*, FSY*, GSY*, UNN, UNY, WTA**

Gross National Product - *UNN, WTA**
National Income - *WTA**

Prices, Production, Employment

Consumer Credit Outstanding - *N/A*
Consumer Prices - *FSM*, FSY*, GSY*, UNY, WTA**
Earnings/Wages - *N/A*
Employment - *N/A*
Production
  Industrial - *WTA**
  Manufacturing - *WTA**
Wholesale/Producer Prices - *N/A*

Securities Markets - *N/A*

Salvadoran Colon - *see* - El Salvador - Exchange Rates

Samoa

Banking, Finance, and Money

Banking Institutions - Assets/Liabilities - *N/A*
Monetary Authorities - Assets/Liabilities - *N/A*
Money Supply - *UNY*

Exchange Rates

Currency - *Samoan Tala*
Cross Rates - *N/A*
Forward Exchange Rate - *N/A*
Per ECU - *N/A*
Per SDR - *N/A*
Per U.S. Dollar - *DRF, UNY*

Government Finance

Debt - *N/A*
Deficit/Surplus - *N/A*
Expenditure - *N/A*
Revenue - *N/A*

Interest Rates

Bank Rate - *N/A*
Discount Rate - *N/A*
Government Bonds - *UNY*
Money Market - *N/A*
Treasury Bills - *N/A*

International Liquidity

Reserves Minus Gold - *UNY*
Gold - *N/A*

International Transactions

Balance of Payments - *UNY*
Exports - *UNN, UNY*
Imports - *UNN, UNY*

National Accounts

Consumption
  Government - *N/A*
  Private - *N/A*
Gross Domestic Product - *UNY*
Gross National Product - *N/A*
National Income - *N/A*

Prices, Production, Employment

Consumer Credit Outstanding - *N/A*
Consumer Prices - *UNY*
Earnings/Wages - *N/A*
Employment - *N/A*
Production - *N/A*
Wholesale/Producer Prices - *N/A*

Securities Markets - *N/A*

Samoan Tala - *see* **- Samoa - Exchange Rates**

Santiago Stock Exchange - *see* **- Chile - Exchange Rates**

Sao Tome and Principe

Banking, Finance, and Money

Banking Institutions - Assets/Liabilities - *N/A*
Monetary Authorities - *N/A*
Money Supply - *WTA**

Exchange Rates

Currency - *Dobra*
Cross Rates - *N/A*
Per ECU - *N/A*
Per SDR - *N/A*
Per U.S. Dollar - *DJN, DRF, UNY*

Government Finance

Debt - *N/A*
Deficit/Surplus - *N/A*
Expenditure - *N/A*
Revenue - *N/A*

Interest Rates

Bank Rate - *N/A*
Discount Rate - *N/A*
Government Bonds - *N/A*
Money Market - *N/A*
Treasury Bills - *N/A*

International Liquidity

Reserves Minus Gold - *N/A*
Gold - *N/A*

International Transactions

Balance of Payments - *BOP*, UNY, WTA**
Exports - *UNN, WTA**
Imports - *UNN, WTA**

National Accounts

Consumption
  Government - *UNN, WTA**
  Private - *UNN, WTA**
Gross Domestic Product - *UNN, UNY, WTA**
Gross National Product - *WTA**
National Income - *WTA**

Prices, Production, Employment

Consumer Credit Outstanding - *N/A*
Consumer Prices - *N/A*
Earnings/Wages - *N/A*
Employment - *N/A*
Production - *N/A*
Wholesale/Producer Prices - *N/A*

Securities Markets - *N/A*

Saudi Arabia

Banking, Finance, and Money

Banking Institutions - Assets/Liabilities - *FSM*, FSY**
Monetary Authorities - Assets/Liabilities - *FSM*, FSY**
Money Supply - *FSM*, FSY*, UNY, WTA**

Exchange Rates

Currency - *Saudi Arabian Riyal*
Cross Rates - *N/A*
Forward Exchange Rate - *N/A*
Per ECU - *N/A*
Per SDR - *FSM*, FSY**
Per U.S. Dollar - *BAR, DJN, DRF, FSM*, FSY*, FTI, NYT, UNY, WSJ*

Government Finance

Debt - *N/A*
Deficit/Surplus - *N/A*
Expenditure - *N/A*
Revenue - *N/A*

Interest Rates

Bank Rate - *N/A*
Discount Rate - *N/A*
Government Bonds - *N/A*
Money Market - *N/A*
Treasury Bills - *N/A*

International Liquidity

Reserves Minus Gold - *FSM*, FSY*, UNY, WTA**
Gold - *FSM*, FSY*, UNY, WTA**

International Transactions

Balance of Payments - *BOP*, FSM*, FSY*, UNY, WDR, WTA**
Exports - *FSM*, FSY*, UNN, UNY, WTA**
Imports - *FSM*, FSY*, UNN, UNY, WTA**

National Accounts

Consumption
  Government - *FSM*, FSY*, UNN*
  Private - *FSM*, FSY*, UNN*

Gross Domestic Product - *FSM*, FSY*, UNN, UNY, WDR, WTA**

Gross National Product - *FSM*, FSY*, UNN, WDR, WTA**

National Income - *UNN, WTA**

Prices, Production, Employment

Consumer Credit Outstanding - *N/A*

Consumer Prices - *FSM*, FSY*, UNY, WDR, WTA**

Earnings/Wages - *N/A*

Employment - *N/A*

Production

Industrial - *WTA**

Manufacturing - *WTA**

Wholesale/Producer Prices - *N/A*

Securities Markets - *N/A*

Saudi Arabian Riyal - *see* **- Saudi Arabia - Exchange Rates**

SBC General Index - *see* **- Switzerland - Securities Markets**

Schilling - *see* **- Austria - Exchange Rates**

SDR - *see* **-Special Drawing Rights**

Securities Exchange of Thailand (SET) - *see* **- Thailand - Securities Markets**

Securities Markets - *see* **- Individual Countries - Securities Markets**

Senegal

Banking, Finance, and Money

Banking Institutions - Assets/Liabilities - *FSM*, FSY**

Monetary Authorities - Assets/Liabilities - *FSM*, FSY**

Money Supply - *FSM*, FSY*, UNY, WTA**

Exchange Rates

Currency - *CFA Franc*

Cross Rates - *N/A*

Forward Exchange Rate - *N/A*

Per ECU - *N/A*

Per SDR - *FSM*, FSY**

Per U.S. Dollar - *DRF, FSM*, FSY*, UNY*

Government Finance

Debt - *FSY*, GSY*, WTA**
Deficit/Surplus - *FSY*, GSY*, WDR, WTA**
Expenditure - *GSY*, WDR, WTA**
Revenue - *GSY*, WDR, WTA**

Interest Rates

Bank Rate - *N/A*
Discount Rate - *FSM*, FSY*, UNY*
Government Bonds - *N/A*
Money Market - *FSM*, FSY**
Treasury Bills - *N/A*

International Liquidity

Reserves Minus Gold - *FSM*, FSY*, UNY, WTA**
Gold - *FSM*, FSY*, UNY, WTA**

International Transactions

Balance of Payments - *BOP*, FSM*, FSY*, UNY, WDR, WTA**
Exports - *FSM*, FSY*, UNN, UNY, WTA**
Imports - *FSM*, FSY*, UNN, UNY, WTA**

National Accounts

Consumption
  Government - *FSM*, FSY*, UNN, WDR, WTA**
  Private - *FSM*, FSY*, UNN, WDR, WTA**
Gross Domestic Product - *FSM*, FSY*, GSY*, UNN, WDR, WTA**
Gross National Product - *UNN, WDR, WTA**
National Income - *UNN, WTA**

Prices, Production, Employment

Consumer Credit Outstanding - *N/A*
Consumer Prices - *FSM*, FSY*, GSY*, UNY, WDR, WTA**
Earnings/Wages - *WTA**
Employment - *N/A*
Production
  Industrial - *WTA**
  Manufacturing - *UNY, WTA**
  Mining - *UNY*
Wholesale/Producer Prices - *N/A*

Securities Markets - *N/A*

SES All Singapore Stock Index - *see* **- Singapore - Securities Markets**

SET (Securities Exchange of Thailand) - *see* **- Thailand - Securities Markets**

Seychelles

Banking, Finance, and Money

Banking Institutions - Assets/Liabilities - *FSM*, FSY**
Monetary Authorities - Assets/Liabilities - *FSM*, FSY**
Money Supply - *FSM*, FSY*, UNY, WTA**

Exchange Rates

Currency - *Seychelles Rupee*
Cross Rates - *N/A*
Forward Exchange Rate - *N/A*
Per ECU - *N/A*
Per SDR - *FSM*, FSY**
Per U.S. Dollar - *DRF, FSM*, FSY*, UNY*

Government Finance

Debt - *FSM*, FSY*, GSY*, WTA**
Deficit/Surplus - *FSM*, FSY*, GSY*, WTA**
Expenditure - *GSY*, WTA**
Revenue - *GSY*, WTA**

Interest Rates

Bank Rate - *N/A*
Discount Rate - *FSM*, FSY*, UNY*
Government Bonds - *N/A*
Money Market - *N/A*
Treasury Bills - *FSM*, FSY*, UNY*

International Liquidity

Reserves Minus Gold - *FSM*, FSY*, UNY, WTA**
Gold - *N/A*

International Transactions

Balance of Payments - *BOP*, FSM*, FSY*, UNY, WTA**
Exports - *FSM*, FSY*, UNN, UNY, WTA**
Imports - *FSM*, FSY*, UNN, UNY, WTA**

National Accounts

Consumption
  Government - *FSM*, FSY*, UNN, WTA**
  Private - *FSM*, FSY*, UNN, WTA**
Gross Domestic Product - *FSM*, FSY*, GSY*, UNN, UNY, WTA**
Gross National Product - *FSM*, FSY*, UNN, UNY, WTA**
National Income - *UNN, WTA**

Prices, Production, Employment

Consumer Credit Outstanding - *N/A*
Consumer Prices - *FSM*, FSY*, GSY*, UNY, WTA**
Earnings/Wages - *UNY, WTA**
Employment - *UNY*
Production
  Industrial - *WTA**
  Manufacturing - *UNN, WTA**
Wholesale/Producer Prices - *N/A*

Securities Markets - *N/A*

Seychelles Rupee - *see* - **Seychelles - Exchange Rates**

Shanghai Securities Exchange - *see* - **China (People's Republic) - Securities Markets**

Shares - *see* - **Individual Countries - Securities Markets**

Shekel - *see* - **Israel - Exchange Rates**

Sheqalum - *see* - **Israel - Exchange Rates**

Shilling - *see* - **Kenya - Exchange Rates; Somalia - Exchange Rates; Tanzania - Exchange Rates; Uganda - Exchange Rates**

Sierra Leone

Banking, Finance, and Money

Banking Institutions - Assets/Liabilities - *FSM*, FSY**
Monetary Authorities - Assets/Liabilities - *FSM*, FSY**
Money Supply - *FSM*, FSY*, UNY, WTA**

Exchange Rates

Currency - *Sierra Leonean Leone*
Cross Rates - *N/A*

Forward Exchange Rate - *N/A*
Per ECU - *N/A*
Per SDR - *FSM*, FSY**
Per U.S. Dollar - *DRF, FSM*, FSY*, UNY*

Government Finance

Debt - *FSM*, FSY*, GSY*, WTA**
Deficit/Surplus - *FSM*, FSY*, GSY*, WDR, WTA**
Expenditure - *GSY*, WDR, WTA**
Revenue - *GSY*, WDR, WTA**

Interest Rates

Bank Rate - *N/A*
Discount Rate - *UNY*
Government Bonds - *N/A*
Money Market - *N/A*
Treasury Bills - *FSY*, UNY*

International Liquidity

Reserves Minus Gold - *FSM*, FSY*, UNY, WTA**
Gold - *N/A*

International Transactions

Balance of Payments - *BOP*, FSM*, FSY*, UNY, WTA**
Exports - *FSM*, FSY*, UNN, UNY, WTA**
Imports - *FSM*, FSY*, UNN, UNY, WTA**

National Accounts

Consumption
Government - FSM*, FSY*, UNN, WDR, WTA*
Private - FSM*, FSY*, UNN, WDR, WTA*
Gross Domestic Product - *FSM*, FSY*, GSY*, UNN, UNY, WDR, WTA**
Gross National Product - *FSM*, FSY*, UNN, WDR, WTA**
National Income - *FSM*, FSY*, UNN, WTA**

Prices, Production, Employment

Consumer Credit Outstanding - *N/A*
Consumer Prices - *FSM*, FSY*, GSY*, UNY, WDR, WTA**
Earnings/Wages - *UNY*
Employment - *UNY*

Production
Industrial - *WTA**
Manufacturing - *UNN, WTA**
Wholesale/Producer Prices - *FSM*, FSY**

Securities Markets - *N/A*

Sierra Leonean Leone - *see* **- Sierra Leone - Exchange Rates**

Silver - *see* **- Commodities**

Singapore

Banking, Finance, and Money

Banking Institutions - Assets/Liabilities - *FSM*, FSY**
Monetary Authorities - Assets/Liabilities - *FSM*, FSY**
Money Supply - *FSM*, FSY*, UNY, WTA**

Exchange Rates

Currency - *Singapore Dollar*
Cross Rates - *N/A*
Forward Exchange Rate - *N/A*
Per ECU - *N/A*
Per SDR - *FSM*, FSY**
Per U.S. Dollar - *BAR, DJN, DRF, FRB, FSM*, FSY*, FTI, NYT, UNY, WSJ*

Government Finance

Debt - *FSM*, FSY*, GSY**
Deficit/Surplus - *FSM*, FSY*, GSY*, WDR, WTA**
Expenditure - *GSY*, WDR, WTA**
Revenue - *GSY*, WDR, WTA**

Interest Rates

Bank Rate - *N/A*
Discount Rate - *N/A*
Eurodollar - *FSM*, FSY**
Government Bonds - *N/A*
Money Market - *FSM*, FSY**
Treasury Bills - *N/A*

International Liquidity

Reserves Minus Gold - *FSM*, FSY*, UNY, WTA**
Gold - *N/A*

International Transactions

Balance of Payments - *BOP*, FSM*, FSY*, UNY, WDR, WTA**

Exports - *FSM*, FSY*, UNN, UNY, WTA**

Imports - *FSM*, FSY*, UNN, UNY, WTA**

National Accounts

Consumption

Government - *FSM*, FSY*, UNN, WDR, WTA**

Private - *FSM*, FSY*, UNN, WDR, WTA**

Gross Domestic Product - *FSM*, FSY*, GSY*, UNN, UNY, WDR, WTA**

Gross National Product - *FSM*, FSY*, UNN, WDR, WTA**

National Income - *UNN, WTA**

Prices, Production, Employment

Consumer Credit Outstanding - *N/A*

Consumer Prices - *FSM*, FSY*, GSY*, UNY, WDR, WT*A*

Earnings/Wages - *UNY, WDR, WTA**

Employment - *UNY, WTA**

Production

Industrial - *WTA**

Manufacturing - *FSM*, FSY*, UNY, WTA**

Wholesale/Producer Prices - *FSM*, FSY*, UNY*

Securities Markets

Stock Exchange - *Stock Exchange of Singapore, Ltd.*

Indexes

SES All-Singapore Stock Index

Straits Stock Index

Shares

Price Indexes

SES - FTI

Straits - BAR, DJN, DRF, WSJ

Prices - Selected Issues - *BAR, FTI*

Singapore Dollar - *see* **- Singapore - Exchange Rates**

Solomon Island Dollar - *see* **- Solomon Islands - Exchange Rates**

Solomon Islands

Banking, Finance, and Money

Banking Institutions - Assets/Liabilities - *FSM*, FSY**
Monetary Authorities - Assets/Liabilities - *FSM*, FSY**
Money Supply - *FSM*, FSY*, UNY, WTA**

Exchange Rates

Currency - *Solomon Island Dollar*
Cross Rates - *N/A*
Forward Exchange Rate - *N/A*
Per ECU - *N/A*
Per SDR - *FSM*, FSY**
Per U.S. Dollar - *DRF, FSM*, FSY*, UNY*

Government Finance

Debt - *FSM*, FSY*, GSY*, WTA**
Deficit/Surplus - *FSM*, FSY*, GSY*, WTA**
Expenditure - *GSY*, WTA**
Revenue - *GSY*, WTA**

Interest Rates

Bank Rate - *N/A*
Discount Rate - *N/A*
Government Bonds - *FSM*, FSY*, UNY*
Money Market - *N/A*
Treasury Bills - *FSM*, FSY*, UNY*

International Liquidity

Reserves Minus Gold - *FSM*, FSY*, UNY, WTA**
Gold - *N/A*

International Transactions

Balance of Payments - *BOP*, FSM*, FSY*, UNY, WTA**
Exports - *FSM*, FSY*, UNN, UNY, WTA**
Imports - *FSM*, FSY*, UNN, UNY, WTA**

National Accounts

Consumption
  Government - *FSM*, FSY*, UNN, WTA**
  Private - *FSM*, FSY*, UNN, WTA**
Gross Domestic Product - *FSM*, FSY*, GSY*, UNN, UNY, WTA**

Gross National Product - *UNN, WTA**
National Income - *UNN, WTA**

Prices, Production, Employment

Consumer Credit Outstanding - *N/A*
Consumer Prices - *FSM*, FSY*, GSY*, UNY, WTA**
Earnings/Wages - *N/A*
Employment - *UNY*
Production
   Copra - FSM*, FSY*
Wholesale/Producer Prices - *N/A*

Securities Markets - *N/A*

Somalia

Banking, Finance, and Money

Banking Institutions - Assets/Liabilities - *FSM*, FSY**
Monetary Authorities - Assets/Liabilities - *FSM*, FSY**
Money Supply - *FSM*, FSY*, UNY, WTA**

Exchange Rates

Currency - *Somali Shilling*
Cross Rates - *N/A*
Forward Exchange Rate - *N/A*
Per ECU - *N/A*
Per SDR - *FSM*, FSY**
Per U.S. Dollar - *DRF, FSM*, FSY*, UNY*

Government Finance

Debt - *WTA**
Deficit/Surplus - *FSY*, WDR*
Expenditure - *WDR*
Revenue - *WDR*

Interest Rates

Bank Rate - *N/A*
Discount Rate - *FSY*, UNY*
Government Bonds - *N/A*
Money Market - *N/A*
Treasury Bills - *N/A*

International Liquidity

Reserves Minus Gold - *FSM*, FSY*, UNY, WTA**

Gold - *FSM*, FSY*, UNY, WTA**

International Transactions

Balance of Payments - *BOP*, FSM*, FSY*, UNY, WDR, WTA**
Exports - *FSM*, FSY*, UNN, UNY, WTA**
Imports - *FSM*, FSY*, UNN, UNY, WTA**

National Accounts

Consumption
  Government - *UNN, WDR, WTA**
  Private - *UNN, WDR, WTA**
Gross Domestic Product - *UNN, UNY, WDR, WTA**
Gross National Product - *UNN, WDR, WTA**
National Income - *UNN, WTA**

Prices, Production, Employment

Consumer Credit Outstanding - *N/A*
Consumer Prices - *FSM*, FSY*, UNY, WDR, WTA**
Earnings/Wages - *WDR*
Employment - *N/A*
Production
  Industrial - *WTA**
  Manufacturing - *WTA**
Wholesale/Producer Prices - *N/A*

Securities Markets - *N/A*

Somali Shilling - *see* - Somalia - Exchange Rates

South Africa

Banking, Finance, and Money

Banking Institutions - Assets/Liabilities - *FSM*, FSY**
Monetary Authorities - Assets/Liabilities - *FSM*, FSY**
Money Supply - *FSM*, FSY*, UNY, WTA**

Exchange Rates

Currency - *South African Rand*
Cross Rates - *N/A*
Forward Exchange Rate - *N/A*
Per ECU - *N/A*
Per SDR - *FSM*, FSY**

Per U.S. Dollar - *BAR, DJN, DRF, FRB, FSM*, FSY*, FTI, NYT, UNY, WSJ*

Government Finance

Debt - *FSM*, FSY*, GSY**
Deficit/Surplus - *FSM*, FSY*, GSY*, WDR, WTA**
Expenditure - *GSY*, WDR, WTA**
Revenue - *GSY*, WDR, WTA**

Interest Rates

Bank Rate - *N/A*
Discount Rate - *FSM*, FSY*, UNY*
Government Bonds - *FSM*, FSY*, UNY*
Money Market - *FSM*, FSY**
Treasury Bills - *FSM*, FSY*, UNY*

International Liquidity

Reserves Minus Gold - *FSM*, FSY*, UNY, WTA**
Gold - *FSM*, FSY*, UNY, WTA**

International Transactions

Balance of Payments - *BOP*, FSM*, FSY*, UNY, WDR, WTA**
Exports - *FSM*, FSY*, UNN, UNY, WTA**
Imports - *FSM*, FSY*, UNN, UNY, WTA**

National Accounts

Consumption
  Government - *FSM*, FSY*, UNN, WDR, WTA**
  Private - *FSM*, FSY*, UNN, WDR, WTA**
Gross Domestic Product - *FSM*, FSY*, GSY*, UNN, UNY, WDR, WTA**
Gross National Product - *FSM*, FSY*, UNN, WDR, WTA**
National Income - *FSM*, FSY*, UNN, WTA**

Prices, Production, Employment

Consumer Credit Outstanding - *N/A*
Consumer Prices - *FSM*, FSY*, GSY*, UNY, WDR, WTA**
Earnings/Wages - *UNY, WDR, WTA**
Employment - *FSM*, FSY*, UNY, WTA**
Production
  Industrial - *WTA**

Manufacturing - *FSM*, FSY*, UNY, WTA**
Mining - *FSM*, FSY*, UNY*
Wholesale/Producer Prices - *UNY*

Securities Markets

Stock Exchange - *Johannesburg Stock Exchange (JSE)*
Indexes
  JSE Gold
  JSE Industrial
  All Share Index
Shares
  Price Indexes
    JSE Gold - *DJN, DRF, FTI, WSJ*
    JSE Industrial - *DRI, FTI*
    All Share Index - *DRI*
  Prices - *FSM*, FSY*, UNY*
  Prices - Selected Issues - *BAR, FTI, FSM*, FSY*, NYT, UNY*

South African Rand - *see* - South Africa - Exchange Rates

Soybeans - *see* - Commodities

Spain

Banking, Finance, and Money

Banking Institutions - Assets/Liabilities - *FSM*, FSY**
Monetary Authorities - Assets/Liabilities - *FSM*, FSY**
Money Supply - *FSM*, FSY*, MEI*, UNY, WTA**

Exchange Rates

Currency - *Spanish Peseta*
Cross Rates - *FTI, WSJ*
Forward Exchange Rate - *FTI*
Per ECU - *FTI*
Per SDR - *FSM*, FSY*, FTI*
Per U.S. Dollar - *BAR, DJN, DRF, FRB, FSM*, FSY*, MEI*,*
  NYT, UNY, WSJ

Government Finance

Debt - *FSM*, FSY*, GSY**
Deficit/Surplus - *FSM*, FSY*, GSY*, WDR, WTA**
Expenditure - *GSY*, WDR, WTA**
Revenue - *GSY*, WDR, WTA**

Interest Rates

Bank Rate - *FSM*, FSY*, FS1*
Discount Rate - *FS2, UNY*
Government Bonds - *BAR, DRF, FSM*, FSY*, FS1, MEI*, UNY*
Money Market - *FSM*, FSY**
Treasury Bills - *FSM*, FSY*, FS1, UNY*

International Liquidity

Reserves Minus Gold - *FSM*, FSY*, MEI*, UNY, WTA**
Gold - *FSM*, FSY*, UNY, WTA**

International Transactions

Balance of Payments - *BOP*, FSM*, FSY*, MEI*, UNY, WDR, WTA**
Exports - *FSM*, FSY*, MEI*, UNN, UNY, WTA**
Imports - *FSM*, FSY*, MEI*, UNN, UNY, WTA**

National Accounts

Consumption
Government - *FSM*, FSY*, UNN, WTA**
Private - *FSM*, FSY*, UNN, WDR, WTA**
Gross Domestic Product - *FSM*, FSY*, GSY*, MEI*, UNN, UNY, WDR, WTA**
Gross National Product - *FSM*, FSY*, UNN, WDR, WTA**
National Income - *FSM*, FSY*, UNN, WTA**

Prices, Production, Employment

Consumer Credit Outstanding - *FS2*
Consumer Prices - *FSM*, FSY*, FS1, GSY*, MEI, UNY, WDR, WTA**
Earnings/Wages - *FSM*, FSY*, MEI*, UNY, WDR, WTA**
Employment - *FSM*, FSY*, MEI*, UNY, WTA**
Production
Industrial - *FSM*, FSY*, MEI*, UNY*
Manufacturing - *MEI*, UNN, UNY*
Mining - *UNY*
Wholesale/Producer Prices - *FSM*, FSY*, MEI*, UNY*

Securities Markets

Stock Exchange - *Bolsa de Comercio de Madrid (Madrid Stock Exchange)*

Index - *Madrid Stock Exchange Index*
Bonds
  Issue price - *FS2**
  Yield - *FS2**
Eurobonds
  Value of bonds issued - *FS1*
Foreign Bonds
  Value of bonds issued - *FS1*
Shares
  Issue price - *FS2**
  Prices last day of month - *MEI**
  Price/Earnings Ratio - *FS1, FS2**
  Price Index - *BAR, DRF, FTI, FS1, FS2*, FSM*, FSY*, MEI*, UNY, WSJ*
  Prices - *FSM, FSY, FS1, MEI*, UNY*
  Prices - Selected Issues - *BAR, FTI*
  Total Gross - *FS2**
  Yield - *FS2**
Stock Exchange Capitalization - *FS2**
Stock Exchange Capitalization - *FS2**

Spanish Peseta - *see* **- Spain - Exchange Rate**

Special Drawing Rights
Exchange Rates - *BAR, WSJ*
Interest Rates - *FSY**

Special Drawing Rights - *see   also* **- Individual Countries - Exchange Rates**

Sri Lanka

Banking, Finance, and Money
Banking Institutions - Assets/Liabilities - *FSM*, FSY**
Monetary Authorities - Assets/Liabilities - *FSM*, FSY**
Money Supply - *FSM*, FSY*, UNY, WTA**

Exchange Rates
Currency - *Sri Lanka Rupee*
Cross Rates - *N/A*
Forward Exchange Rate - *N/A*
Per ECU - *N/A*

Per SDR - *FSM*, FSY**
Per U.S. Dollar - *DJN, DRF, FRB, FSM*, FSY*, UNY*

Government Finance

Debt - *FSM*, FSY*, GSY*, WTA**
Deficit/Surplus - *FSM*, FSY*, GSY*, WDR, WTA**
Expenditure - *GSY*, WDR, WTA**
Revenue - *GSY*, WDR, WTA**

Interest Rates

Bank Rate - *FSM*, FSY**
Discount Rate - *FSM*, FSY*, UNY*
Government Bonds - *FSM*, FSY*, UNY*
Money Market - *FSM*, FSY*, UNY*
Treasury Bills - *FSM*, FSY*, UNY*

International Liquidity

Reserves Minus Gold - *FSM*, FSY*, UNY, WTA**
Gold - *FSM*, FSY*, UNY, WTA**

International Transactions

Balance of Payments - *BOP*, FSM*, FSY*, UNN, UNY, WDR, WTA**
Exports - *FSM*, FSY*, UNN, UNY, WTA**
Imports - *FSM*, FSY*, UNN, UNY, WTA**

National Accounts

Consumption
  Government - *FSM*, FSY*, UNN, WDR, WTA**
  Private - *FSM*, FSY*, UNN, WDR, WTA**
Gross Domestic Product - *FSM*, FSY*, GSY*, UNN, UNY, WTA**
Gross National Product - *FSM*, FSY*, UNN, WDR, WTA**
National Income - *FSY*, UNN, WTA**

Prices, Production, Employment

Consumer Credit Outstanding - *N/A*
Consumer Prices - *FSM*, FSY*, GSY*, UNY, WDR, WTA**
Earnings/Wages - *FSM*, FSY*, UNY, WDR, WTA**
Employment - *UNY, WTA**
Production
  Industrial - *WTA**

Manufacturing - *UNN, UNY, WTA**
Wholesale/Producer Prices - *FSM*, FSY*, UNY*
Securities Markets - *N/A*

Sri Lanka Rupee - *see* - Sri Lanka - Exchange Rates

Stock Exchange Capitalization - *see* - Individual Countries - Securities Markets

Stock Exchange of Hong Kong Limited - *see* - Hong Kong - Securities Markets

Stock Exchange of Singapore - *see* - Singapore - Securities Markets

Stock Exchange Turnover - *see* - Individual Countries - Securities Markets

Stockholm Stock Exchange - *see* - Sweden - Securities Markets

Støckholms Føndbørs (Stockholm Stock Exchange) - *see* - Sweden - Securities Markets

Straits Stock Index - *see* - Singapore - Securities Markets

Sucre - *see* - Ecuador - Exchange Rates

Sudan

    Banking, Finance, and Money

        Banking Institutions - Assets/Liabilities - *FSM*, FSY**
        Monetary Authorities - Assets/Liabilities - *FSM*, FSY**
        Money Supply - *FSM*, FSY*, UNY, WTA**

    Exchange Rates

        Currency - *Sudanese Pound*
        Cross Rates - *N/A*
        Forward Exchange Rates - *N/A*
        Per ECU - *N/A*
        Per SDR - *FSM*, FSY**
        Per U.S. Dollar - *FSM*, FSY*, UNY*

    Government Finance

        Debt - *FSY*, WTA**
        Deficit/Surplus - *FSY*, WDR, WTA**

Expenditure - *WDR, WTA**
Revenue - *WDR, WTA**

Interest Rates

Bank Rate - *N/A*
Discount Rate - *N/A*
Government Bonds - *N/A*
Money Market - *N/A*
Treasury Bills - *N/A*

International Liquidity

Reserves Minus Gold - *FSM*, FSY*, UNY, WTA**
Gold - *N/A*

International Transactions

Balance of Payments - *BOP*, FSM*, FSY*, UNY, WDR, WTA**
Exports - *FSM*, FSY*, UNN, UNY, WTA**
Imports - *FSM*, FSY*, UNN, UNY, WTA**

National Accounts

Consumption
    Government - *FSY*, UNN, WDR, WTA**
    Private - *FSY*, UNN, WDR, WTA**
Gross Domestic Product - *FSM*, FSY*, UNN, UNY, WDR, WTA**
Gross National Product - *FSY*, UNN, WDR*
National Income - *FSY*, UNN, WTA**

Prices, Production, Employment

Consumer Credit Outstanding - *N/A*
Consumer Prices - *FSM*, FSY*, UNY, WDR, WTA**
Earnings/Wages - *N/A*
Employment - *N/A*
Production
    Industrial - *WTA**
    Manufacturing - *UNN, WTA**
Wholesale/Producer Prices - *N/A*

Securities Markets - *N/A*

Sudanese Pound - *see* **- Sudan - Exchange Rates**

Sugar - *see* **- Commodities**

Suriname

Banking, Finance, and Money

Banking Institutions - Assets/Liabilities - *FSM*, FSY**
Monetary Authorities - Assets/Liabilities - *FSM*, FSY**
Money Supply - *FSM*, FSY*, UNY, WTA**

Exchange Rates

Currency - *Suriname Guilder*
Cross Rates - *N/A*
Forward Exchange Rate - *N/A*
Per ECU - *N/A*
Per SDR - *FSM*, FSY**
Per U.S. Dollar - *DJN, DRF, FSM*, FSY*, UNY*

Government Finance

Debt - *FSM*, FSY*, GSY**
Deficit/Surplus - *FSM*, FSY*, GSY*, WTA**
Expenditure - *GSY*, WTA**
Revenue - *GSY*, WTA**

International Liquidity

Reserves Minus Gold - *FSM*, FSY*, UNY, WTA**
Gold - *FSM*, FSY*, UNY, WTA**

International Transactions

Balance of Payments - *BOP*, FSM*, FSY*, UNY, WTA**
Exports - *FSM*, FSY*, UNN, WTA**
Imports - *FSM*, FSY*, UNN, WTA**

National Accounts

Consumption
  Government - *FSM*, FSY*, UNN*
  Private - *FSM*, FSY*, UNN*
Gross Domestic Product - *FSM*, FSY*, GSY*, UNN, UNY, WTA**
Gross National Product - *FSM*, FSY*, UNN, WTA**
National Income - *FSY*, UNN*

Prices, Production, Employment

Consumer Credit Outstanding - *N/A*
Consumer Prices - *FSM*, FSY*, GSY*, UNY, WTA**
Earnings/Wages - *N/A*

Employment - *UNY*
Production
  Industrial - *WTA**
  Manufacturing - *WTA**
  Wholesale/Producer Prices - *N/A*

Securities Markets - *N/A*

Suriname Guilder - *see* **- Suriname - Exchange Rates**

Swaziland

Banking, Finance, and Money

Banking Institutions - Assets/Liabilities - *FSM*, FSY**
Monetary Authorities - Assets/Liabilities - *FSM*, FSY**
Money Supply - *FSM*, FSY*, UNY, WTA**

Exchange Rates

Currency - *Swaziland Emalangeni*
Cross Rates - *N/A*
Forward Exchange Rate - *N/A*
Per ECU - *N/A*
Per SDR - *FSM*, FSY**
Per U.S. Dollar - *DRF, FSM*, FSY**

Government Finance

Debt - *FSM*, FSY*, GSY*, WTA**
Deficit/Surplus - *FSM*, FSY*, GSY*, WTA**
Expenditure - *GSY*, WTA**
Revenue - *GSY*, WTA**

Interest Rates

Bank Rate - *N/A*
Discount Rate - *FSM*, FSY*, UNY*
Money Market - *FSM*, FSY**
Treasury Bills - *FSM*, FSY*, UNY*

International Liquidity

Reserves Minus Gold - *FSM*, FSY*, UNY, WTA**
Gold - *N/A*

International Transactions

Balance of Payments - *BOP*, FSM*, FSY*, UNY, WTA**
Exports - *FSM*, FSY*, UNN, WTA**

Imports - *FSM*, FSY*, UNN, WTA**

National Accounts

Consumption
Government - *FSM*, FSY*, UNN, WTA**
Private - *FSM*, FSY*, UNN, WTA**
Gross Domestic Product - *FSM*, FSY*, GSY*, UNN, UNY, WTA**
Gross National Product - *FSY*, UNN, WTA**
National Income - *FSY*, WTA**

Prices, Production, Employment

Consumer Credit Outstanding - *N/A*
Consumer Prices - *FSM*, FSY*, GSY*, UNY, WTA**
Earnings/Wages - *UNY*
Employment - *UNY*
Production
Industrial - *WTA**
Manufacturing - *UNN, WTA**
Wholesale/Producer Prices - *N/A*

Securities Markets - *N/A*

Swaziland Emalangeni - *see* - Swaziland - Exchange Rates

Sweden

Banking, Finance, and Money

Banking Institutions - Assets/Liabilities - *FSM*, FSY**
Monetary Authorities - Assets/Liabilities - *FSM*, FSY**
Money Supply - *FSM*, FSY*, MEI*, UNY, WTA**

Exchange Rates

Currency - *Krona*
Cross Rates - *N/A*
Forward Exchange Rate - *FTI*
Per ECU - *FTI*
Per SDR - *FSM*, FSY*, FTI*
Per U.S. Dollar - *DJN, DRF, FRB, FSM*, FSY*, MEI*, NYT, WSJ*

Government Finance

Debt - *FSM*, FSY*, GSY**
Deficit/Surplus - *FSM*, FSY*, GSY*, WDR, WTA**

Expenditure - *GSY*, *WDR*, *WTA**
Revenue - *GSY*, *WDR*, *WTA**

Interest Rates

Bank Rate - *N/A*
Discount Rate - *FSM*, *FSY*, *FS1*, *FS2*, *MEI*, *UNY*
Government Bonds - *BAR*, *FSM*, *FSY*, *FS1*, *MEI*, *UNY*
Money Market - *FSM*, *FSY**
Treasury Bills - *FSM*, *FSY*, *FS1*, *MEI*, *UNY*

International Liquidity

Reserves Minus Gold - *FSM*, *FSY*, *MEI*, *UNY*, *WTA**
Gold - *FSM*, *FSY*, *UNY*, *WTA**

International Transactions

Balance of Payments - *BOP*, *FSM*, *FSY*, *MEI*, *UNY*, *WDR*, *WTA**
Exports - *FSM*, *FSY*, *MEI*, *UNN*, *UNY*, *WTA**
Imports - *FSM*, *FSY*, *MEI*, *UNN*, *UNY*, *WTA**

National Accounts

Consumption
  Government - *FSM*, *FSY*, *UNN*, *WDR*, *WTA**
  Private - *FSM*, *FSY*, *UNN*, *WDR*, *WTA**
Gross Domestic Product - *FSM*, *FSY*, *GSY*, *MEI*, *UNN*, *UNY*, *WTA**
Gross National Product - *FSM*, *FSY*, *UNN*, *WDR*, *WTA**
National Income - *FSM*, *FSY*, *UNN*, *WTA**

Prices, Production, Employment

Consumer Credit Outstanding - *FS2**
Consumer Prices - *FSM*, *FSY*, *FS1*, *GSY*, *MEI*, *UNY*, *WDR*, *WTA**
Earnings/Wages - *FSM*, *FSY*, *MEI*, *UNY*, *WDR*
Employment - *FSM*, *FSY*, *MEI*, *UNY*, *WTA**
Production
  Industrial - *FSM*, *FSY*, *MEI*, *UNY*
  Manufacturing - *MEI*, *UNN*, *UNY*
  Mining - *UNY*
Wholesale/Producer Prices - *FSY*, *MEI*, *UNY*

Securities Markets

Stock Exchange - *Støckholms Føndbørs (Stockholm Stock Exchange)*
Index - *Affarsvariden General*
Bonds
Yield - *FS2**
Eurobonds
Value of bonds issued - *FS1*
Foreign Bonds
Value of bonds issued - *FS1*
Shares
Share last day of month - *MEI**
Price/Earnings Ratio - *FS1, FS2**
Price Index - *BAR, FTI, WSJ, FS2*, DJN, DRI, FSM, FS1, MEI*, UNY*
Prices - *FSM, FS1, MEI*, UNY*
Prices - Selected Issues - *BAR, FTI, NYT, WSJ*
Stock Exchange Capitalization - *FS2**

Swedish Krona - *see* - **Sweden - Exchange Rates**

Swiss Bank Corp General Index - *see* - **Switzerland - Securities Markets**

Swiss Franc - *see* - **Switzerland - Exchange Rates;** *see also* - **Commodities**

Swiss Market Index - *see* - **Switzerland - Securities Markets;** *see also* - **Commodities**

Switzerland

Banking, Finance, and Money

Banking Institutions - Assets/Liabilities - *FSM*, FSY**
Monetary Authorities - Assets/Liabilities - *FSM*, FSY**
Money Supply - *FSM*, FSY*, MEI*, UNY, WTA**

Exchange Rates

Currency - *Swiss Franc*
Cross Rates - *FTI, WSJ*
Currency Futures - *BAR, NYT, WSJ*
Currency Options - *NYT*
Forward Exchange Rate - *FTI, MEI**

Per ECU - *FTI*
Per SDR - *FSM*, FSY*, FTI*
Per U.S. Dollar - *BAR, DJN, DRF, FRB, FSM*, FSY*, MEI*, NYT, UNY, WSJ*

Government Finance

Debt - *FSM*, FSY*, GSY**
Deficit/Surplus - *FSM*, FSY*, GSY*, WDR, WTA**
Expenditure - *GSY*, WDR, WTA**
Revenue - *GSY*, WDR, WTA**

Interest Rates

Bank Rate - *N/A*
Discount Rate - *DRF, FRB, FSM*, FSY*, FS1, FS2*, MEI*, UNY*
Government Bonds - *FSM*, FSY*, FS1, UNY*
Money Market - *FSM*, FSY**
Prime Rate - *BAR, DJN, DRF, WSJ*
Treasury Bills - *FSM*, FSY*, UNY*

International Liquidity

Reserves Minus Gold - *FSM*, FSY*, MEI*, UNY, WTA**
Gold - *FSM*, FSY*, UNY, WTA**

International Transactions

Balance of Payments - *BOP*, FSM*, FSY*, UNY, WDR, WTA**
Exports - *FSM*, FSY*, MEI*, UNN, UNY, WTA**
Imports - *FSM*, FSY*, MEI*, UNN, UNY, WTA**

National Accounts

Consumption
  Government - *FSM*, FSY*, UNN, WDR, WTA**
  Private - *FSM*, FSY*, UNN, UNY, WTA**
Gross Domestic Product - *FSM*, FSY*, GSY*, MEI, UNN, UNY, WDR, WTA**
Gross National Product - *FSM*, FSY*, UNN, WDR, WTA**
National Income - *FSM*, FSY*, UNN, WTA**

Prices, Production, Employment

Consumer Credit Outstanding - *FS2**

Consumer Prices - *FSM*, FSY*, FS1, GSY*, MEI*, UNY, WDR, WTA**
Earnings/Wages - *FSM*, FSY*, UNY*
Employment - *FSM*, FSY*, MEI*, UNY, WTA**
Production
   Industrial - *FSM*, FSY*, MEI*, UNY*
   Manufacturing - *FSM*, MEI*, UNY*
   Wholesale/Producer Prices - *FSY*, MEI*, UNY*

Securities Markets

Stock Exchange - *Zürchen Böise (Zurich Stock Exchange)*
Indexes
   Swiss Bank Industrial Index
   SBC General Index
   Swiss Market Index
   Credit Suisse Stock Index
Bonds
   Issue price - *FS2**
   Yield - *FS2**
Eurobonds
   Value of bonds issued - *FS1*
Foreign Bonds
   Value of bonds issued - *FS1*
Money Market Instruments Issued - *FS2**
Shares
   Issue price - *FS2**
   Price/Earnings Ratio - *FS1, FS2**
   Price Indexes
      Credit Suisse Index - *BAR, DJN, DRI, NYT*
      Swiss Bank - *FTI, DRI*
      Swiss Market - *DRI, NYT, WSJ*
      SBC General - *FTI, DRI, FSM*, FSY*, FS1, MEI*, UNY*
   Prices - Selected Issues - *BAR, FTI, NYT, WSJ*
   Total Gross - *FS2*
   Yield - *FS1, FS2**
Stock Exchange Capitalization - *FS2**

Syrian Arab Republic

Banking, Finance, and Money

Banking Institutions - Assets/Liabilities - *FSM*, FSY**

Monetary Authorities - Assets/Liabilities - *FSM*, FSY**
Money Supply - *FSM*, FSY*, WTA**

Exchange Rates

Currency - *Syrian Pound*
Cross Rates - *N/A*
Forward Exchange Rate - *N/A*
Per ECU - *N/A*
Per SDR - *FSM*, FSY**
Per U.S. Dollar - *DRF, FSM*, FSY**

Government Finance

Debt - *GSY*, WTA**
Deficit/Surplus - *FSM*, FSY*, GSY*, WDR, WTA**
Expenditure - *GSY*, WDR, WTA**
Revenue - *GSY*, WDR, WTA**

Interest Rates

Bank Rate - *N/A*
Discount Rate - *FSM*, FSY**
Government Bonds - *N/A*
Money Market - *N/A*
Treasury Bills - *N/A*

International Liquidity

Reserves Minus Gold - *FSM*, FSY*, WTA**
Gold - *FSM*, FSY*, WTA**

International Transactions

Balance of Payments - *BOP*, FSM*, FSY*, WDR, WTA**
Exports - *FSM*, FSY*, UNN, WTA**
Imports - *FSM*, FSY*, UNN, WTA**

National Accounts

Consumption
  Government - *FSM*, FSY*, UNN, WDR, WTA**
  Private - *FSM*, FSY*, UNN, WDR, WTA**
Gross Domestic Product - *FSM*, FSY*, GSY*, UNN, UNY, WDR, WTA**
Gross National Product - *FSM*, WDR, WTA**
National Income - *WTA**

Prices, Production, Employment

Consumer Credit Outstanding - *N/A*
Consumer Prices - *FSM*, FSY*, GSY*, UNY, WDR, WTA**
Earnings/Wages - *WDR, WTA**
Employment - *WTA**
Production
   Industrial - FSM*, FSY*, UNY, WTA*
   Manufacturing - UNN, UNY
   Mining - UNY
   Wholesale/Producer Prices - *FSM*, FSY**

Securities Markets - *N/A*

Syrian Pound - *see* - Syria - Exchange Rates

T

Taiwan - *see* - China (Republic of)

Taiwan Dollar - *see* - China (Republic of) - Exchange Rates

Taiwan Stock Exchange Corporation - *see* - China (Republic of) - Securities Markets

Taiwan Stock Exchange Weighted Price Index - *see* - China (Republic of) - Securities Markets

Tala - *see* - Samoa - Exchange Rates; Western Samoa - Exchange Rates

Tanzania

Banking, Finance, and Money

Banking Institutions - Assets/Liabilities - *FSM**, *FSY**
Monetary Authorities - Assets/Liabilities - *FSM**, *FSY**
Money Supply - *FSM**, *FSY**, *UNY*, *WTA**

Exchange Rates

Currency - *Tanzania Shilling*
Cross Rates - *N/A*
Forward Exchange Rate - *N/A*
Per ECU - *N/A*
Per SDR - *FSM**, *FSY**
Per U.S. Dollar - *DJN, DRF, FSM*, FSY*, UNY*

Government Finance

Debt - *GSY*, WTA**
Deficit/Surplus - *FSM*, FSY*, GSY*, WDR, WTA**
Expenditure - *GSY*, WDR, WTA**

Revenue - *GSY*, WDR, WTA**

Interest Rates

Bank Rate - *N/A*
Discount Rate - *FSM*, FSY*, UNY*
Government Bonds - *N/A*
Money Market - *N/A*
Treasury Bills - *N/A*

International Liquidity

Reserves Minus Gold - *FSM*, FSY*, UNY, WTA**
Gold - *N/A*

International Transactions

Balance of Payments - *BOP*, FSM*, FSY*, UNY, WDR, WTA**
Exports - *FSM*, FSY*, UNN, UNY, WTA**
Imports - *FSM*, FSY*, UNN, UNY, WTA**

National Accounts

Consumption
Government - *FSM*, FSY*, UNN, WDR, WTA**
Private - *FSM*, FSY*, UNN, WDR, WTA**
Gross Domestic Product - *FSM*, FSY*, GSY*, UNN, UNY, WDR, WTA**
Gross National Product - *FSM*, FSY*, UNN, WDR, WTA**
National Income - *FSM*, FSY*, UNN, WDR, WTA**

Prices, Production, Employment

Consumer Credit Outstanding - *FSM*, FSY*, GSY*, WDR, WTA**
Consumer Prices - *FSM*, FSY*, GSY*, UNY, WDR, WTA**
Earnings/Wages - *WDR, WTA**
Employment - *UNY*
Production
Industrial - *WTA**
Manufacturing - *WTA**

Securities Markets - *N/A*

Tanzania Shilling - *see* - **Tanzania - Exchange Rates**

Taxa - *see* - **Bangladesh - Exchange Rates**

Tel Aviv Stock Exchange - *see* - **Israel** - **Securities Markets**

TASE (Tel Aviv Stock Exchange) General Share Index - *see* - **Israel** - **Securities Markets**

Thai Baht - *see* - **Thailand** - **Exchange Rates**

Thailand

Banking, Finance, and Money

Banking Institutions - Assets/Liabilities - *FSM**, *FSY**
Monetary Authorities - Assets/Liabilities - *FSM**, *FSY**
Money Supply - *FSM**, *FSY**, *UNY, WTA**

Exchange Rates

Currency - *Thai Baht*
Cross Rates - *N/A*
Forward Exchange Rate - *N/A*
Per ECU - *N/A*
Per SDR - *FSM**, *FSY**
Per U.S. Dollar - *BAR, DJN, DRF, FRB, FSM**, *FSY**, *NYT, UNY, WSJ*

Government Finance

Debt - *FSM**, *FSY**, *GSY**, *WTA**
Deficit/Surplus - *FSM**, *FSY**, *GSY**, *WDR, WTA**
Expenditure - *GSY**, *WDR, WTA**
Revenue - *GSY**, *WDR, WTA**

Interest Rates

Bank Rate - *N/A*
Discount Rate - *FSM**, *FSY**, *UNY*
Government Bonds - *FSM**, *FSY**, *UNY*
Money Market - *FSM**, *FSY**
Treasury Bills - *FSM**, *FSY**, *UNY*

International Liquidity

Reserves Minus Gold - *FSM**, *FSY**, *UNY, WDR*
Gold - *FSM**, *FSY**, *UNY, WTA**

International Transactions

Balance of Payments - *BOP**, *FSM**, *FSY**, *UNY, WDR, WTA**
Exports - *FSM**, *FSY**, *UNN, UNY, WTA**

Imports - *FSM*, FSY*, UNN, UNY, WTA**

National Accounts

Consumption
Government - *FSM*, FSY*, UNN, WDR, WTA**
Private - *FSM*, FSY*, UNN, WDR, WTA**
Gross Domestic Product - *FSM*, FSY*, GSY*, UNN, UNY, WDR, WTA**
Gross National Product - *FSM*, FSY*, UNN, WDR, WTA**
National Income - *FSM*, FSY*, UNN, WTA**

Prices, Production, Employment

Consumer Credit Outstanding - *N/A*
Consumer Prices - *FSM*, FSY*, GSY*, UNY, WDR, WTA**
Earnings/Wages - *UNY, WDR, WTA**
Employment - *UNY*
Production
Industrial - *WTA**
Manufacturing - *UNN, WTA**
Wholesale/Producer Prices - *FSM*, FSY*, UNY*

Securities Markets

Stock Exchange - *Securities Exchange of Thailand (SET)*
Index - *Bangkok SET Index*
Foreign Bonds
Value of bonds issued - *FS1*
Shares
Price Index - *BAR, DRF, FTI*

Tin - *see* - Commodities

Togo

Banking, Finance, and Money

Banking Institutions - Assets/Liabilities - *FSM*, FSY**
Monetary Authorities - Assets/Liabilities - *FSM*, FSY**
Money Supply - *FSM*, FSY*, UNY, WTA**

Exchange Rates

Currency - *CFA Franc*
Cross Rates - *N/A*
Forward Exchange Rate - *N/A*
Per ECU - *N/A*

Per SDR - *FSM*, FSY**
Per U.S. Dollar - *DRF, FSM*, FSY*, UNY*

Government Finance

Debt - *FSM*, FSY*, GSY*, WTA**
Deficit/Surplus - *FSM*, FSY*, GSY*, WTA**
Expenditure - *GSY*, WTA**
Revenue - *GSY*, WTA**

Interest Rates

Bank Rate - *N/A*
Discount Rate - *FSM*, FSY*, UNY*
Government Bonds - *N/A*
Money Market - *FSM*, FSY**
Treasury Bills - *N/A*

International Liquidity

Reserves Minus Gold - *FSM*, FSY*, UNY, WTA**
Gold - *FSM*, FSY*, UNY, WTA**

International Transactions

Balance of Payments - *BOP*, FSM*, FSY*, UNY, WDR, WTA**
Exports - *FSM*, FSY*, UNN, UNY, WTA**
Imports - *FSM*, FSY*, UNN, UNY, WTA**

National Accounts

Consumption
  Government - *FSM*, FSY*, UNN, WDR, WTA**
  Private - *FSM*, FSY*, UNN, WDR, WTA**
Gross Domestic Product - *FSM*, FSY*, GSY*, UNN, UNY, WDR, WTA**
Gross National Product - *UNN, WDR, WTA**
National Income - *FSM*, FSY*, UNN, WTA**

Prices, Production, Employment

Consumer Credit Outstanding - *N/A*
Consumer Prices - *FSM*, FSY*, GSY*, UNY, WDR, WTA**
Earnings/Wages - *N/A*
Employment - *UNY*
Production
  Industrial - *WTA**

Manufacturing - *WTA**
Wholesale/Producer Prices - *N/A*

Securities Markets - *N/A*

Tokyo Stock Exchange (TSE) - *see* **- Japan - Securities Markets**

Tokyo Stock Exchange Stock Price Index (TOPIX) - *see* **- Japan - Securities Markets**

Tonga

Banking, Finance, and Money

Banking Institutions - Assets/Liabilities - *FSM*, FSY**
Monetary Authorities - Assets/Liabilities - *FSM*, FSY**
Money Supply - *FSM*, FSY*, UNY*

Exchange Rates

Currency - *Tongan Pa'anga*
Cross Rates - *N/A*
Forward Exchange Rate - *N/A*
Per ECU - *N/A*
Per SDR - *FSM*, FSY**
Per U.S. Dollar - *DRF, FSM*, FSY*, UNY*

Government Finance

Debt - *FSY*, WTA**
Deficit/Surplus - *FSM*, FSY*, WTA**
Expenditure - *WTA**
Revenue - *WTA**

International Liquidity

Reserves Minus Gold - *FSM*, FSY*, UNY, WTA**
Gold - *N/A*

International Transactions

Balance of Payments - *BOP*, FSM*, UNY, WTA**
Exports - *FSM*, FSY*, UNN, UNY, WTA**
Imports - *FSM*, FSY*, UNN, UNY, WTA**

National Accounts

Consumption
  Government - *UNN*
  Private - *UNN*
Gross Domestic Product - *FSM*, FSY*, UNN, UNY, WTA**

Gross National Product - *UNN, WTA**
National Income - *UNN*

Prices, Production, Employment

Consumer Credit Outstanding - *N/A*
Consumer Prices - *FSM*, FSY*, UNY, WTA**
Earnings/Wages - *UNY*
Employment - *N/A*
Production
  Industrial - *WTA**
  Manufacturing - *WTA**
  Wholesale/Producer Prices - *N/A*

Securities Markets - *N/A*

Tongan Pa' anga - *see* **- Tonga - Exchange Rates**

TOPIX Index (Tokyo Stock Exchange Stock Price Index) - *see* **- Japan - Securities Markets;** *see also* **- Commodities**

Toronto Stock Exchange (TSE) - *see* **- Canada - Securities Markets**

Toronto 300 Composite Index - *see* **- Canada - Securities Markets**

Treasury Bills - *see* **- Individual Countries - Interest Rates**

TSE (Tokyo Stock Exchange) - *see* **- Japan - Securities Markets**

TSE (Toronto Stock Exchange) - *see* **- Canada - Securities Markets**

Trinidad and Tobago

Banking, Finance, and Money

Banking Institutions - Assets/Liabilities - *FSM*, FSY**
Monetary Authorities - Assets/Liabilities - *FSM*, FSY**
Money Supply - *FSM*, FSY*, UNY, WTA**

Exchange Rates

Currency - *Trinidad and Tobago Dollar*
Cross Rates - *N/A*
Forward Exchange Rate - *N/A*
Per ECU - *N/A*
Per SDR - *FSM*, FSY**
Per U.S. Dollar - *DJN, DRF, FSM*, FSY*, UNY*

Government Finance

Debt - *FSM*, *FSY*, *GSY*, *WTA**
Deficit/Surplus - *FSM*, *FSY*, *GSY*, *WTA**
Expenditure - *GSY*, *WTA**
Revenue - *GSY*, *WTA**

Interest Rates

Bank Rate - *N/A*
Discount Rate - *UNY*
Government Bonds - *FSM*, *FSY*, *UNY*
Money Market - *N/A*
Treasury Bills - *FSM*, *FSY*, *UNY*

International Liquidity

Reserves Minus Gold - *FSM*, *FSY*, *UNY, WTA**
Gold - *FSM*, *FSY*, *UNY, WTA**

International Transactions

Balance of Payments - *BOP*, *FSM*, *FSY*, *UNY, WDR, WTA**
Exports - *FSM*, *FSY*, *UNN, UNY, WTA**
Imports - *FSM*, *FSY*, *UNN, UNY, WTA**

National Accounts

Consumption
    Government - FSM*, FSY*, UNN, WDR, WTA*
    Private - FSM*, FSY*, UNN, WDR, WTA*
Gross Domestic Product - *FSM*, *FSY*, *GSY*, *UNN, UNY, WDR, WTA**
Gross National Product - *FSM*, *FSY*, *UNN, WDR, WTA**
National Income - *FSM*, *FSY*, *UNN, WTA**

Prices, Production, Employment

Consumer Credit Outstanding - *N/A*
Consumer Prices - *FSM*, *FSY*, *GSY*, *UNY, WDR, WTA**
Earnings/Wages - *WDR, WTA**
Employment - *UNY, WTA**
Production
    Crude Petroleum - *FSM*, *FSY**
    Industrial - *FSM*, *FSY*, *UNY, WTA**
    Manufacturing - *UNY, WTA**
    Mining - *UNY*

Wholesale/Producer Prices - *FSM*, UNY*

Securities Markets - *N/A*

Trinidad and Tobago Dollar - *see* - **Trinidad and Tobago - Exchange Rates**

Tunisia

Banking, Finance, and Money

Banking Institutions - Assets/Liabilities - *FSM*, FSY**
Monetary Authorities - Assets/Liabilities - *FSM*, FSY**
Money Supply - *FSM*, FSY*, UNY, WTA**

Exchange Rates

Currency - *Tunisian Dinar*
Cross Rates - *N/A*
Forward Exchange Rate - *N/A*
Per ECU - *N/A*
Per SDR - *FSM*, FSY**
Per U.S. Dollar - *DRF, FSM*, FSY*, UNY*

Government Finance

Debt - *FSM*, FSY*, GSY*, WTA**
Deficit/Surplus - *FSM*, FSY*, GSY*, WTA**
Expenditure - *GSY*, WDR, WTA**
Revenue - *GSY*, WDR, WTA**

Interest Rates

Bank Rate - *N/A*
Discount Rate - *FSM*, FSY*, UNY, WDR*
Government Bonds - *N/A*
Money Market - *FSM*, FSY**
Treasury Bills - *N/A*

International Liquidity

Reserves Minus Gold - *FSM*, FSY*, UNY, WTA**
Gold - *FSM*, FSY*, UNY, WTA**

International Transactions

Balance of Payments - *BOP*, FSM*, FSY*, UNY, WDR, WTA**
Exports - *FSM*, FSY*, UNN, UNY, WTA**
Imports - *FSM*, FSY*, UNN, UNY, WTA**

National Accounts

Consumption
  Government - *FSM*, FSY*, UNN, WDR, WTA**
  Private - *FSM*, FSY*, UNN, UNY, WDR, WTA**
  Gross Domestic Product - *FSM*, FSY*, GSY*, UNN, WDR, WTA**
  Gross National Product - *FSM*, FSY*, UNN, WDR, WTA**
  National Income - *FSM*, FSY*, UNN, WTA**

Prices, Production, Employment

Consumer Credit Outstanding - *N/A*
Consumer Prices - *FSM*, FSY*, GSY*, UNY, WDR, WTA**
Earnings/Wages - *WDR*
Employment - *N/A*
Production
  Crude Petroleum - *FSM*, FSY**
  Industrial - *UNY, WTA**
  Manufacturing - *UNY, WTA**
  Mining - *FSM*, FSY*, UNY*
Wholesale/Producer Prices - *FSM*, FSY*, UNY*

Securities Markets - *N/A*

Tunisian Dinar - *see* - Tunisia - Exchange Rates

Turkey

Banking, Finance, and Money

Banking Institutions - Assets/Liabilities - *FSM*, FSY**
Monetary Authorities - Assets/Liabilities - *FSM*, FSY**
Money Supply - *FSM*, FSY*, MEI*, WTA**

Exchange Rates

Currency - *Turkish Lira*
Cross Rates - *N/A*
Forward Exchange Rate - *N/A*
Per ECU - *N/A*
Per SDR - *FSM*, FSY**
Per U.S. Dollar - *BAR, DJN, DRF, FSM*, FSY*, MEI*, NYT, UNY, WSJ*

Government Finance

Debt - *FSM*, FSY*, GSY*, WTA**

Deficit/Surplus - *FSM*, FSY*, GSY*, WDR, WTA**
Expenditure - *GSY*, WDR, WTA**
Revenue - *GSY*, WDR, WTA**

Interest Rates

Bank Rate - *N/A*
Discount Rate - *UNY*
Government Bonds - *N/A*
Money Market - *N/A*
Treasury Bills - *FSM*, FSY*, UNY*

International Liquidity

Reserves Minus Gold - *FSM*, FSY*, MEI*, UNY, WTA**
Gold - *FSM*, FSY*, UNY, WTA**

International Transactions

Balance of Payments - *BOP*, FSM*, FSY*, MEI*, UNY, WDR, WTA**
Exports - *FSM*, FSY*, MEI*, UNN, UNY, WTA**
Imports - *FSM*, FSY*, MEI*, UNN, UNY, WTA**

National Accounts

Consumption
  Government - *FSM*, FSY*, MEI*, UNN, WTA**
  Private - *FSM*, FSY*, MEI*, UNN, UNY, WTA**
Gross Domestic Product - *FSM*, FSY*, GSY*, MEI*, UNN, UNY, WDR, WTA**
Gross National Product - *FSM*, FSY*, UNN, WDR, WTA**
National Income - *FSM*, FSY*, UNN, WTA**

Prices, Production, Employment

Consumer Credit Outstanding - *N/A*
Consumer Prices - *FSM*, FSY*, GSY*, MEI*, UNY, WDR, WTA**
Earnings/Wages - *UNY, WDR, WTA**
Employment - *MEI*, UNY, WTA**
Production
  Industrial - *MEI*, UNY, WTA**
  Manufacturing - *MEI*, UNY, WTA**
  Mining - *UNY*
Wholesale/Producer Prices - *FSM*, FSY*, MEI, UNY*

Securities Markets

Stock Exchange - *Instanbul Menkulklymetler Borsasi* (*Istanbul Stock Exchange*)
Eurobonds
Value of bonds issued - *FS1*
Foreign Bonds
Value of bonds issued - *FS1*
Shares
Price Index - *BAR, FTI*

Turkish Lira - *see* - **Turkey - Exchange Rates**

U

UAE - *see* - **United Arab Emirates**

UAE Dirham - *see* - **United Arab Emirates - Exchange Rates**

Uganda

Banking, Finance, and Money

Banking Institutions - Assets/Liabilities - *FSM*, FSY**
Monetary Authorities - Assets/Liabilities - *FSM*, FSY**
Money Supply - *FSM*, FSY*, UNY, WTA**

Exchange Rates

Currency - *Uganda Shilling*
Cross Rates - *N/A*
Forward Exchange Rate - *N/A*
Per ECU - *N/A*
Per SDR - *FSM*, FSY**
Per U.S. Dollar - *DJN, DRF, FSM*, FSY*, UNY*

Government Finance

Debt - *FSM*, FSY*, GSY*, WTA**
Deficit/Surplus - *FSM*, FSY*, GSY*, WDR, WTA**
Expenditure - *GSY*, WDR, WTA**
Revenue - *GSY*, WDR, WTA**

Interest Rates

Bank Rate - *N/A*
Discount Rate - *UNY*
Government Bonds - *FSY*, UNY*
Money Market - *N/A*
Treasury Bills - *FSM*, FSY*, UNY*

International Liquidity

Reserves Minus Gold - *FSM*, FSY*, UNY, WTA**
Gold - *FSM*, FSY**

International Transactions

Balance of Payments - *BOP*, FSM*, FSY*, UNY, WTA**
Exports - *FSM*, FSY*, UNN, UNY, WTA**
Imports - *FSM*, FSY*, UNN, UNY, WTA**

National Accounts

Consumption
  Government - *UNN, WDR*
  Private - *FSY*, WDR*
Gross Domestic Product - *FSM*, FSY*, GSY*, UNN, UNY, WDR, WTA**
Gross National Product - *WDR, WTA**
National Income - *N/A*

Prices, Production, Employment

Consumer Credit Outstanding - *N/A*
Consumer Prices - *FSM*, FSY*, GSY*, UNY, WDR, WTA**
Earnings/Wages - *N/A*
Employment - *N/A*
Production
  Industrial - *WTA**
  Manufacturing - *WTA**
Wholesale/Producer Prices - *N/A*

Securities Markets - *N/A*

Uganda Shilling - *see* - Uganda - Exchange Rates

Union of Soviet Socialist Republics

Banking, Finance, and Money

Banking Institutions - Assets/Liabilities - *N/A*
Monetary Authorities - Assets/Liabilities - *N/A*
Money Supply - *N/A*

Exchange Rates

Currency - *USSR Ruble*
Cross Rates - *N/A*
Forward Exchange Rate - *N/A*

Per ECU - *N/A*
Per SDR - *N/A*
Per U.S. Dollar - *UNY*

Government Finance

Debt - *N/A*
Deficit/Surplus - *N/A*
Expenditure - *N/A*
Revenue - *N/A*

Interest Rates

Bank Rate - *N/A*
Discount Rate - *N/A*
Government Bonds - *N/A*
Money Market - *N/A*
Treasury Bills - *N/A*

International Liquidity

Reserves Minus Gold - *N/A*
Gold - *N/A*

International Transactions

Balance of Payments - *N/A*
Exports - *UNN, UNY*
Imports - *UNN, UNY*

National Accounts

Consumption
  Government - *UNN*
  Private - *UNN*
Gross Domestic Product - *UNN, UNY*
Gross National Product - *N/A*
National Income - *N/A*

Prices, Production, Employment

Consumer Credit Outstanding - *N/A*
Consumer Prices - *UNY*
Earnings/Wages - *UNY*
Employment - *UNY*
Production
  Industrial - *UNY*
  Manufacturing - *UNY*

Mining - *UNY*
Wholesale/Producer Prices - *N/A*

Securities Markets - *N/A*

United Arab Emirates

Banking, Finance, and Money

Banking Institutions - Assets/Liabilities - *FSM*, FSY**
Monetary Authorities - Assets/Liabilities - *FSM*, FSY**
Money Supply - *FSM*, FSY*, UNY, WTA**

Exchange Rates

Currency - *UAE Dirham*
Cross Rates - *N/A*
Forward Exchange Rate - *N/A*
Per ECU - *N/A*
Per SDR - *FSM*, FSY**
Per U.S. Dollar - *BAR, DJN, DRF, FSM*, FSY*, FTI, NYT, UNY, WSJ*

Government Finance

Debt - *GSY**
Deficit/Surplus - *FSM*, FSY*, GSY*, WDR, WTA**
Expenditure - *GSY*, WDR, WTA**
Revenue - *GSY*, WDR, WTA**

Interest Rates

Bank Rate - *N/A*
Discount Rate - *N/A*
Government Bonds - *N/A*
Money Market - *N/A*
Treasury Bills - *N/A*

International Liquidity

Reserves Minus Gold - *FSM*, FSY*, UNY, WTA**
Gold - *FSM*, FSY*, UNY, WTA**

International Transactions

Balance of Payments - *WDR, WTA**
Exports - *FSM*, FSY*, UNN, UNY, WTA**
Imports - *FSM*, FSY*, UNN, UNY, WTA**

National Accounts

Consumption
  Government - *FSM*, FSY*, UNN, WDR, WTA**
  Private - *FSM*, FSY*, UNN, WDR, WTA**
Gross Domestic Product - FSM*, FSY*, GSY*, UNN, UNY, WDR, WTA*
Gross National Product - *UNN, WDR, WTA**
National Income - *UNN, WTA**

Prices, Production, Employment

Consumer Credit Outstanding - *N/A*
Consumer Prices - *WDR*
Earnings/Wages - *WTA**
Employment - *N/A*
Production
  Crude Petroleum - *FSM*, FSY**
  Industrial - *GSY*, WTA**
  Manufacturing - *UNN, UNY, WTA**
Wholesale/Producer Prices - *N/A*

Securities Markets - *N/A*

United Kingdom

Banking, Finance, and Money

Banking Institutions - Assets/Liabilities - *FSM*, FSY**
Monetary Authorities - Assets/Liabilities - *FSM*, FSY**
Money Supply - *FSM*, FSY*, MEI*, UNY, WTA**

Exchange Rates

Currency - *Pound Sterling*
Cross Rates - *FTI, WSJ*
Currency Futures - *NYT*
Currency Options - *BAR, NYT, WSJ*
Forward Exchange Rate - *FTI, MEI**
Per ECU - *FTI*
Per Eurodollar - *FSM*, WSJ*
Per SDR - FSM*, FSY*, FTI
Per U.S. Dollar - *BAR, DJN, DRF, FRB, FSM*, FSY*, MEI*, NYT, UNY, WSJ*

Government Finance

Debt - *FSM*, FSY*, GSY**
Deficit/Surplus - *FSM*, FSY*, GSY*, WDR, WTA**
Expenditure - *GSY*, WDR, WTA**
Revenue - *GSY*, WDR, WTA**

Interest Rates

Bank Rate - *N/A*
Discount Rate - *DRF, FRB, FS2*
Government Bonds - *BAR, DRF, FSM*, FSY*, FS1, FTI, MEI**
Libor - *BAR, FS2, FSY*, NYT, WSJ*
Money Market - *FSM*, FSY*, UNY*
Prime Rate - *BAR, DJN, DRF, WSJ*
Treasury Bills - *DRF, FSM*, FSY*, UNY*

International Liquidity

Reserves Minus Gold - *FSM*, FSY*, MEI*, UNY, WTA**
Gold - *FSM*, FSY*, UNY, WTA**

International Transactions

Balance of Payments - *BOP*, FSM*, FSY*, MEI*, UNY, WDR, WTA**
Exports - *FSM*, FSY*, MEI*, UNN, UNY, WDR, WTA**
Imports - *FSM*, FSY*, MEI*, UNN, UNY, WTA**

National Accounts

Consumption
　Government - *FSM*, FSY*, UNN, WDR, WTA**
　Private - *FSM*, FSY*, UNN, WDR, WTA**
Gross Domestic Product - *FSM*, FSY*, GSY*, MEI*, UNN, UNY, WDR, WTA**
Gross National Product - *FSM*, FSY*, UNN, WDR, WTA**
National Income - *UNN, WTA**

Prices, Production, Employment

Consumer Credit Outstanding - *FS2**
Consumer Prices - *ECI, FSM*, FSY*, FS1, GSY*, MEI*, UNY, WDR, WTA**
Earnings/Wages - *FSM*, FSY*, MEI*, UNY, WTA**
Employment - *FSM*, FSY*, MEI*, UNY, WTA**
Production
　Industrial - *ECI, FSM*, FSY*, MEI*, UNY*

Manufacturing - *MEI*, UNY*
Mining - *UNY*
Wholesale/Producer Prices - *MEI*, UNY*

Securities Markets

Stock Exchange - *London Stock Exchange*
Indexes
  FTSE 100
  FTSE 30 Index
  London Gold Mines
  FTSE Mid 250
  FTSE All Share
  FTSE Actuaries 350
Bonds
  Issue price - *FS2**
  Prices - Selected Issues - *NYT*
  Yield - *FS2**
Eurobonds
  Value of bonds Issued - *FS1*
  Financial Futures and Options - *FTI*
Foreign Bonds
  Value of bonds Issued - *FS1*
  Money Market Instruments Issued - *FS2**
Shares
  Issue price - *FS2**
  Share price last day of month - *MEI**
  Price/Earnings Ratio - *FS1, FS2**
  Price Indexes
    FT All Share - *FTI, NYT*
    FT 250 - *FTI, FSM*, FSY*, FS1, MEI*, UNY*
    FT 100 - *FTI, BAR, DJN, DRF, WSJ*
    FT 30 - *DJN, DRF, NYT, WSJ*
    Gold Mines - *WSJ, DJN, DRF*
    FT Actuaries 350 - *FTI*
  Prices - *FSM, FSY, FS1, MEI*, UNY*
  Prices - Selected Issues - *BAR, FTI, NYT, WSJ*
  Yield - *FS1, FS2**
Stock Exchange Capitalization - *FS2**
Stock Exchange Turnover - *FS2**
Stock Market Instruments Issued - *FS2**

Trading Volume - *FTI*

United States

Banking, Finance, and Money

Banking Institutions - Assets/Liabilities - *FRB, FSM*, FSY**
Monetary Authorities - Assets/Liabilities - *FSM*, FSY**
Money Supply - *ECI, FRB, FSM*, FSY*, MEI*, UNY, WTA**

Exchange Rates

Currency - *US Dollar*
Cross Rates - *FTI, WSJ*
Currency Options - *WSJ*
Forward Exchange Rate - *N/A*
Per ECU - *FTI*
Per SDR - *FSM*, FSY**
Spot Forward Rate - *FTI*

Government Finance

Debt - *ECI, FRB, FSM*, FSY*, GSY**
Deficit/Surplus - *ECI, FSM*, FSY*, GSY*, WDR, WTA**
Expenditure - *ECI, FRB, GSY*, WDR*
Revenue - *ECI, FRB, GSY*, WDR*

Interest Rates

Bank Rate - *N/A*
Discount Rate - *BAR, DRF, FSM*, FSY*, FS1, FS2*, MEI*, UNY, WSJ*
Government Bonds - *BAR, DRF, FSM*, FSY*, FS1, FTI, MEI*, NYT, UNY*
Money Market - *BAR, FSM*, FSY*, NYT, WSJ*
Prime Rate - *BAR, DJN, DRF, ECI, FRB, FS1, FTI, MEI*, WSJ*
Treasury Bills - *BAR, ECI, FRB, FSM*, FSY*, FS1, UNY, WSJ*

International Liquidity

Reserves Minus Gold - *FSM*, FSY*, UNY, WTA**
Gold - *FRB, FSM*, FSY*, UNY, WTA**

International Transactions

Balance of Payments - *BOP*, FRB, FSM*, FSY*, MEI*, UNY, WDR, WTA**
Exports - *ECI, FRB, FSM*, FSY*, MEI*, UNN, UNY, WTA**
Imports - *ECI, FRB, FSM*, FSY*, MEI*, UNN, UNY, WTA**

National Accounts

Consumption
   Government - *FRB, FSM*, FSY*, UNN, WDR, WTA**
   Private - *ECI, FRB, FSM*, FSY*, UNN, UNY, WDR, WTA**
Gross Domestic Product - *ECI, FRB, FSM*, FSY*, GSY*, MEI*, UNN, UNY, WDR, WTA**
Gross National Product - *FSM*, FSY*, UNN, WDR, WTA**
National Income - *ECI, FRB, FSM*, FSY*, UNN, WTA**

Prices, Production, Employment

Consumer Credit Outstanding - *FS2**
Consumer Prices - *DJN, ECI, FRB, FSM*, FSY*, FS2*, GSY*, MEI*, UNY, WDR, WTA**
Earnings/Wages - *ECI, FRB, FSM*, FSY*, MEI*, UNY, WDR, WTA**
Employment - *ECI, FRB, FSM*, MEI*, UNY, WTA**
Production
   Crude Petroleum - *FSM*, FSY*, UNN, UNY*
   Industrial - *ECI, FRB, FSM*, FSY*, MEI*, UNY, WTA**
   Manufacturing - *ECI, FRB, MEI*, UNY, WTA**
   Mining - *UNY*
Wholesale/Producer Prices - DJN, ECI, FRB, FSM*, FSY*, MEI*, UNY

Securities Markets

Stock Exchanges
   American Stock Exchange (AMEX)
   Boston Stock Exchange (BSE)
   Midwest Stock Exchange (MSE)
   New York Stock Exchange (NYSE)
   Over-The-Counter Market (NASDAQ)
   Pacific Stock Exchange (PSE)
   Philadelphia Stock Exchange (PHLX)
Indexes
   Amex Value Index
   Dow Jones Average
   S&P 500
   S&P 400
   NASDAQ Composite
   NYSE Composite

Bonds
  Issue price (NYSE) - *FS2**
  Yield (NYSE) - *FS2**
Eurobonds
  Value of bonds issued (NYSE) - *FS1*
Foreign Bonds
  Value of bonds issued (NYSE) - *FS1*
Money Market Instruments Issued (NYSE) - *FS2**
Shares
  American Stock Exchange
    Most Active - *BAR, NYT, WSJ*
    Prices - *BAR, DJN, FTI, NYT, WSJ*
    Volume - *BAR, DJN, FRB, FTI, NYT, WSJ*
  Boston Stock Exchange
    Prices (Selected Issues) - *BAR, NYT, WSJ*
    Volume - *DJN, NYT*
  Midwest Stock Exchange
    Prices (Selected Issues) - *BAR, NYT, WSJ*
    Volume - *DJN, NYT*
  New York Stock Exchange
    Most Active - *BAR, NYT, WSJ*
    Prices - *BAR, FTI, NYT, WSJ*
    Volume - *BAR, DJN, FRB, NYT, WSJ*
  Over the Counter (NASDAQ)
    Most Active - *BAR, NYT, WSJ*
    Prices - *BAR, FTI, NYT, WSJ*
    Volume - *BAR, DJN, FTI, NYT, WSJ*
  Pacific Stock Exchange
    Prices (Selected Issues) - *BAR, NYT, WSJ*
    Volume - *DJN, NYT*
  Philadelphia Stock Exchange
    Prices (Selected Issues) - *BAR, NYT, WSJ*
    Volume - *DJN, NYT*
  Financial Futures and Options
    Chicago - BAR, FTI, NYT, WSJ
    New York - BAR, FTI, NYT, WSJ
    Philadelphia - BAR, FTI, NYT, WSJ
  Issue price (NYSE) - *FS2*
  Price/Earnings Ratio (NYSE) - *FS1, FS2*

Price Indexes
Amex - *BAR, DJN, DRI, FTI, NYT, WSJ*
Dow Jones
Composite - *BAR, DJN, DRI, NYT, WSJ*
Industrials - *BAR, DJN, DRI, NYT, WSJ*
Transportation - *BAR, DJN, DRI, NYT, WSJ*
Utilities - *BAR, DJN, DRI, NYT, WSJ*
NASDAQ Composite - *BAR, DJN, DRI, FTI, NYT, WSJ*
NYSE Composite - *BAR, DJN, DRI, FTI, FSM, FSY, FS1, FS2, MEI*, NYT, UNY, WSJ*
Standard & Poor's 500 - *BAR, DJN, DRI, FTI, NYT, WSJ*
Standard & Poor's 400 - *BAR, DJN, DRI, FTI, NYT, WSJ*
Yield (NYSE) - *FS1*
Stock Exchange Capitalization (NYSE) - *FS2**
Stock Exchange Turnover (NYSE) - *FS2**

United States Dollar - *see -* **United States - Exchange Rates**

United States Treasury Bills - *see -* **Commodities**

United States Treasury Bonds - *see -* **Commodities**

United States Treasury Notes - *see -* **Commodities**

Upper Volta - *see -* **Burkina Faso**

Uruguay

Banking, Finance, and Money

Banking Institutions - Assets/Liabilities - *FSM*, FSY**
Monetary Authorities - Assets/Liabilities - *FSM*, FSY**
Money Supply - *FSM*, FSY*, UNY, WTA**

Exchange Rates

Currency - *Uruguayan New Peso*
Cross Rates - *N/A*
Forward Exchange Rate - *N/A*
Per ECU - *N/A*
Per SDR - *FSM*, FSY**
Per U.S. Dollar - *BAR, DJN, DRF, FSM*, FSY*, NYT, UNY, WSJ*

Government Finance

Debt - *FSM*, FSY*, GSY*, WTA**
Deficit/Surplus - *FSM*, FSY*, GSY*, WDR, WTA**
Expenditure - *GSY*, WDR, WTA**
Revenue - *GSY*, WDR, WTA**

Interest Rates

Bank Rate - *N/A*
Discount Rate - *FSM*, FSY*, UNY*
Government Bonds - *N/A*
Money Market - *N/A*
Treasury Bills - *N/A*

International Liquidity

Reserves Minus Gold - *FSM*, FSY*, UNY, WTA**
Gold - *FSM*, FSY*, UNY, WTA**

International Transactions

Balance of Payments - *BOP*, FSM*, FSY*, UNY, WDR, WTA**
Exports - *FSM*, FSY*, UNN, UNY, WTA**
Imports - *FSM*, FSY*, UNN, UNY, WTA**

National Accounts

Consumption
Government - *FSM*, FSY*, UNN, WDR, WTA**
Private - *FSM*, FSY*, UNN, WDR, WTA**
Gross Domestic Product - *FSM*, FSY*, GSY*, UNN, UNY, WDR, WTA**
Gross National Product - *FSM*, FSY*, UNN, WDR, WTA**
National Income - *FSM*, FSY*, UNN, WTA**

Prices, Production, Employment

Consumer Prices - *FSM*, FSY*, GSY*, UNY, WDR, WTA**
Earnings/Wages - *UNY, WDR, WTA**
Employment - *UNY, WTA**
Production
Industrial - *UNY, WTA**
Manufacturing - *UNN, UNY, WTA**
Wholesale/Producer Prices - *FSM*, FSY*, UNY*

Securities Markets - *N/A*

Uruguayan New Peso - *see* - **Unuguay - Exchange Rates**

USSR - *see* - **Union of Soviet Socialist Republics**

USSR Ruble - *see* - **Union of Soviet Socialist Republics - Exchange Rates**

V

Vanuatu

Banking, Finance, and Money
Banking Institutions - Assets/Liabilities - *FSM*, FSY**
Monetary Authorities - Assets/Liabilities - *FSM*, FSY**
Money Supply - *FSM*, FSY*, UNY, WTA**

Exchange Rates
Currency - *Vanuatu Vatu*
Cross Rates - *N/A*
Forward Exchange Rate - *N/A*
Per ECU - *N/A*
Per SDR - *FSM*, FSY**
Per U.S. Dollar - *DJN, DRF, FSM*, FSY*, UNY*

Government Finance
Debt - *FSM*, FSY*, GSY*, WTA**
Deficit/Surplus - *FSM*, FSY*, GSY*, WTA**
Expenditure - *GSY*, WTA**
Revenue - *GSY*, WTA**

Interest Rates
Bank Rate - *N/A*
Discount Rate - *N/A*
Government Bonds - *FSM*, FSY*, UNY*
Money Market - *FSM*, FSY**
Treasury Bills - *N/A*

International Liquidity
Reserves Minus Gold - *FSM*, FSY*, UNY, WTA**
Gold - *N/A*

International Transactions

Balance of Payments - *BOP*, FSM*, FSY*, UNY, WTA**
Exports - *FSM*, FSY*, UNN, UNY, WTA**
Imports - *FSM*, FSY*, UNN, UNY, WTA**

National Accounts

Consumption
　Government - *FSM*, UNN, WTA**
　Private - *FSM*, UNN, WTA**
　Gross Domestic Product - *FSM*, GSY*, UNN, UNY, WTA**
　Gross National Product - *FSM*, UNN, WTA**
　National Income - *UNN, WTA**

Prices, Production, Employment

Consumer Credit Outstanding - *N/A*
Consumer Prices - *FSM*, FSY*, GSY*, UNY, WTA**
Earnings/Wages - *N/A*
Employment - *N/A*
Production
　Industrial - *WTA**
　Manufacturing - *WTA**
Wholesale/Producer Prices - *N/A*

Securities Markets - *N/A*

Vanuatu Vatu - *see* **- Vanuatu - Exchange Rates**

Vatu - *see* **- Vanuatu - Exchange Rates**

Venezuela

Banking, Finance, and Money

Banking Institutions - Assets/Liabilities - *FSM*, FSY**
Monetary Authorities - Assets/Liabilities *FSM*, FSY**
Money Supply - *FSM*, FSY*, UNY, WTA**

Exchange Rates

Currency - *Venezuelan Bolivar*
Cross Rates - *N/A*
Forward Exchange Rate - *N/A*
Per ECU - *N/A*
Per SDR - *FSM*, FSY**

Per U.S. Dollar - *BAR, DJN, DRF, FSM*, FSY*, NYT, UNY, WSJ*

Government Finance

Debt - *FSM*, FSY*, GSY*, WTA**
Deficit/Surplus - *FSM*, FSY*, GSY*, WDR, WTA**
Expenditure - *GSY*, WDR, WTA**
Revenue - *GSY*, WDR, WTA**

Interest Rates

Bank Rate - *N/A*
Discount Rate - *FSM*, FSY*, UNY*
Government Bonds - *FSM*, FSY*, UNY*
Money Market - *N/A*
Treasury Bills - *N/A*

International Liquidity

Reserves Minus Gold - *FSM*, FSY*, UNY, WTA**
Gold - *FSM*, FSY*, UNY, WTA**

International Transactions

Balance of Payments - *BOP*, FSM*, FSY*, UNY, WDR, WTA**
Exports - *FSM*, FSY*, UNN, UNY, WTA**
Imports - *FSM*, FSY*, UNN, UNY, WTA**

National Accounts

Consumption
  Government - *FSM*, FSY*, UNN, WDR, WTA**
  Private - *FSM*, FSY*, UNN, WDR, WTA**
Gross Domestic Product - *FSM*, FSY*, GSY*, UNN, UNY, WDR, WTA**
Gross National Product - *FSM*, FSY*, UNN, WDR, WTA**
National Income - *FSM*, FSY*, UNN, WTA**

Prices, Production, Employment

Consumer Credit Outstanding - *N/A*
Consumer Prices - *FSM*, FSY*, GSY*, UNY, WDR, WTA**
Earnings/Wages - *FSM*, FSY*, UNY, WDR*
Employment - *FSM*, FSY*, UNY*
Production
  Crude Petroleum - *FSM*, FSY*, UNN, UNY*

Industrial - *UNY, WTA**
Manufacturing - *UNN, UNY, WTA**
Mining - *UNY*
Wholesale/Producer Prices - *UNY*

Securities Markets

Stock Exchange - *N/A*
Index - *N/A*
Bonds
  Issue price - *N/A*
  Yield - *N/A*
Eurobonds
  Value of bonds issued - *N/A*
Foreign Bonds
  Value of bonds issued - *N/A*
Shares
  Dividend yield - *N/A*
  Issue price - *N/A*
  Last day of month - *N/A*
  Price/Earnings Ratio - *N/A*
  Price Index - *BAR, FTI, UNY*
  Prices - *UNY*
  Prices - Selected Issues - *N/A*
  Total Gross - *N/A*
  Yield - *N/A*
Stock Exchange Capitalization - *N/A*
Stock Exchange Turnover - *N/A*

Venezuelan Bolivar - *see* **- Venezula - Exchange Rates**

Vibor - *see* **- Austria - Interest Rates**

Vienna Stock Exchange - *see* **- Austria - Securities Markets**

Vietnam

Banking, Finance, and Money

Banking Institutions - Assets/Liabilities - *N/A*
Monetary Authorities - Assets/Liabilities - *N/A*
Money Supply - *N/A*

Exchange Rates

Currency - *Dong*

Cross Rates - *N/A*
Forward Exchange Rate - *N/A*
Per ECU - *N/A*
Per SDR - *N/A*
Per U.S. Dollar - *DRF, UNY*

Government Finance

Debt - *N/A*
Deficit/Surplus - *N/A*
Expenditure - *N/A*
Revenue - *N/A*

Interest Rates

Bank Rate - *N/A*
Discount Rate - *N/A*
Government Bonds - *N/A*
Money Market - *N/A*
Treasury Bills - *N/A*

International Liquidity

Reserves Minus Gold - *N/A*
Gold - *N/A*

International Transactions

Balance of Payments - *BOP*
Exports - *N/A*
Imports - *N/A*

National Accounts

Consumption
  Government - *N/A*
  Private - *N/A*
Gross Domestic Product - *UNN, UNY*
Gross National Product - *N/A*
National Income - *N/A*

Prices, Production, Employment

Consumer Credit Outstanding - *N/A*
Consumer Prices - *N/A*
Earnings/Wages - *N/A*
Employment - *N/A*
Production - *N/A*

Share Prices - *N/A*
Wholesale/Producer Prices - *N/A*
Securities Markets - *N/A*

W

Wages - *see* - **Individual Countries - Earnings/Wages**

Weiner Borse (Vienna Stock Exchange) - *see* - **Austria - Securities Markets**

Wellington Barclays Stock Index (NZSE 40 Cap) - *see* - **New Zealand - Securities Markets**

Western Samoa

Banking, Finance, and Money

Banking Institutions - Assets/Liabilities - *FSM*, FSY**
Monetary Authorities - Assets/Liabilities - *FSM*, FSY**
Money Supply - *FSM*, FSY*, WTA**

Exchange Rates

Currency - *Western Samoa Tala*
Cross Rates - *N/A*
Forward Exchange Rate - *N/A*
Per ECU - *N/A*
Per SDR - *FSM*, FSY**
Per U.S. Dollar - *DRF, FSM*, FSY**

Government Finance

Debt - FSY*, WTA*
Deficit/Surplus - FSY*
Expenditure - N/A
Revenue - N/A

Interest Rates

Bank Rate - *N/A*
Discount Rate - *N/A*

Government Bonds - *FSM*, FSY**
Money Market - *N/A*
Treasury Bills - *N/A*

International Liquidity

Reserves Minus Gold - *FSM*, FSY*, WTA**
Gold - *N/A*

International Transactions

Balance of Payments - *BOP*, FSM*, FSY*, WTA**
Exports - *FSM*, FSY*, WTA**
Imports - *FSM*, FSY*, WTA**

National Accounts

Consumption
  Government - *WTA**
  Private - *WTA**
Gross Domestic Product - *WTA**
Gross National Product - *WTA**
National Income - *WTA**

Prices, Production, Employment

Consumer Credit Outstanding - *N/A*
Consumer Prices - *FSM*, FSY*, WTA**
Earnings/Wages - *N/A*
Employment - *N/A*
Production - *N/A*
Wholesale/Producer Prices - *N/A*

Securities Markets - *N/A*

Western Samoa Tala - *see* **- Western Samoa - Exchange Rates**

Wheat - *see* **- Commodities**

Wholesale/Producer Prices - *see* **- Prices, Production, Employment**

Won - *see* **- Korea (Republic of South) - Exchange Rates**

Y

Yemen (People's Democratic Republic)

Banking, Finance, and Money

Banking Institutions - Assets/Liabilities - *FSM*, FSY**
Monetary Authorities - Assets/Liabilities - *FSM*, FSY**
Money Supply - *FSM*, FSY**

Exchange Rates

Currency - *Dinar*
Cross Rates - *N/A*
Forward Exchange Rate - *N/A*
Per ECU - *N/A*
Per SDR - *FSM*, FSY**
Per U.S. Dollar - *DRF, FSM*, FSY**

Government Finance

Debt - *N/A*
Deficit/Surplus - *FSY**
Expenditure - *N/A*
Revenue - *N/A*

International Liquidity

Reserves Minus Gold - *FSM*, FSY**
Gold - *FSM*, FSY**

International Transactions

Balance of Payments - *BOP*, FSM*, FSY**
Exports - *FSM*, FSY*, UNN*
Imports - *FSM*, FSY*, UNN*

National Accounts

Consumption

Government - *UNN*
Private - *UNN*
Gross Domestic Product - *UNN*
Gross National Product - *UNN*
National Income - *UNN*

Prices, Production, Employment

Consumer Credit Outstanding - *N/A*
Consumer Prices - *FSM*, FSY**
Wholesale/Producer Prices - *FSM*, FSY**

Securities Markets - *N/A*

Yemen (Republic of)

Banking, Finance, and Money

Banking Institutions - Assets/Liabilities - *N/A*
Monetary Authorities - Assets/Liabilities - *N/A*
Money Supply - *N/A*

Exchange Rates

Currency - *Yemeni Dinar*
Cross Rates - *N/A*
Forward Exchange Rate - *N/A*
Per ECU - *N/A*
Per SDR - *N/A*
Per U.S. Dollar - *UNY*

International Liquidity

Reserves Minus Gold - *UNY*
Gold - *UNY*

International Transactions

Balance of Payments - *UNY*
Exports - *UNN, UNY*
Imports - *UNN, UNY*

National Accounts

Consumption
Government - *UNY*
Private - *UNN*
Gross Domestic Product - *UNN, UNY*
Gross National Product - *UNN*
National Income - *UNN*

Prices, Production, Employment

Consumer Credit Outstanding - *N/A*
Consumer Prices - *N/A*
Earnings/Wages - *N/A*
Employment - *N/A*
Production - *N/A*
Wholesale/Producer Prices - *N/A*
Securities Markets - *N/A*

Yemen Arab Republic

Banking, Finance, and Money

Banking Institutions - Assets/Liabilities - *FSM*, FSY**
Monetary Authorities - Assets/Liabilities - *FSM*, FSY**
Money Supply - *FSM*, FSY*, UNY*

Exchange Rates

Currency - *Yemeni Rial*
Cross Rates - *N/A*
Forward Exchange Rate - *N/A*
Per ECU - *N/A*
Per SDR - *FSM*, FSY**
Per U.S. Dollar - *DRF, FSM*, FSY**

Government Finance

Debt - *FSY*, GSY**
Deficit/Surplus - *FSM*, FSY*, GSY**
Expenditure - *N/A*
Revenue - *N/A*

International Liquidity

Reserves Minus Gold - *FSM*, FSY**
Gold - *FSM*, FSY**

International Transactions

Balance of Payments - *BOP*, FSM*, FSY*, WDR*
Exports - *FSM*, FSY*, UNN*
Imports - *FSM*, FSY*, UNN*

National Accounts

Consumption
  Government - *FSM*, FSY*, UNN*
  Private - *FSM*, FSY*, UNN*
Gross Domestic Product - *FSM*, FSY*, GSY*, UNN, WDR*
Gross National Product - *FSM*, FSY*, UNN*

National Income - *FSM*, FSY*, UNN*
Prices, Production, Employment
Consumer Credit Outstanding - *N/A*
Consumer Prices - *FSM*, FSY*, GSY*, UNY*
Earnings/Wages - *N/A*
Employment - *N/A*
Production
  Manufacturing - *UNN*
Wholesale/Producer Prices - *UNY*
Securities Markets - *N/A*

Yemeni Dinar - *see* **- Yemen (People's Democratic Republic) - Exchange Rates; Yemen (Republic of) - Exchange Rates**

Yemeni Rial - *see* **- Yemen Arab Republic - Exchange Rates**

Yen - *see* **- Japan - Exchange Rates**

Yuan - *see* **- China (People's Republic) - Exchange Rates**

Yugoslav Dinar - *see* **- Yugoslavia - Exchange Rates**

Yugoslavia
  Banking, Finance, and Money
    Banking Institutions - Assets/Liabilities - *FSM*, FSY**
    Monetary Authorities - Assets/Liabilities - *FSM*, FSY**
    Money Supply - *FSM*, FSY*, UNY, WTA**
  Exchange Rates
    Currency - *Yugoslav Dinar*
    Cross Rates - *N/A*
    Forward Exchange Rate - *N/A*
    Per ECU - *N/A*
    Per SDR - *FSM*, FSY**
    Per U.S. Dollar - *DJN, DRF, FSM*, FSY*, NYT, UNY*
  Government Finance
    Debt - *FSY*, GSY*, WTA**
    Deficit/Surplus - *FSM*, FSY*, GSY*, WDR, WTA**
    Expenditure - *GSY*, WDR, WTA**
    Revenue - *GSY*, WDR, WTA**
  Interest Rates
    Bank Rate - *N/A*

Discount Rate - *FSM*, FSY*, UNY*
Government Bonds - *N/A*
Money Market - *FSM*, FSY**
Treasury Bills - *N/A*

International Liquidity

Reserves Minus Gold - *FSM*, FSY*, UNY, WTA**
Gold - *FSM*, FSY*, UNY, WTA**

International Transactions

Balance of Payments - *BOP*, FSM*, FSY*, UNY, WDR, WTA**
Exports - *FSM*, FSY*, UNN, UNY, WTA**
Imports - *FSM*, FSY*, UNN, UNY, WTA**

National Accounts

Consumption
  Government - *FSM*, FSY*, UNN, WDR, WTA**
  Private - *FSM*, FSY*, UNN, WDR, WTA**
Gross Domestic Product - *FSM*, FSY*, GSY*, UNN, UNY, WDR, WTA**
Gross National Product - *UNN, WDR, WTA**
National Income - *UNN, WTA**

Prices, Production, Employment

Consumer Credit Outstanding - *N/A*
Consumer Prices - *FSM*, FSY*, GSY*, UNY, WDR, WTA**
Earnings/Wages - *FSM*, FSY*, UNY, WDR, WTA**
Employment - *FSM*, FSY*, UNY, WTA**
Production
  Industrial - *FSM*, FSY*, UNY, WTA**
  Manufacturing - *UNY*
  Mining - *UNY*
Wholesale/Producer Prices - *FSM*, FSY*, UNY*

Securities Markets - *N/A*

Z

Zaire

Banking, Finance, and Money

Banking Institutions - Assets/Liabilities - *FSM*, FSY**
Monetary Authorities - Assets/Liabilities - *FSM*, FSY**
Money Supply - *FSM*, FSY*, UNY, WTA**

Exchange Rates

Currency - *Zairian Zaire*
Forward Exchange Rate - *N/A*
Per ECU - *N/A*
Per SDR - *FSM*, FSY**
Per U.S. Dollar - *DRF, FSM*, FSY*, UNY*

Government Finance

Debt - *FSM*, FSY*, GSY*, WTA**
Deficit/Surplus - *FSM*, FSY*, GSY*, WDR, WTA**
Expenditure - *GSY*, WDR, WTA**
Revenue - *GSY*, WDR, WTA**

Interest Rates

Bank Rate - *N/A*
Discount Rate - *FSM*, FSY*, UNY*
Government Bonds - *N/A*
Money Market - *N/A*
Treasury Bills - *N/A*

International Liquidity

Reserves Minus Gold - *FSM*, FSY*, UNY, WTA**
Gold - *FSM*, FSY*, UNY, WTA**

International Transactions

Balance of Payments - *BOP*, FSM*, FSY*, UNY, WDR, WTA**

Exports - *FSM*, FSY*, UNN, UNY, WTA**

Imports - *FSM*, FSY*, UNN, UNY, WTA**

National Accounts

Consumption
  Government - *FSM*, FSY*, UNN, WDR, WTA**
  Private - *FSM*, FSY*, UNN, WDR, WTA**
Gross Domestic Product - *FSM*, FSY*, UNN, UNY, WDR, WTA**
Gross National Product - *UNN, WDR, WTA**
National Income - *FSY*, UNN, WTA**

Prices, Production, Employment

Consumer Credit Outstanding - *N/A*
Consumer Prices - *FSM*, FSY*, GSY*, WDR, WTA**
Earnings/Wages - *N/A*
Employment - *N/A*
Production
  Industrial - *WTA**
  Manufacturing - *WTA**
  Mining - *FSY**
Wholesale/Producer Prices - *N/A*

Securities Markets - *N/A*

Zairian Zaire - *see* - Zaire - Exchange Rates

Zambia

Banking, Finance, and Money

Banking Institutions - Assets/Liabilities - *FSM*, FSY**
Monetary Authorities - Assets/Liabilities - *FSM*, FSY**
Money Supply - *FSM*, FSY*, UNY, WTA**

Exchange Rates

Currency - *Zambian Kwacha*
Cross Rates - *N/A*
Forward Exchange Rate - *N/A*
Per ECU - *N/A*
Per SDR - *FSM*, FSY**

Per U.S. Dollar - *DJN, DRF, FSM*, FSY*, UNY*

Government Finance

Debt - *FSM*, FSY*, GSY*, WTA**
Deficit/Surplus - *FSM*, FSY*, GSY*, WDR, WTA**
Expenditure - *GSY*, WDR, WTA**
Revenue - *GSY*, WDR, WTA**

Interest Rates

Bank Rate - *N/A*
Discount Rate - *FSM*, FSY*, UNY*
Government Bonds - *N/A*
Money Market - *N/A*
Treasury Bills - *FSM*, FSY*, UNY*

International Liquidity

Reserves Minus Gold - *FSM*, FSY*, UNY, WTA**
Gold - *FSM*, FSY*, UNY, WTA**

International Transactions

Balance of Payments - *BOP*, FSM*, FSY*, UNY, WDR, WTA**
Exports - *FSM*, FSY*, UNN, UNY, WTA**
Imports - *FSM*, FSY*, UNN, UNY, WTA**

National Accounts

Consumption
Government - *FSM*, FSY*, UNN, WDR, WTA**
Private - *FSM*, FSY*, UNN, WDR, WTA**
Gross Domestic Product - *FSM*, FSY*, GSY*, UNN, UNY, WDR, WTA**
Gross National Product - *FSM*, FSY*, UNN, WDR, WTA**
National Income - *FSM*, FSY*, UNN, WTA**

Prices, Production, Employment

Consumer Credit Outstanding - *N/A*
Consumer Prices - *FSM*, FSY*, GSY*, UNY, WDR, WTA**
Earnings/Wages - *WDR*
Employment - *UNY*
Production
Industrial - *FSM*, FSY*, UNY, WTA**
Manufacturing - *UNN, UNY, WTA**

Mining - *FSM*, FSY*, UNN, UNY*
Wholesale/Producer Prices - *FSM*, FSY*, UNY*
Securities Markets - *N/A*

Zambian Kwacha - *see* - Zambia - Exchange Rates

Zimbabwe

Banking, Finance, and Money

Banking Institutions - Assets/Liabilities - *FSM*, FSY**
Monetary Authorities - Assets/Liabilities - *FSM*, FSY**
Money Supply - *FSM*, FSY*, WTA**

Exchange Rates

Currency - *Zimbabwean Dollar*
Cross Rates - *N/A*
Forward Exchange Rate - *N/A*
Per ECU - *N/A*
Per SDR - *FSM*, FSY**
Per U.S. Dollar - *DJN, DRF, FSM*, FSY*, UNY*

Government Finance

Debt - *FSY*, GSY*, WTA**
Deficit/Surplus - *FSY*, GSY*, WDR, WTA**
Expenditure - *GSY*, WDR, WTA**
Revenue - *GSY*, WDR, WTA**

Interest Rates

Bank Rate - *FSY**
Discount Rate - *UNY*
Government Bonds - *FSM*, FSY*, UNY*
Money Market - *FSM*, FSY**
Treasury Bills - *FSM*, FSY*, UNY*

International Liquidity

Reserves Minus Gold - *FSM*, FSY*, UNY, WTA**
Gold - *FSM*, FSY*, UNY, WTA**

International Transactions

Balance of Payments - *BOP*, FSM*, FSY*, UNY, WDR, WTA**
Exports - *FSM*, FSY*, UNN, UNY, WTA**
Imports - *FSM*, FSY*, UNN, UNY, WTA**

National Accounts

Consumption

Government - *FSM*, FSY*, UNN, WDR, WTA**

Private - *FSM*, FSY*, UNN, WDR, WTA**

Gross Domestic Product - FSM*, FSY*, GSY*, UNN, UNY, WDR, WTA*

Gross National Product - *FSM*, FSY*, UNN, WDR, WTA**

National Income - *UNN, WTA**

Prices, Production, Employment

Consumer Credit Outstanding - *N/A*

Consumer Prices - *FSM*, FSY*, GSY*, UNY, WDR, WTA**

Earnings/Wages - *UNY, WDR, WTA**

Employment - *UNY, WTA**

Production

Industrial - *UNY, WTA**

Manufacturing - *FSM*, FSY*, UNN, UNY, WTA**

Mining - *UNY*

Securities Markets - *N/A*

Zimbabwean Dollar - *see* - **Zimbabwe - Exchange Rates**

Zinc - *see* - **Commodities**

Zloty - *see* - **Poland - Exchange Rates**

Zürchen Böise (The Zurich Stock Exchange) - *see* - **Switzerland - Securities Markets**

Zurich Stock Exchange - *see* - **Switzerland - Securities Markets**

Appendix

Directory of World Securities Markets

Argentina (Buenos Aires)
Mercado de Valores de Buenos Aires
25 de Mayo 367
Buernos Aires 1002
    Telephone: (54-1) 313-4522
    Fax: (54-1) 313-4472
    Telex: (390) 17445 MERBA A

Argentina (Rosario)
Bolsa de Comercio de Rosario
Córdoba Esquina Corrientes
Rosario AR-2000
    Telephone: (54-41) 213-470
    Fax: (54-41) 241-019
    Telex: 41824

Australia
Australian Stock Exchange Ltd.
Level 9, 87-89 Pitt Street
Sydney, NSW2000
    Telephone: (02)227-0000
    Fax: (02) 235-0056
    Telex: 24628

Austria
Vienna Stock Exchange
1011 Vienna
Wipplinger Str. 34
    Telephone: (0222) 53-4-99
    Fax: (0222) 535-68-57
    Telex: 132447

Bahrain
Bahrain Stock Exchange
c/o Bahrain Monetary Agency
POB 27 Manama
    Telephone: 535535
    Fax: 534170
    Telex: 9191

Bangladesh
Dhaka Stock Exchange Ltd.
Stock Exchange Building
9F, Motijheel Commercial Area
Dhaka 1000
    Telephone: (880-2) 239-882/231-935
    Fax: (880-2) 231-935
    Telex: 632150 DSE BJ

Barbados
Securities Exchange
6th Floor
Central Bank Building
Church Village
St. Michel
    Telephone: (809) 436-9871
    Fax: (809) 429-8942

Belgium
Societe de la Bourse de Valeurs Mobilieres de Bruxelles
2 Rue Henri Maus
1000 Brussels
    Telephone: (02) 509-12-11
    Fax: (02) 511-95-00
    Telex: 21374

Bolivia (La Paz)
Bolsa Boliviana de Valores S.A.
Ayacucho y Mercado No. 308
Casilla 12521
La Paz
    Telephone: (591-2) 32-2422
    Fax: (591-2) 37-6240

Bolivia (Santa Cruz)
Bolsa de Valores de Santa Cruz de la Sierra, S.A.
Velazco 308
Santa Cruz

Botswana
Stockbrokers Botswana Ltd.
5th Floor, Barclays House
Khama Cresent
Gaborone
    Telephone: (267) 357900
    Fax: (2766) 357901

Brazil (Belo Horizonte)
Bolsa de Valores Minas-Espirito Santo e Brasilia
Rua dos Carijos, 126 3 Andar
Belo Horizonte MG 30120
    Telephone: (55-31) 219-9000
    Fax: (55-31) 273-1202
    Telex: 1428

Brazil (Rio de Janeiro)
Bolsa de Valores de Rio de Janeiro
Praca XV de Novembro
No. 20 3rd Floor
Rio de Janeiro 20010
    Telephone: (55-21) 271-1001
    Fax: (55-21) 221-2151
    Telex: 31500

Brazil (Sao Paulo)
Bolsa de Valores de Saõ Paulo
Rua Alvares Pentecado, 151
Sao Paulo 01012
    Telephone: (55-11) 258-7222
    Fax: (55-11) 36 0871
    Telex: (391) 34088

Bulgaria
First Bulgarian Stock Exchange
3 Angel Kanchev Str.
BG- Sofia
    Telephone: (359-2) 813-527

Fax: (359-2) 810-057
Telex: 24019inbg

Canada
Alberta Stock Exchange
300 Fifth Avenue SW
21st Floor
Calgary, AB T2P 3C4
Telephone: (403) 262-7791
Fax: (403) 237-0450

Montreal Stock Exchange/Bourse de Montréal
Tour de la Bourse
800 Square Victoria
CP61, Montreal, PQH4Z1A9
Telephone: (514) 871-2424
Fax: (514) 871-3533

Toronto Stock Exchange
The Exchange Tower
2 First Canadian Place
Toronto, ON M5X 1J2
Telephone: (416) 947-4700
Fax: (416) 947-4585
Telex: 0662-17759

Vancouver Stock Exchange
Stock Exchange Tower
609 Granville Street
POB 10333
Vancouver, BC V7Y 1H1
Telephone: (604) 689-3334
Fax: (604) 688-6051

Winnepeg Stock Exchange
One Lombard Place
Suite 2901
Winnepeg, MB R3B 0Y2
Telephone: (204) 942-8431
Fax: (204) 947-9536

Chile
Bolsa de Comercio de Santiago

La Bolsa 64
Santiago
    Telephone: (56-2) 698-2001
    Fax: (56-2) 672-8046
    Telex: (352) 340531 BOLCOM

China, People's Republic (Shanghai)
Shanghai Securities Exchange
15 Huang Pu Road
Shanghai 200080
    Telephone: (86-21) 306-3195
    Fax: (86-21) 306-3076

China, People's Republic (Shenzhen)
Shenzhen Stock Exchange
15/F International Trust and Investment Building
Hong Ling Zhong Road
Shenzhen 518001
    Telephone: (86-755) 583927
    Fax: (86-755) 583931
    Telex: 420592 SZSELCN

China (Taiwan)
Taiwan Stock Exchange
City Building 10th Floor
85 Yen-Ping South Road
Taipei 10034
    Telephone: (02) 3114020
    Fax: (02) 3114004
    Telex: 22914

Colombia (Bogota)
Bolsa de Bogotá S.A.
Carrera 8A, No. 13-82, 8
Apartado Aéreo 3584
Bogotá
    Telephone: (57-1) 243-65 01
    Fax: (57-1) 281-3170
    Telex: (396) 044807

Colombia (Cali)
Bolsa de Occidente
Calle 8a. No. 3-14 piso17

Cali
>   Telephone: (572) 381-7022
>   Fax: (572) 382-1072
>   Telex: 351217

Colombia (Medellin)
Bolsa de Medellín S.A..
Carrera 50, No. 50-48, Piso 2
Apartado Aéreo 3535
Medellín
>   Telephone: (57-4) 2603000
>   Fax: (57-4) 2511981
>   Telex: (396) 666788

Commonwealth of Independent States (Moscow)
Moscow International Stock Exchange
Minishy of Finance
9 Klubyshev Street
Moscow 103097
>   Telephone: (7-095) 251-0392/ 251-1576
>   Fax: (7-095) 925-0889

Costa Rica
Costa Rica Stock Exchange
Central Street, AV. 1st, 3th
San Jose 1000
>   Telephone: (506) 22 8011
>   Fax: (506) 55 0131
>   Telex: BONAVA 2863

Côte d'Ivoire
Abidjan Stock Exchange
Avenue Joseph Anoma
Abidjan 01
Mailing Address:
>   Telephone: (225) 21-5742
>   Fax: (225) 22-1657
>   Telex: 2221 Bourse Abidjan

Cyprus [No Official Stock Exchange—Over the Counter Market]
Cyprus Investment Security Corp.
P.O. Box 597
Nicosia

Telephone:	(357-2) 451535
Telex:	4449CISCO CY

The Czech Republic (Bratislava)
Bratislava Stock Exchange
Hlavne Nam, 8
Bratislava 81101

Telephone:	(42-7) 335839
Fax:	(42-7) 335725

Czech Republic (Prague)
Stock Exchange of Prague
Na Mustku 3
Praha 1110 00

Telephone:	(42-2) 26 1146
Fax:	(42-2) 23 56233

Denmark
Copenhagen Stock Exchange
Nikolaj Plads 66
POB 1040
1007 Copenhagen K

Telephone:	33-93-33-66
Fax:	33-12-86-13
Telex:	16496

Ecuador
Bolsa de Valores
Av. Río Amazonas 540
Jeronimo Carrión 8piso
Quito

Telephone:	(593-2) 526805
Fax:	(593-2) 500942

Egypt (Alexandria)
Alexandria Stock Exchange
11 Talat Harb Street
Menshia
Alexandria

Telephone:	(20-3) 483-5432

Egypt (Cario)
Cairo Stock Exchange

4 Sherifien Street
Cairo
    Telephone: (20-1) 392-8526

El Salvador
El Salvador Stock Exchange
6 piso, Edificio La Centroamericana
Alameda Roosevelt #3107
San Salvador
    Telephone: (503) 23-3721 / 23-2215
    Fax: (503) 23-2898

Finland
Helsinki Stock Exchange
Fabianinkatu 14
POB 361
00101 Helsinki
    Telephone: (90) 173301
    Fax: (90) 17330399
    Telex: 123460

France
La Bourse de Paris
Palais de la Bourse
4 Place de la Bourse, 75080
Paris Cedex 02
    Telephone: (1) 40-26-85-90

Germany (Berlin)
Berliner Wertpapierbörse
1000 Berlin 12
Fasanenstr. 3
    Telephone: (030) 311091-0
    Fax: (030) 311091-79

Germany (Bremen)
Bremer Wertpapierbörse
2800 Bremen 1
Obernstr. 2-12
Postfach 10 07 26
    Telephone: (0421) 323037
    Fax: (0421) 323123
    Telex: 246331

Germany (Düsseldorf)
Rheinisch-Westfälische Borse zu Düsseldorf
4000 Düsseldorf 1
Ernst-Schneider Platz 1
    Telephone: (0211) 1389-0
    Fax: (0211) 133287
    Telex: 8582600

Germany (Frankfurt)
Frankfurter Wertpapierbörse
6000 Frankfurt am Main
Borsenplatz 4
    Telephone: (069) 29977-0
    Fax: (069) 29990330
    Telex: (069) 411412

Germany (Hamburg)
Hanseatische Wertpapierbörse Hamburg
2000 Hamburg 1
Schauenburgerstr. 47-49
    Telephone: (040) 361302-0
    Fax: (040) 361302-23

Germany (Hannover)
Niedersächsische Börse zu Hannover
3000 Hannover 1
Rathenaustr. 2
    Telephone: (0511) 327661
    Fax: (0511) 324915

Germany (München)
Bayerische Börse
8000 München 2
Lenbachplatz 2A/1
    Telephone: (089) 5990-0
    Fax: (089) 599032
    Telex: 523515

Germany (Stuttgart)
Baden-Württembergische Wertpapierbörse zu Stuttgart
7000 Stuttgart 1
Königstr. 28

Telephone: (0711) 290183
Fax: (0711) 2268119

Ghana
Ghana Stock Exchange
Kwame Nkrumah Avenue
Kingsway Bldg.—2nd Floor
Accra
Telephone: (233-21) 666 99 08/ 669935
Fax: (233-21) 66 9913
Telex: 2722

Greece
Athens Stock Exchange
10 Sophocleous Street
Athens 105 59
Telephone: (30-1) 3211301
Fax: (30-1) 3213938
Telex: (863) 215820 BURS GR

Honduras
Bolsa Hondurena de Valores S.A.
Edi Ficio Martinez Valenzuela
1 Piso, 2 Calle 3 Ave S.O.
San Pedro Sula
Telephone: (504) 53-4410
Fax: (504) 53-4480

Hungary
Budapest Stock Exchange
Deak Ferenc Utca 5
Budapest H-1052
Telephone: (36-1) 1175-226
Fax: (36-1) 1181-737

India (Bangalore)
Bangalore Stock Exchange Ltd.
1st Floor
Block Unity Bldg. J.C. Road
Bangalore 560-002
Telephone: (918-12) 2201631 / 236567
Telex: 8452874 BSEIN

India (Bombay)
The Bombay Stock Exchange
Phiroze Jeejeebhoy Towers
Dalal Street
Bombay 400 001
     Telephone: (91-22) 275860/61
     Fax: (91-22) 202-8121
     Telex: (953) 011859 STEX IN

India (Calcutta)
The Calcutta Stock Exchange Association, Ltd.
7 Lyons Range
Calcutta 700 00 1
     Telephone: (91-33) 20-9366 / 201488
     Telex: 021-7414 CSEA IN

India (New Delhi)
The Delhi Stock Exchange Association, Ltd.
3 and 4/4B Asaf Ali Road
New Delhi 110 002
     Telephone: (91-11) 327-9000
     Fax: (91-11) 326-7112
     Telex: (953) 3165317 DSEAIN

India (Madras)
Madras Stock Exchange
11 Second Line Beach
Madras 600 001
     Telephone: (91-44) 521071
     Fax: (91-44) 514897
     Telex: 953-0418050 MSEXIN

Indonesia (Jakarta)
The Jakarta Stock Exchange
Jl Merdeka Selatan 14
Jakarta 10110
Gedung Bursa 2nd Floor
     Telephone: (62-21) 360-649
     Fax: (62-21) 384-019

Indonesia (Surabaya)
Surabaya Stock Exchange
Jl Pemuda No. 29-31

Bank Exim Building 5th Floor Surabaya
    Telephone: (031) 510646/512716/513869
    Fax   (031) 510823

Iran
Tehran Stock Exchange
Avenue Saadi 521
Taghinia Building
Tehran
    Telephone: (98-21) 311149-501/316 292
    Fax: (98-21) 310765

Iraq
Capital Market Authority
Baghdad

Ireland
The Stock Exchange (Irish Unit)
24-28 Anglesea Street
Dublin 2
    Telephone: (01) 778808
    Telex: 93437

Italy (Genova)
Borsa Valori
Via G. Boccardo 1
    Telephone: (010) 2094400

Italy (Milan)
Borsa Valori
Via Camperio 4
20123 Milan
    Telephone: (02) 85344627
    Fax: 878090
    Telex: 321430

Italy (Naples)
Borsa Valori
Palazzo Borsa
Piazza Bovio
    Telephone: (081) 269151

Italy (Rome)
Borsa Valori
Via dei Burro 147
    Telephone: (06) 6792701

Italy (Turin)
Borsa Valori
Via San Francesco da Paola 28
    Telephone: (011) 547743
    Fax: 5612193
    Telex: 220614

Jamaica
Jamaica Stock Exchange
Bank of Jamaica Tower
Nethersole Place
Kingston
    Telephone: (809) 922-0806/ 0807
    Fax: (809) 922-6966
    Telex: 2165/2167

Japan (Osaka)
Osaka Securities Exchange
8-16 Kitahama 1-chome
Chuo-ku
Osaka 541
    Telephone: (06) 229-86643
    Fax: (06) 231-2639
    Telex: 22215

Japan (Tokyo)
Tokyo Stock Exchange
2-1 Nihonbashi-Kabuto-cho
Chuo-ku
Tokyo 103
    Telephone: (03) 3666-0141
    Fax: (03) 3663-0625
    Telex: 22759

Jordan
Amman Financial Market
P.O. Box 8802
Amman

Telephone: (962-6) 663170
Fax: (962-6) 686830
Telex: (925) 21711

Kenya
The Nairobi Stock Exchange
IPS Building, 2nd Floor
Kirmathi Street
Nairobi
    Telephone: (254-2) 230692
    Fax: (254-2) 224200

Korea
Korea Stock Exchange
33 Yoido-Dong
Yongdeungpo-ku
Seoul 150-010
    Telephone: (82-2) 780-2271
    Fax: (82-2) 786-0263
    Telex: K 28384 (KOSTEX)

Kuwait
Kuwait Stock Exchange
Mubarak Al Kabir Street
Safat 13063
    Telephone: (965) 24 23 130
    Fax: (965) 2420779/2558832
    Telex: 44105—44028

Luxembourg
Société de la Bourse de Luxembourg SA
11 Ave de la Porte-Neuve, BP 165
2011 Luxembourg
    Telephone: 47-79-366-1
    Fax: 47-32-98
    Telex: 2559

Malaysia
The Kuala Lumpur Stock Exchange
3rd-5th Floor Exchange Square
Off Jalan Semantan
Damansara Heights
Kuala Lumpur 50490

Telephone:	(60-3) 2546433
Fax:	(60-3) 2557463/2561291
Telex:	KLSE MA (784) 30241

Malta
The Maltese Stock Exchange
Pope Pius V Street
Valletta
| Telephone: | (3566) 244051 |
| Fax: | (3566) 244071 |

Mauritius
Stock Exchange Commission
9th Floor Sicom Building
Sir Celicourt Antelme Street
Port Louis
Telephone:	(230) 208-8735
Fax:	(230) 208-86766
Telex:	5291

Mexico
Bolsa Mexicana de Valores, S.A. de C.V.
Paseo de la Reforma, 255
Col. Cuauhtemoc
Mexico D.F. 06500
Telephone:	(52-2) 208-3131
Fax:	(52-2) 208-8972
Telex:	(383) 1762233

Morocco
Casablanca Stock Exchange
98, Boulevard Mohammed V
Casablanca 01
Telephone:	(212-2) 2041 10 / 31 28 88
Fax:	(212-2) 20 03 65
Telex:	23698 BOURSVAL

Nepal
Securities Exchange Center Ltd.
Dillibazar, Kathmandu
    Telephone: 411031

Netherlands
Amsterdam Stock Exchange
Beursplein 5
1012 JW Amsterdam
    Telephone: (020) 5234567
    Fax: (020) 6248062
    Telex: 12302

New Zealand
New Zealand Stock Exchange
Caltex Tower
286-292 Lambton Quay
POB 2959, Wellington 1
    Telephone: (04) 472-7599
    Fax: (04) 473-1470
    Telex: 3424

New Zealand (Dunedin)
Dunedin Stock Exchange
POB 12664 Dunedin
    Telephone: (03) 477-5900
    Telex: 5610

Nigeria
Nigerian Stock Exchange
Stock Exchange House 8-9 Floors
2-4 Customs Street
Lagos
    Telephone: (234-1) 660287
    Fax: (234-1) 668724
    Telex: (961) 23567 STEX NG

Norway
Oslo Børs
Tollbught 2
POB 4660 Sentrum
0105 Oslo
    Telephone: (2) 42-38-80
    Fax: (2) 41-65-90
    Telex: 77242

Oman
Muscat Securities Market
    Telephone: (968) 702-760

Fax: (968) 702-691
Telex: 3220 ON

Pakistan (Karachi)
Karachi Stock Exchange Guarantee Ltd.
Stock Exchange Building
Stock Exchange Road
Karachi 2
Telephone: (92-21) 241-91466
Fax: (22-21) 241-0825
Telex: (952) 2746

Pakistan (Lahore)
Lahore Stock Exchange
Lahore
Telephone: (42-92) 368-111

Panama
Bolsa de Valores de Panama, S.A.
Calle Elvira Mendez y Calle 52
Edificio Vallarino, Planta Baja
Apdo. Postal 87-0878
Panama
Telephone: (507) 69-1966
Fax: (507) 69-2457

Paraguay
Bolsa de Valores y Productos de Asunción S.A.
Calle Estrella 540
Asuncion
Telephone: (595-21) 490-359
Fax: (595-21) 490-356
Telex: 144PY

Peru
Lima Stock Exchange
Pasaje Acuña 191
Lima 1
Telephone: (51-14) 286-280
Fax: (51-14) 337-650
Telex: 25856

Philippines (Makati)
Makati Stock Exchange Inc.
Makati Stock Exchange Building
Ayala Avenue, Makati
Metro Manila
>   Telephone: (63-2) 810 1145
>   Fax: (63-2) 810 5710
>   Telex: 45074 MKSE PM

Philippines (Manila)
Manila Stock Exchange
Prensa St.
cor Muelle de la Industria
Binondo
Manila
>   Telephone: (63-2) 47-33-82
>   Fax: (63-2) 471125 / 408867
>   Telex: (722) 40503 MSE PM

Poland
Glelda Papierow Wartosciowych
Nowy _wiat 6 / 12
Warszawa 00-920
>   Telephone: (48-22) 628-32—32
>   Fax: (48-22) 628 17541 / 628 8191

Portugal (Lisbon)
Bolsa de Valores de Lisboa
Rua dos Fanqueiros, 10
Lisbon 1100
>   Telephone: (351-1) 888.27.38 / 29.17
>   Fax: (351-1) 864-231/877-402
>   Telex: (832) 44751 BVLISB P

Portugal (Oporto)
Bolsa de Valores Do Porto
Palacio da Bolsa
Rua de Ferreira Borges
4000 Porto
>   Telephone: (351-2) 200-2476
>   Fax: (351-2) 200-2475
>   Telex: 28522

Singapore
Stock Exchange of Singapore
1 Raffles Place
24-00 OUB Centre
Singapore 0104
    Telephone: 5353788
    Fax: 5350985
    Telex: 21853

South Africa
Johannesburg Stock Exchange
POB 1174
Johannesburg 2000
    Telephone: 83366580
    Telex: 487663

Spain (Barcelona)
Bolsa de Barcelona
Paseo Isabel II, 1
08003 Barcelona
    Telephone: (93) 4013555
    Telex: 54131

Spain (Biblao)
Bolsa de Bilbao
Calle José M. Olabarri 1
48001 Bilbao
    Telephone: (94) 4237400
    Telex: 32709

Spain (Madrid)
Bolsa de Madrid
Palacio de la Bolsa
Plaza de la Lealtad 1
28014 Madrid
    Telephone: (91) 5892600
    Telex: 49184

Spain (Valencia)
Bolsa de Valencia
San Vincente 23
46002 Valencia
    Telephone: (96) 3870100

| Fax: | (96) 3870160 |
| Telex: | 62880 |

Sri Lanka
Colombo Stock Exchange
2nd Floor, MacKinnons Bldg.
York Street
Colombo 1

Telephone:	(94-1) 44 6581
Fax:	(94-1) 44 7603
Telex:	21124 MACKINON CE

Sweden
Stockholm Stock Exchange
Källargränd 2
POB 1256
11182 Stockholm

Telephone:	(8) 613-88-00
Fax:	(8) 10-81-10
Telex:	13551

Switzerland (Basel)
Basel Stock Exchange
Aeschenplatz 7
4002 Basel

Telephone:	(061) 2720555
Fax:	(061) 2720626
Telex:	962524

Switzerland (Berne)
Berne Stock Exchange
Aarbergergasse 36
3011 Berne

| Telephone: | (031) 224042 |
| Fax: | (031) 225309 |

Switzerland (Geneva)
Geneva Stock Exchange
8 rue de la Confederation
1211 Geneva 11

| Telephone: | (022) 280684 |

Switzerland (Zurich)
Zurich Stock Exchange
Selnaustr. 30
8021 Zurich
    Telephone: (01) 2292111
    Fax: (01) 2292233

Thailand
Securities Exchange of Thailand
Sinthon Building, 2nd Floor
132 Wireless Road
Bangkok 10330
    Telephone: (66-2) 254-0440
    Fax: (66-2) 254-3040
    Telex: (788) 20126 BEJARATH

Trinidad and Tobago
Trinidad & Tovago Stock Exchange
65 Independence Square
Port of Spain
    Telephone: (809) 625-5107-9
    Fax: (809) 623-0089
    Telex: CBTRIN 22532

Tunisia
Tunis Stock Exchange
19 bis, rue Kamel Ataturk
Tunis 1001
    Telephone: (216-1) 259-411
    Fax: (216-1) 347-256
    Telex: 14931

Turkey
Istanbul Stock Exchange
Rihtim Caddesi No. 245
Karakoy-Istanbul 80030
    Telephone: (90-1) 152 48 00
    Fax: (90-1) 143 7425 / 152 4915
    Telex: (821) 22748 IMKB TR

Uganda
Kampala Stock Exchange

P.O. Box 8223
Kampala

United Kingdom (London)
The London Stock Exchange
Old Broad Street
London, EC2N 1HP
    Telephone: (071) 797-1000
    Telex: 886557

United Kingdom (Northern Ireland)
Stock Exchange
10 High Street
Belfast BT1 2BP
    Telephone: (0232) 321094
    Fax: (0232) 328149

United States
American Stock Exchange
86 Trinity Place
New York, New York 10006
    Telephone: (212) 306-1000
    Fax: (212) 306-1802
    Telex: 129297

Boston Stock Exchange
One Boston Place
Boston, Massachusetts 02108
    Telephone: (617) 723-9500
    Fax: (617) 723-2474

Midwest Stock Exchange
440 South LaSalle Street
Chicago, Illinois 60605
    Telephone: (312) 663-2222
    Fax: (312) 347-7743

New York Stock Exchange
11 Wall Street
New York, New York 10005
    Telephone: (212) 656-3000
    Fax: (212) 656-5646
    Telex: 710-5815464

Pacific Stock Exchange
301 Pine Street
San Francisco, California
 Telephone: (415) 393-4000
 Fax: (415) 393-4202
 Telex: 203025

Philadelphia Stock Exchange
Stock Exchange Building
1900 Market Street
Philadelphia, Pennsylvania 19103
 Telephone: (215) 496-5000
 Fax: (215) 496-6729

Uruguay
Volsa de Valores de Montevideo
Misiones 1400
Montevideo
 Telephone: (598-12) 95 49 21
 Fax: (598-12) 96 19 00
 Telex: BOLSA UY 26996

Venezuela
Bolsa de Valores de Caracas
Edificio Atrium
Calle Sorocaima Urbanizacion
El Rosal, Pisol
Caracas
 Telephone: (58-2) 905-5511
 Fax: (58-2) 905-5829
 Telex: (395) 26536

Yugoslavia (Belgrade)
Belgrade Stock Exchange
Vladimira Popovica 6 B 02
Belgrade 11070
 Telephone: (38-11) 222 40 49
 Fax: (38-11) 222 43 55

Yugoslavia (Ljubljana)
Yugoslav Stock Exchange, Inc.
Ajdovscina 4
Ljubljana 61000

Telephone:	(38-11) 301-959
Fax:	(38-11) 61-301-950
Telex:	31606

Yugoslavia (Zagreb)

Zagreb Stock Exchange
Ksaver 208
Zagreb / Croatia 41000

Telephone:	(38-41) 420293
Fax:	(38-41) 42 0002

Zimbabwe Stock Exchange

8th Floor, Southampton Place
Union Avenue
Harare

Telephone:	(263-4) 736861
Fax:	(263-4) 791045
Telex:	(987) 24196 ZW